VOL. 36
VIZ Media Edition

Story and Art by
RUMIKO TAKAHASHI

English Adaptation by Gerard Jones

Translation/Mari Morimoto
Touch-up Art & Lettering/Bill Schuch
Cover and Interior Graphic Design/Yuki Ameda
Editor/Ian Robertson

Editor in Chief, Books/Alvin Lu
Editor in Chief, Magazines/Marc Weidenbaum
VP, Publishing Licensing/Rika Inouye
VP, Sales & Product Marketing/Gonzalo Ferreyra
VP, Creative/Linda Espinosa
Publisher/Hyoe Narita

INUYASHA 36 by Rumiko TAKAHASHI
© 2004 Rumiko TAKAHASHI
All rights reserved. Original Japanese edition
published in 2004 by Shogakukan Inc., Tokyo. The
stories, characters and incidents mentioned in this
publication are entirely fictional.

Printed in the U.S.A.

Published by VIZ Media, LLC
P.O. Box 77010
San Francisco, CA 94107

VIZ Media Edition
10 9 8 7 6 5 4 3 2 1
First printing, January 2009

www.viz.com   store.viz.com

INUYASHA

VOL. 36

VIZ Media Edition

STORY AND ART BY

RUMIKO TAKAHASHI

CONTENTS

Long ago, in the "Warring States" era of Japan's Muromachi period (Sengoku-jidai, approximately 1467-1568 CE), a legendary dog-like half-demon called "Inuyasha" attempted to steal the Shikon Jewel—or "Jewel of Four Souls"—from a village, but was stopped by the enchanted arrow of the village priestess, Kikyo. Inuyasha fell into a deep sleep, pinned to a tree by Kikyo's arrow, while the mortally wounded Kikyo took the Shikon Jewel with her into the fires of her funeral pyre. Years passed.

Fast-forward to the present day. Kagome, a Japanese high school girl, is pulled into a well one day by a mysterious centipede monster and finds herself transported into the past—only to come face-to-face with the trapped Inuyasha. She frees him, and Inuyasha easily defeats the centipede monster.

The residents of the village, now 50 years older, readily accept Kagome as the reincarnation of their deceased priestess Kikyo, a claim supported by the fact that the Shikon Jewel emerges from a cut on Kagome's body. Unfortunately, the jewel's rediscovery means that the village is soon under attack by a variety of demons in search of this treasure. Then, the jewel is accidentally shattered into many shards, each of which may have the fearsome power of the entire jewel.

Although Inuyasha says he hates Kagome because of her resemblance to Kikyo, the woman who "killed" him, he is forced to team up with her when Kaede, the village leader, binds him to Kagome with a powerful spell. Now the two grudging companions must fight to reclaim and reassemble the shattered shards of the Shikon Jewel before they fall into the wrong hands...

THIS VOLUME Inuyasha and the gang are holding fort at a temple with the weakened Goryomaru. Kagura attacks the temple while searching for the infant with Naraku's heart, while Inuyasha remains unsure whether Goryomaru is an enemy of Naraku. Kagura becomes seriously wounded. Is this the end for her? Perhaps Naraku

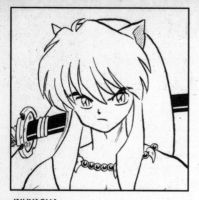

INUYASHA
Half-demon hybrid, son of a human mother and demon father. His necklace is enchanted, allowing Kagome to control him with a word.

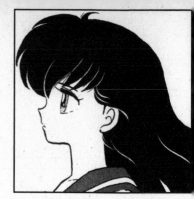

KAGOME
Modern-day Japanese schoolgirl who can travel back and forth between the past and present through an enchanted well.

NARAKU
Enigmatic demon-mastermind behind the miseries of nearly everyone in the story.

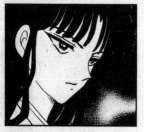

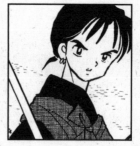

MIROKU
Lecherous Buddhist priest cursed with a mystical "hellhole" in his hand that's slowly killing him.

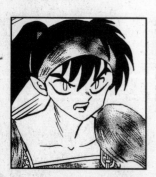

KOGA
Leader of the Wolf Clan, Koga is himself a Wolf Demon and, because of several Shikon shards in his legs, possesses super speed. Enamored of Kagome, he quarrels with Inuyasha frequently.

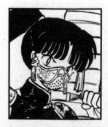

SANGO
"Demon Exterminator" or slayer from the village where the Shikon Jewel was first born.

SCROLL 1

THE SWARM OF CORPSES

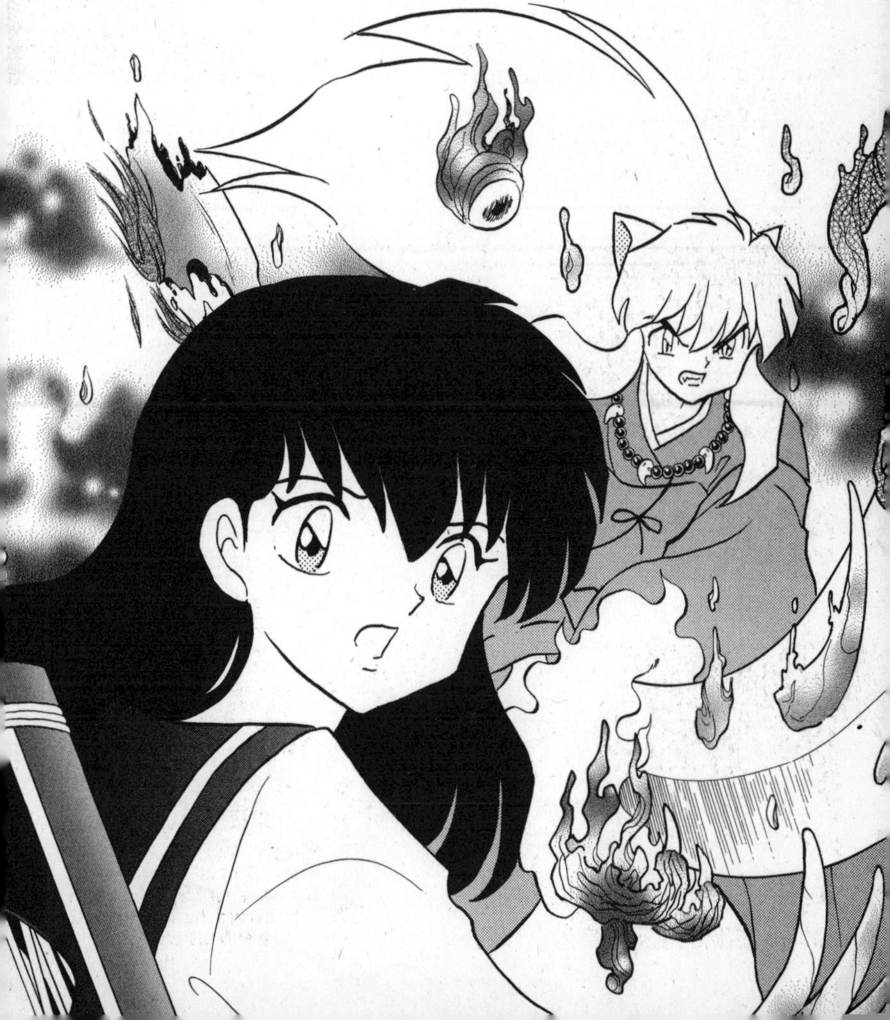

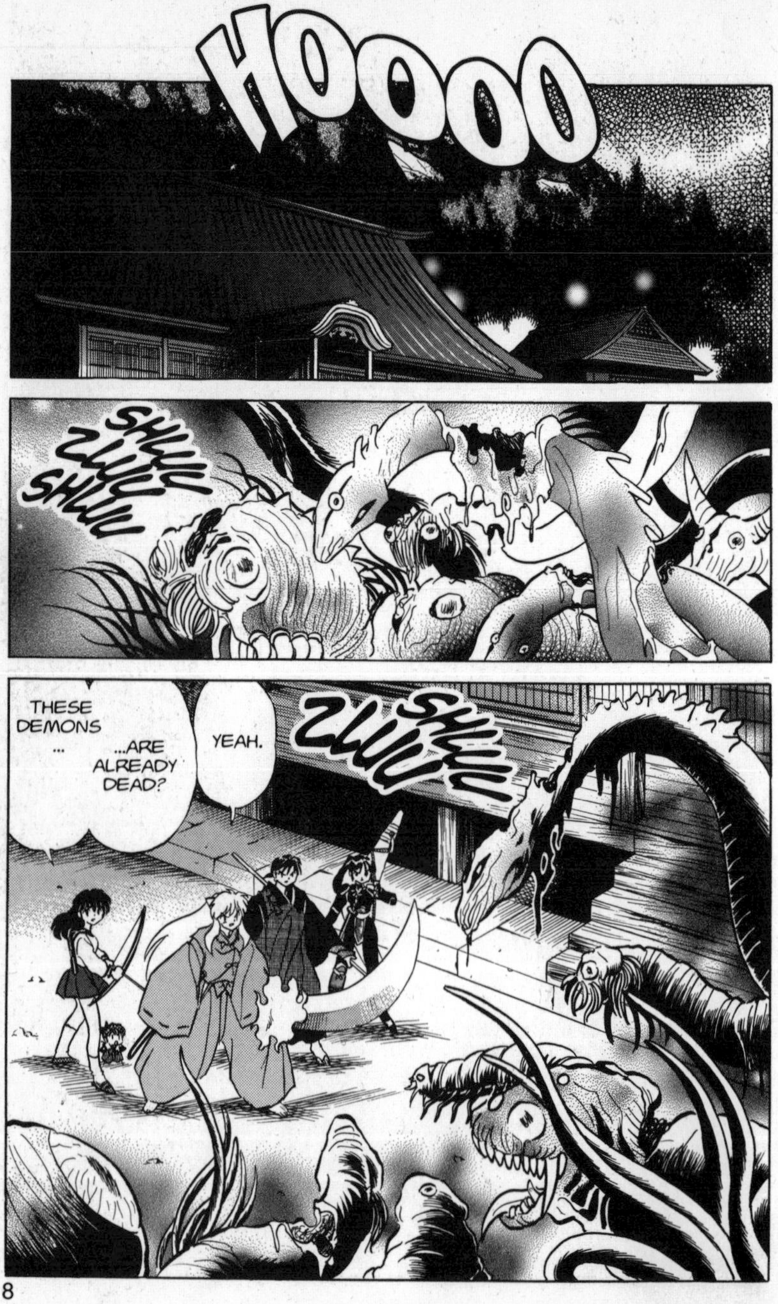
HOOOO
SHUUU
ZUUU
SHUUU
THESE DEMONS ...
...ARE ALREADY DEAD?
YEAH.
SHUUU
ZUUU

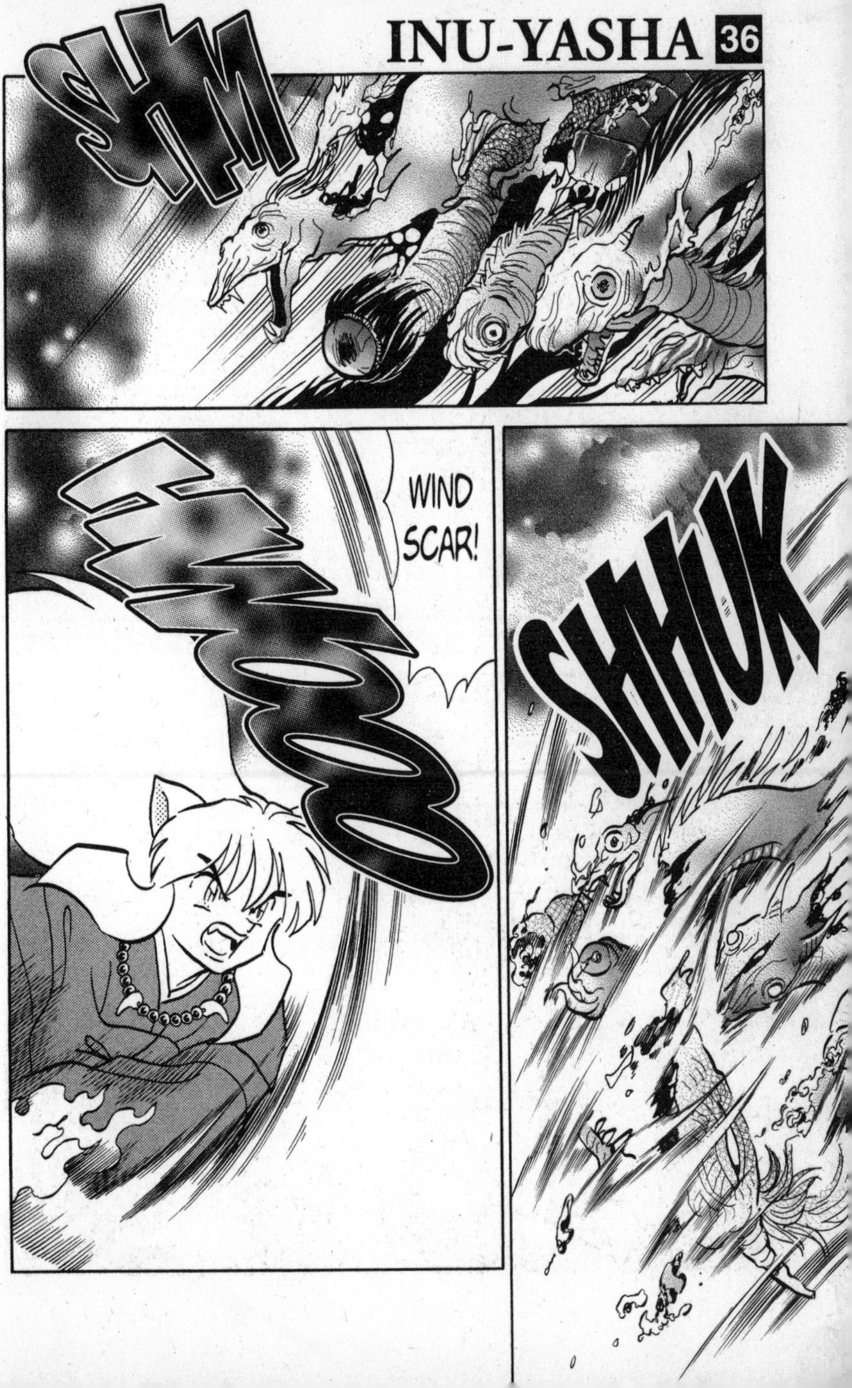
SHIM
WIND SCAR!
SHWOOOO
SHHUK

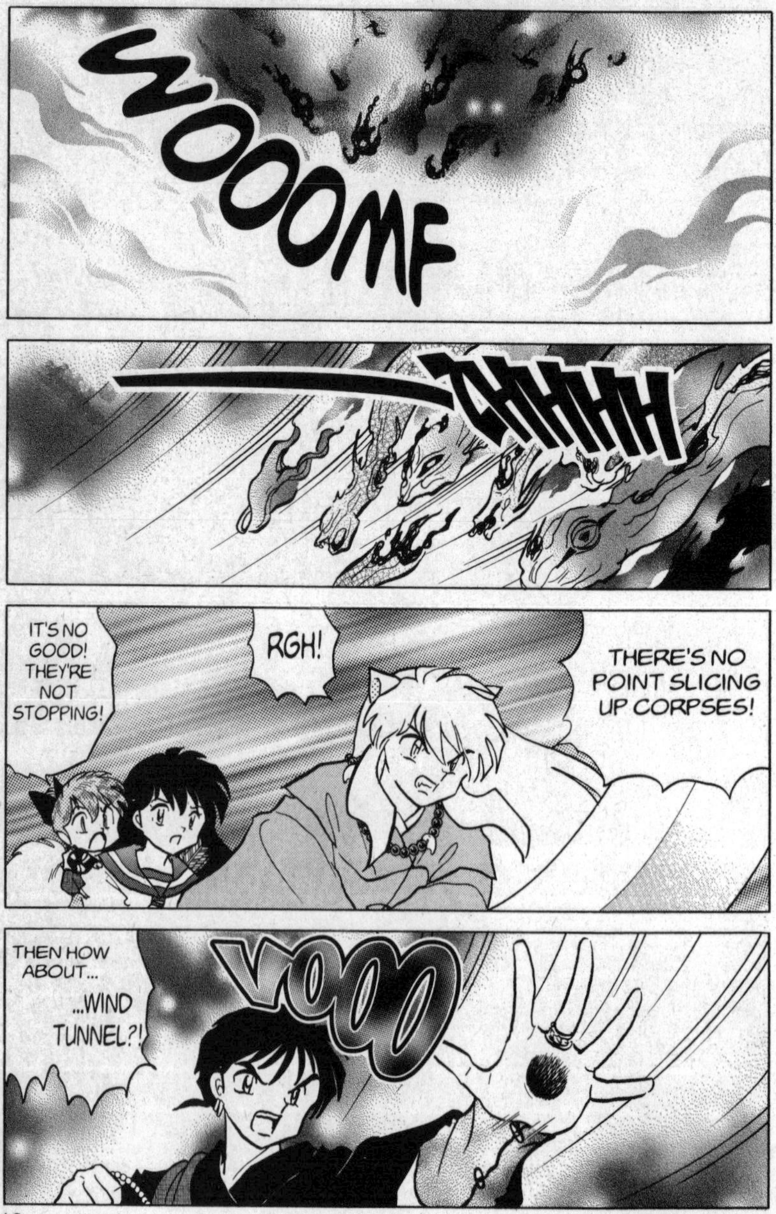
WOOOMF
CHHHH
IT'S NO GOOD! THEY'RE NOT STOPPING!
RGH!
THERE'S NO POINT SLICING UP CORPSES!
THEN HOW ABOUT...
...WIND TUNNEL?!
VOOO

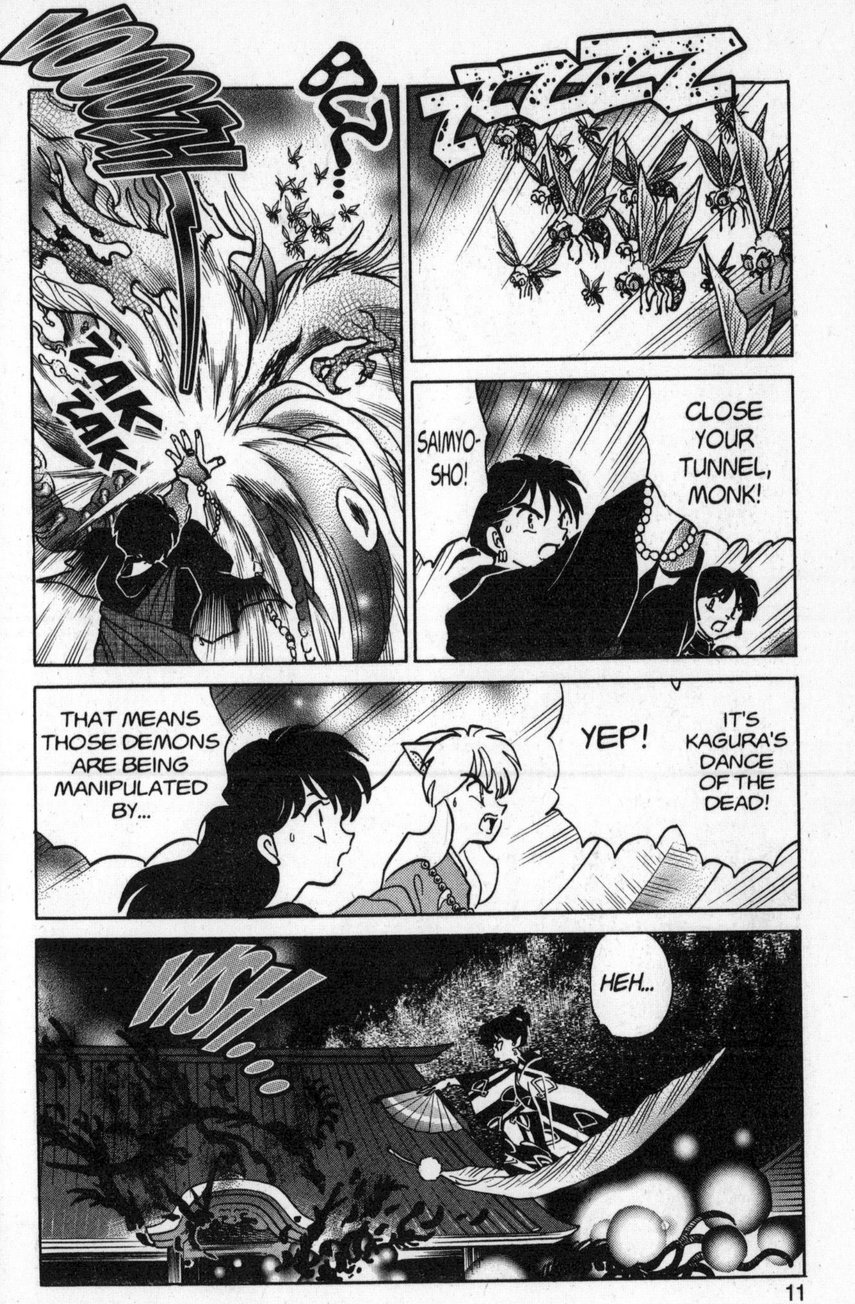
VOOOOM
BZZ...
ZAK ZAK
SAIMYO-SHO!
CLOSE YOUR TUNNEL, MONK!
THAT MEANS THOSE DEMONS ARE BEING MANIPULATED BY...
YEP!
IT'S KAGURA'S DANCE OF THE DEAD!
VSH...
HEH...

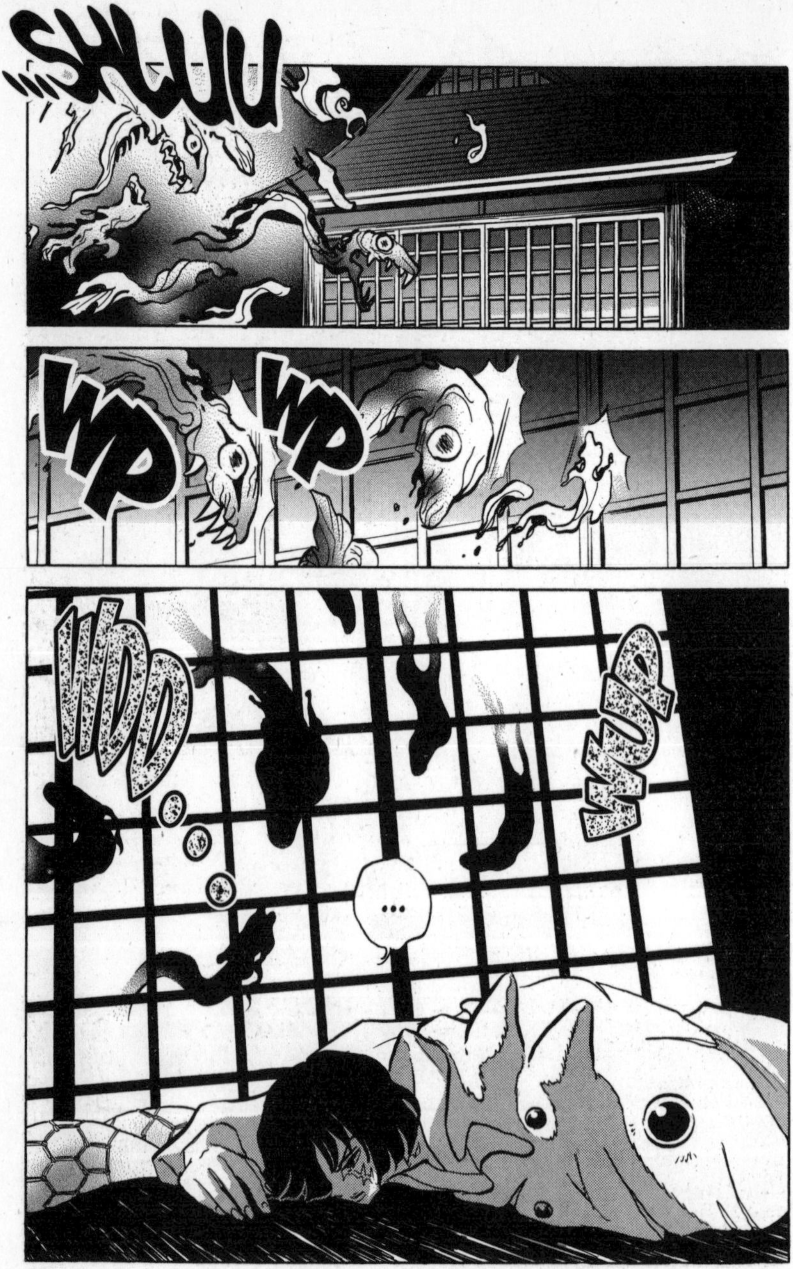
SHUU
WP
WP
WOO
WUP
...

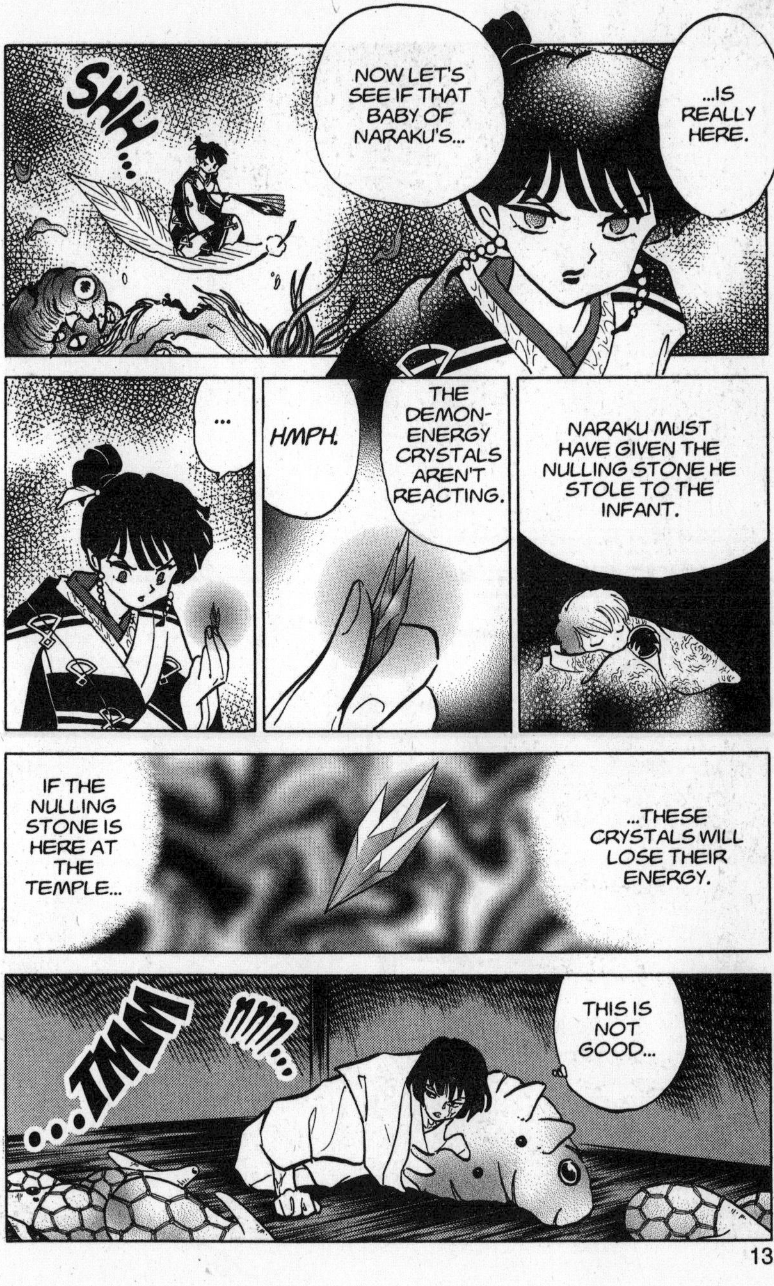
SHH...
NOW LET'S SEE IF THAT BABY OF NARAKU'S...
...IS REALLY HERE.
...
HMPH.
THE DEMON-ENERGY CRYSTALS AREN'T REACTING.
NARAKU MUST HAVE GIVEN THE NULLING STONE HE STOLE TO THE INFANT.
IF THE NULLING STONE IS HERE AT THE TEMPLE...
...THESE CRYSTALS WILL LOSE THEIR ENERGY.
...ZMM
MMM...
THIS IS NOT GOOD...

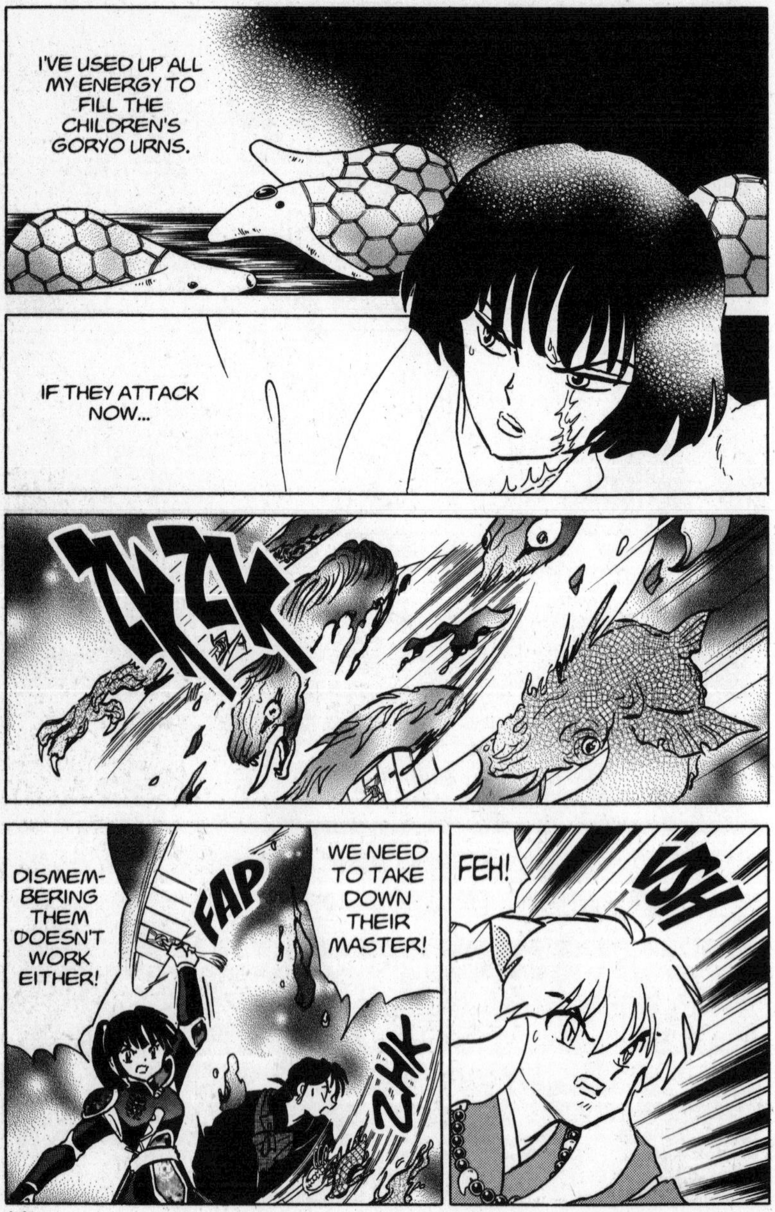

I'VE USED UP ALL MY ENERGY TO FILL THE CHILDREN'S GORYO URNS.
IF THEY ATTACK NOW...
DISMEMBERING THEM DOESN'T WORK EITHER!
FAP
WE NEED TO TAKE DOWN THEIR MASTER!
ZHK
FEH!
ISH

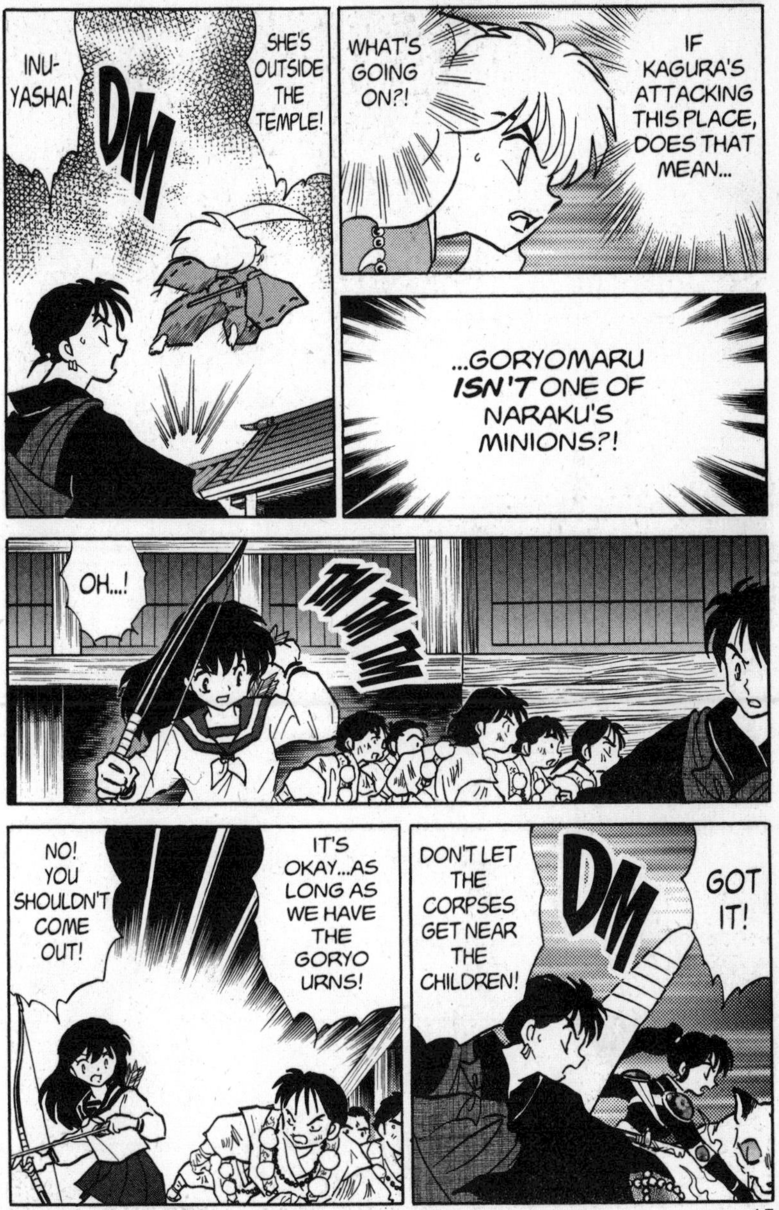
INU-YASHA!
DM
SHE'S OUTSIDE THE TEMPLE!
WHAT'S GOING ON?!
IF KAGURA'S ATTACKING THIS PLACE, DOES THAT MEAN...
...GORYOMARU ISN'T ONE OF NARAKU'S MINIONS?!
OH...!
TM TM TM
NO! YOU SHOULDN'T COME OUT!
IT'S OKAY...AS LONG AS WE HAVE THE GORYO URNS!
DON'T LET THE CORPSES GET NEAR THE CHILDREN!
DM
GOT IT!

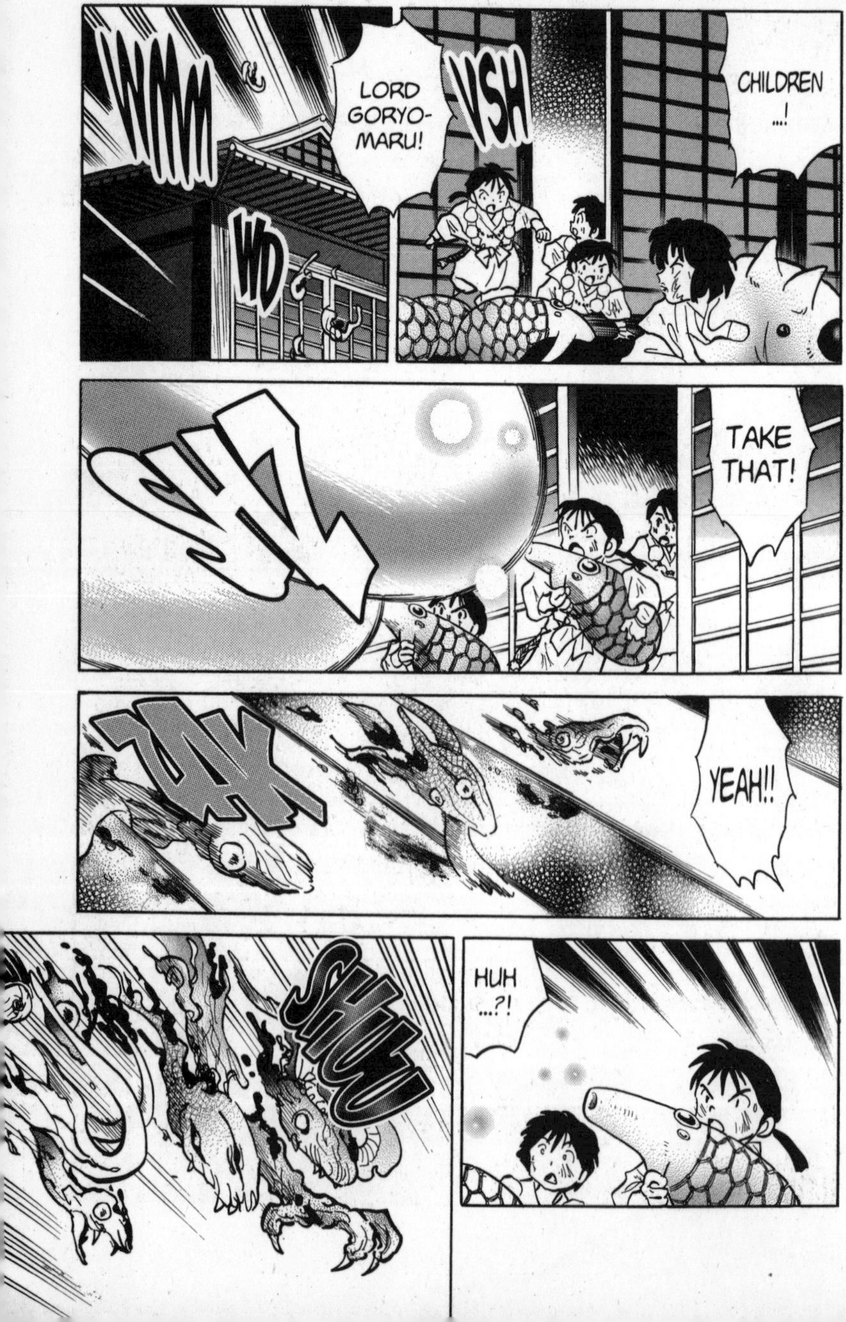

WMMM
WD
LORD GORYO-MARU!
VSH
CHILDREN ...!
SHZ
TAKE THAT!
ZAK
YEAH!!
SHUW
HUH ...?!

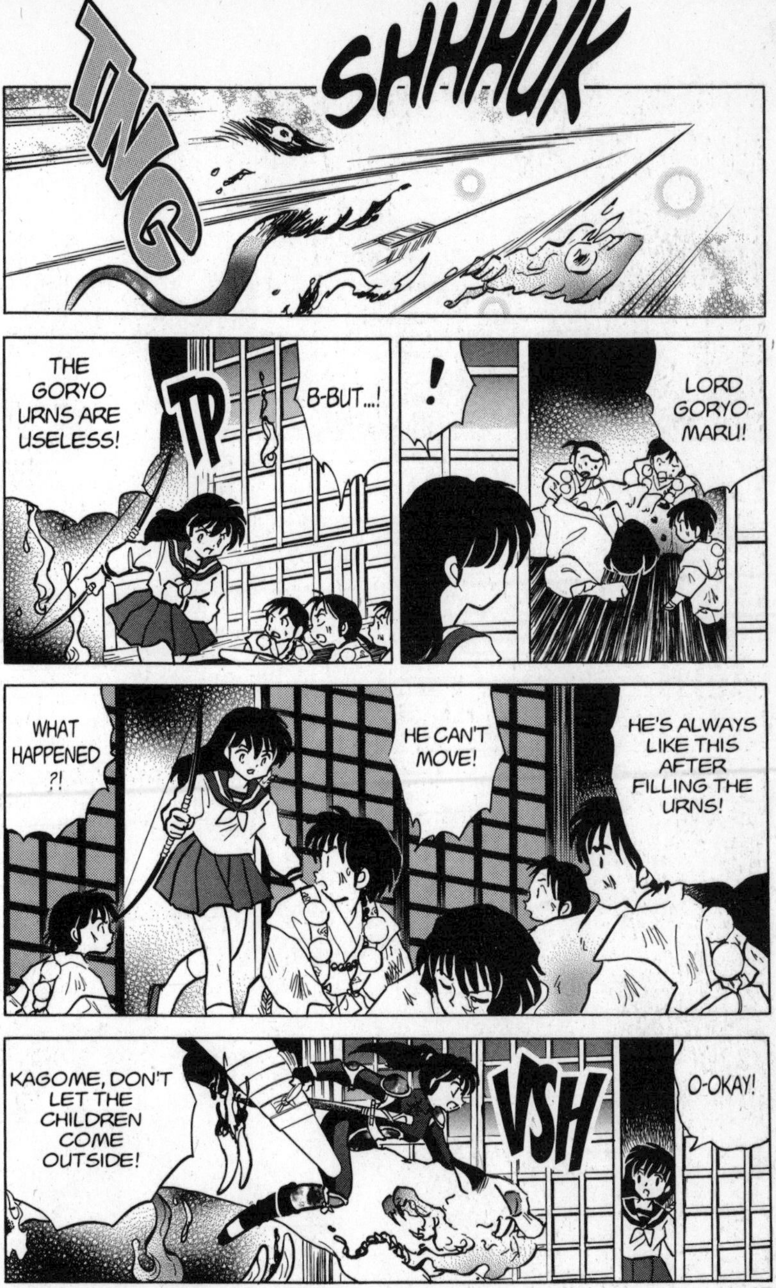
TING
SHHHUK
THE GORYO URNS ARE USELESS!
TP
B-BUT...!
!
LORD GORYO-MARU!
WHAT HAPPENED?!
HE CAN'T MOVE!
HE'S ALWAYS LIKE THIS AFTER FILLING THE URNS!
KAGOME, DON'T LET THE CHILDREN COME OUTSIDE!
VSH
O-OKAY!

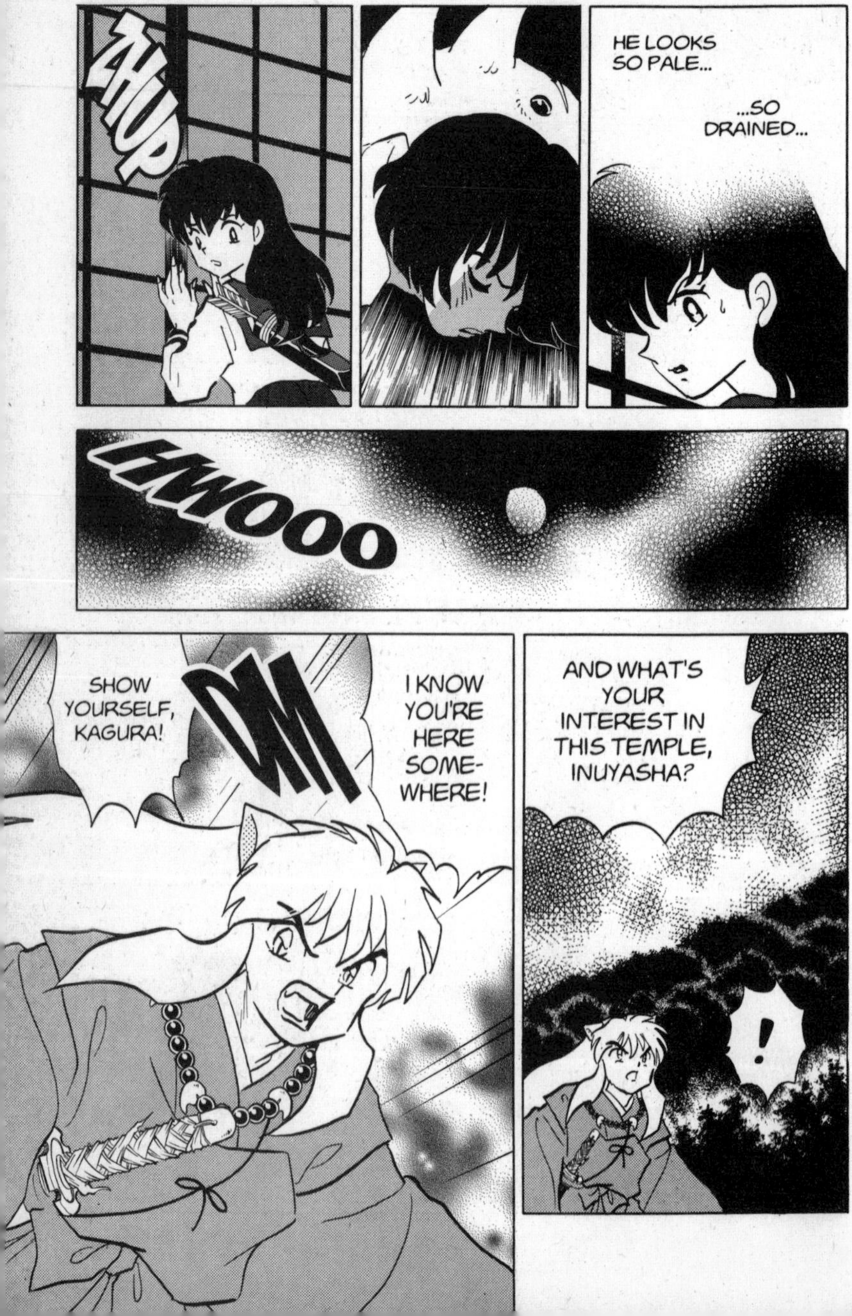
ZHUP
HE LOOKS SO PALE...
...SO DRAINED...
FWOOO
SHOW YOURSELF, KAGURA!
VM
I KNOW YOU'RE HERE SOMEWHERE!
AND WHAT'S YOUR INTEREST IN THIS TEMPLE, INUYASHA?
!

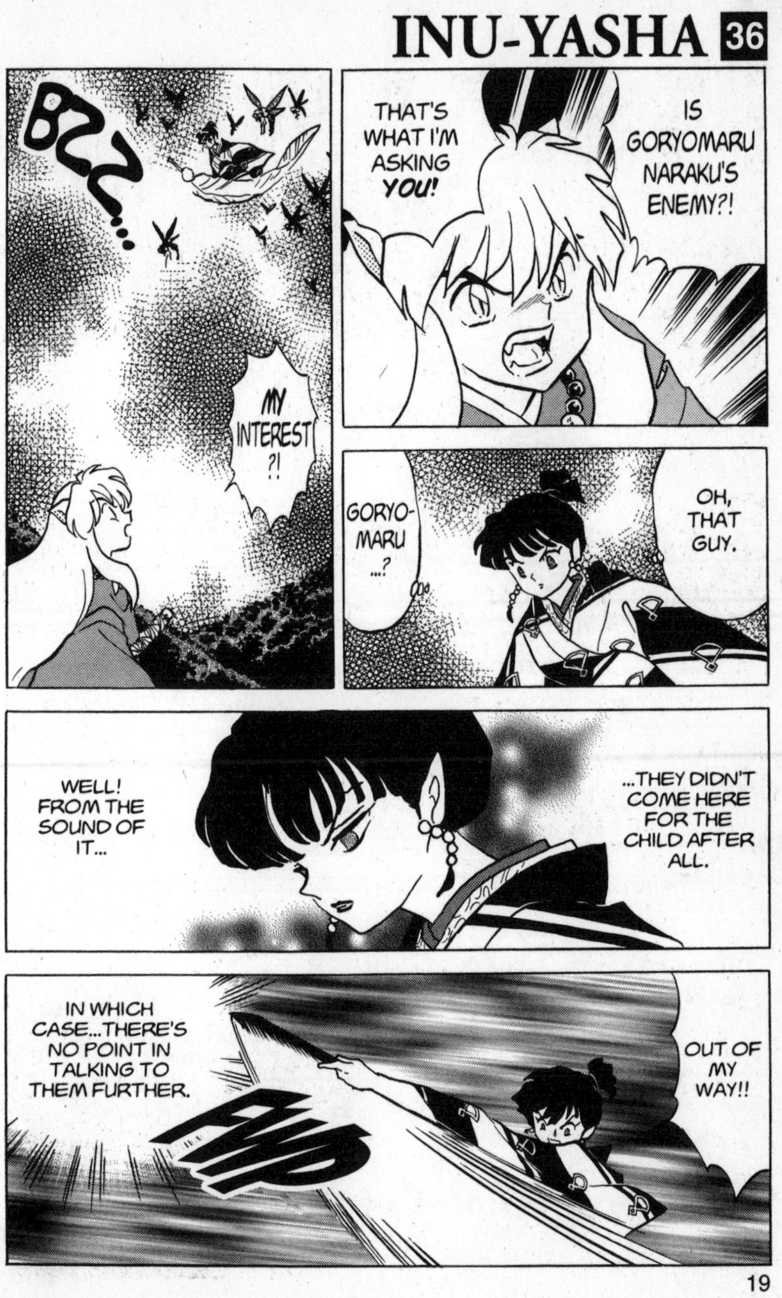
BZZ...
MY INTEREST ?!
THAT'S WHAT I'M ASKING YOU!
IS GORYOMARU NARAKU'S ENEMY?!
GORYO-MARU ...?
OH, THAT GUY.
WELL! FROM THE SOUND OF IT...
...THEY DIDN'T COME HERE FOR THE CHILD AFTER ALL.
IN WHICH CASE...THERE'S NO POINT IN TALKING TO THEM FURTHER.
FWP
OUT OF MY WAY!!

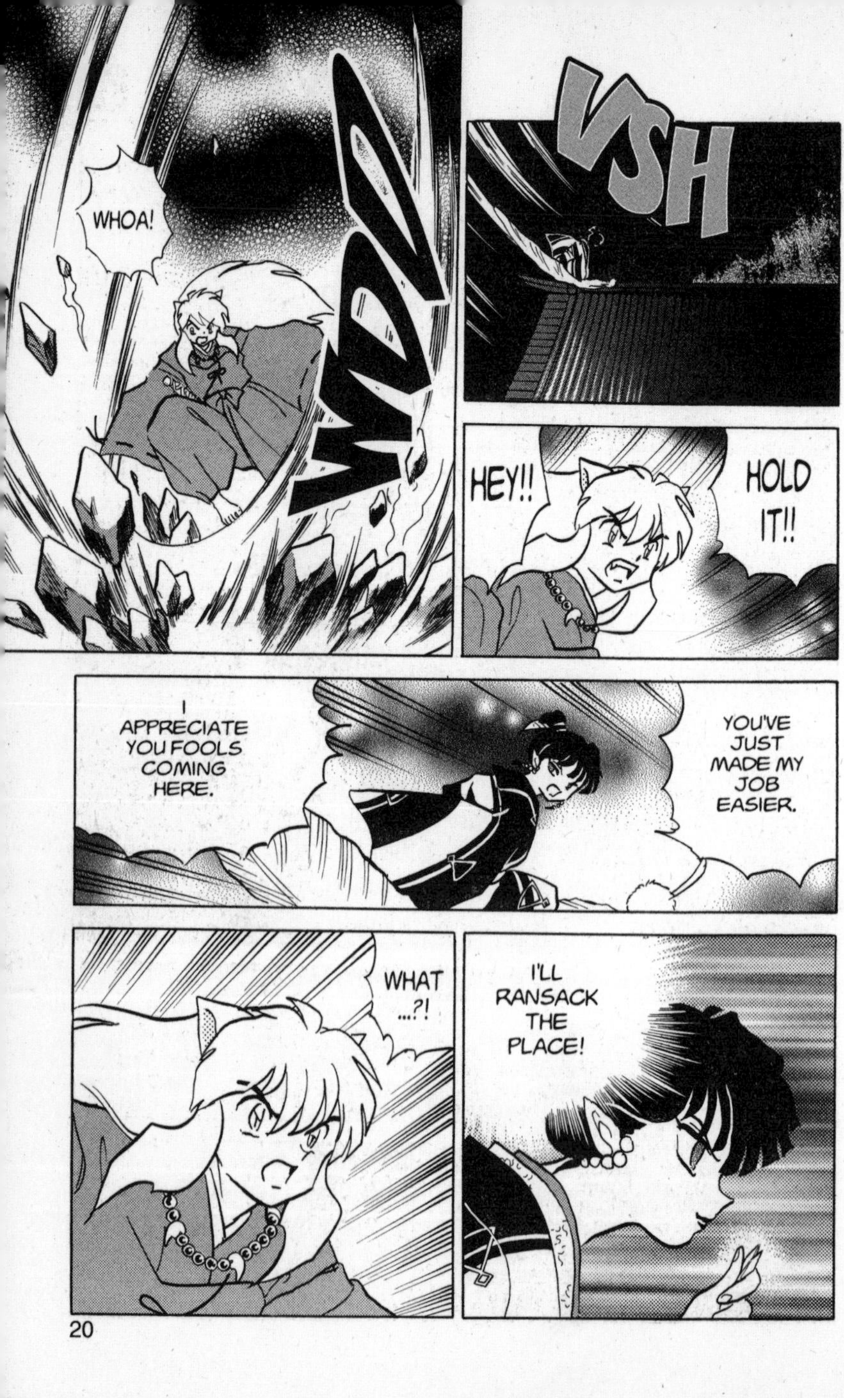
WHOA!
VSH
HEY!!
HOLD IT!!
I APPRECIATE YOU FOOLS COMING HERE.
YOU'VE JUST MADE MY JOB EASIER.
WHAT ...?!
I'LL RANSACK THE PLACE!

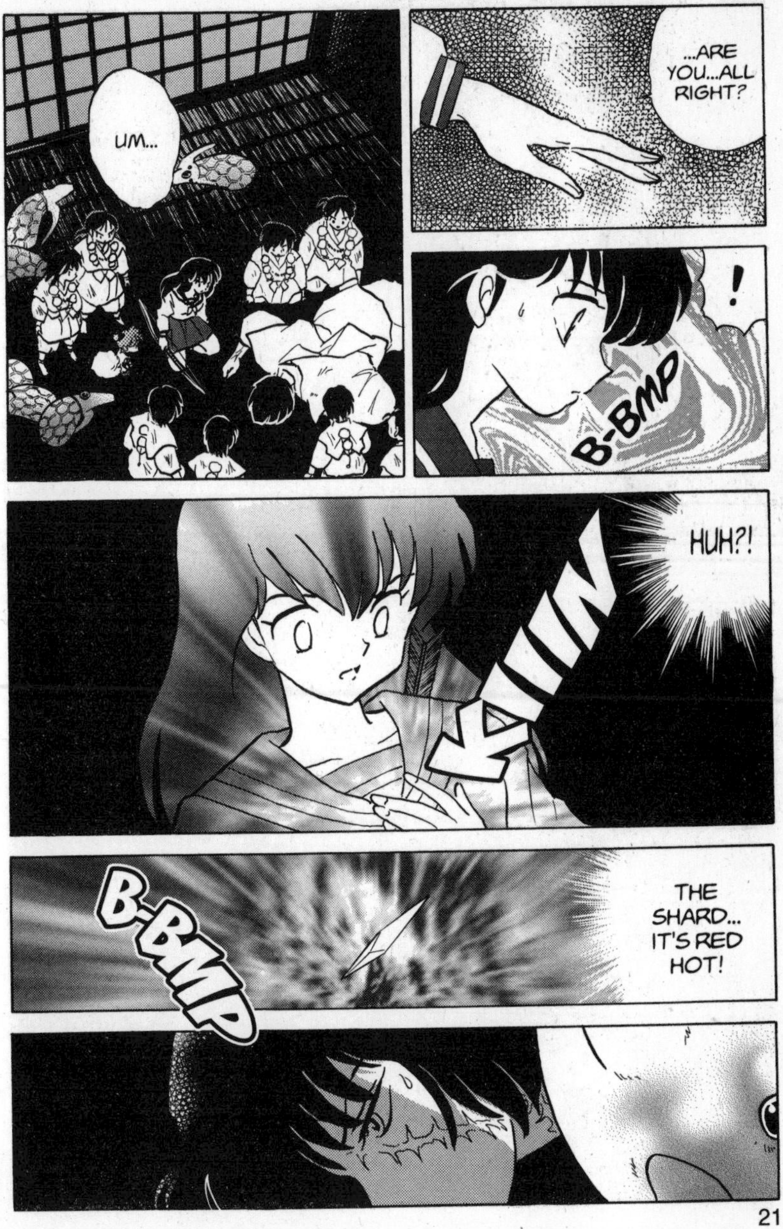
UM...
...ARE YOU...ALL RIGHT?
!
B-BMP
KIIIN
HUH?!
B-BMP
THE SHARD... IT'S RED HOT!

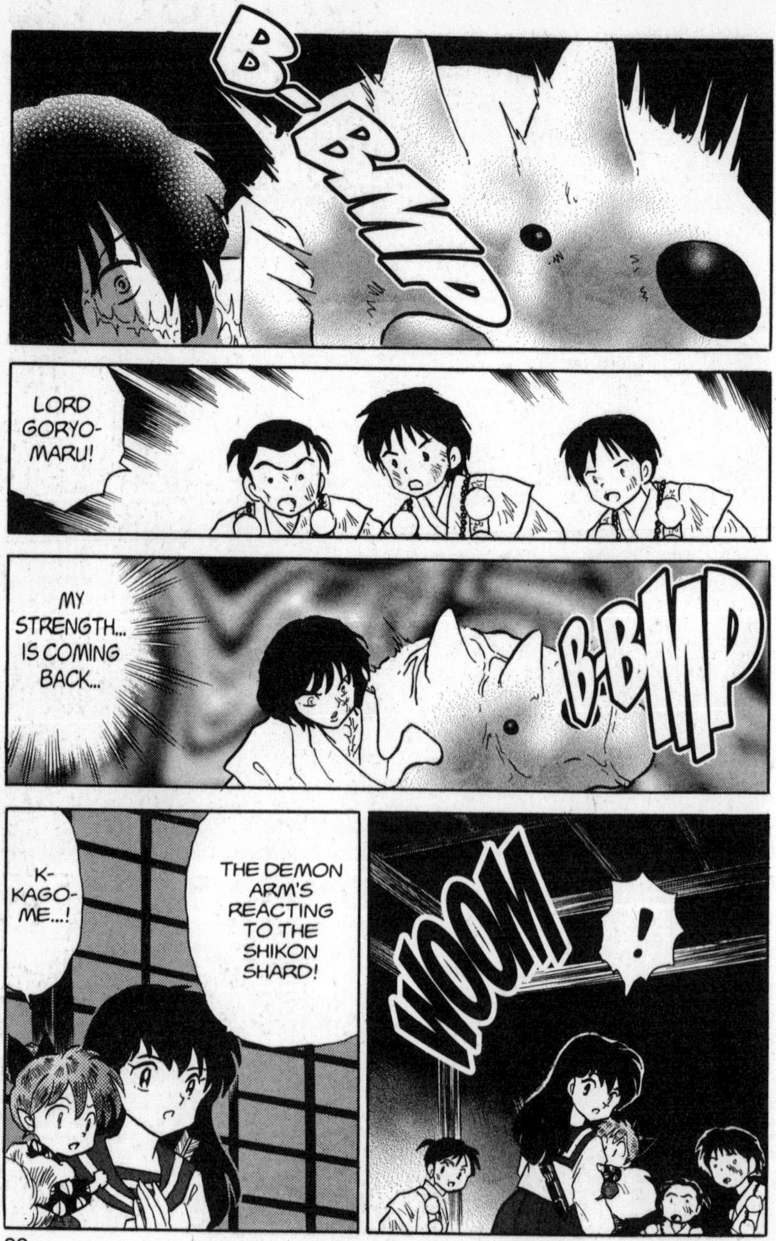
B-BMP
LORD GORYO-MARU!
MY STRENGTH... IS COMING BACK...
B-BMP
K-KAGO-ME...!
THE DEMON ARM'S REACTING TO THE SHIKON SHARD!
WOOM
!

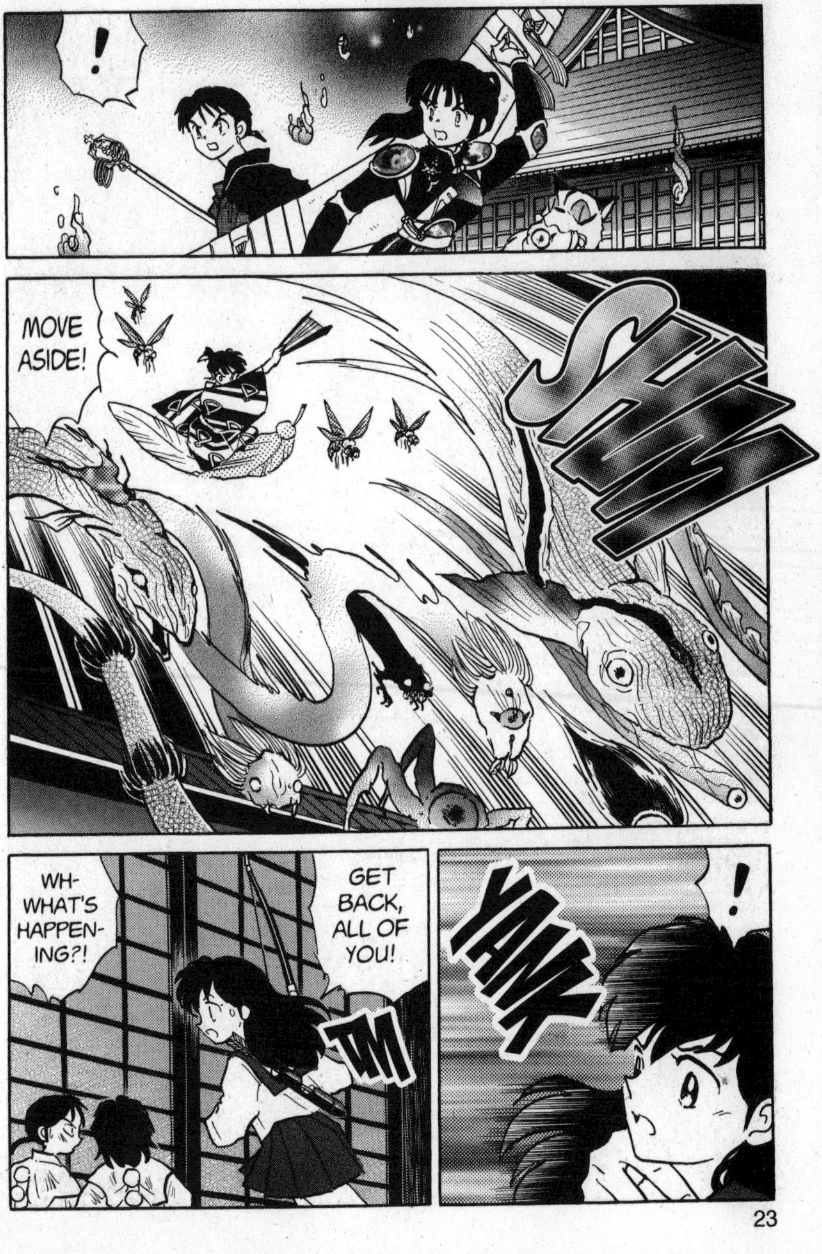
!
MOVE ASIDE!
WH- WHAT'S HAPPEN- ING?!
GET BACK, ALL OF YOU!
YANK
!

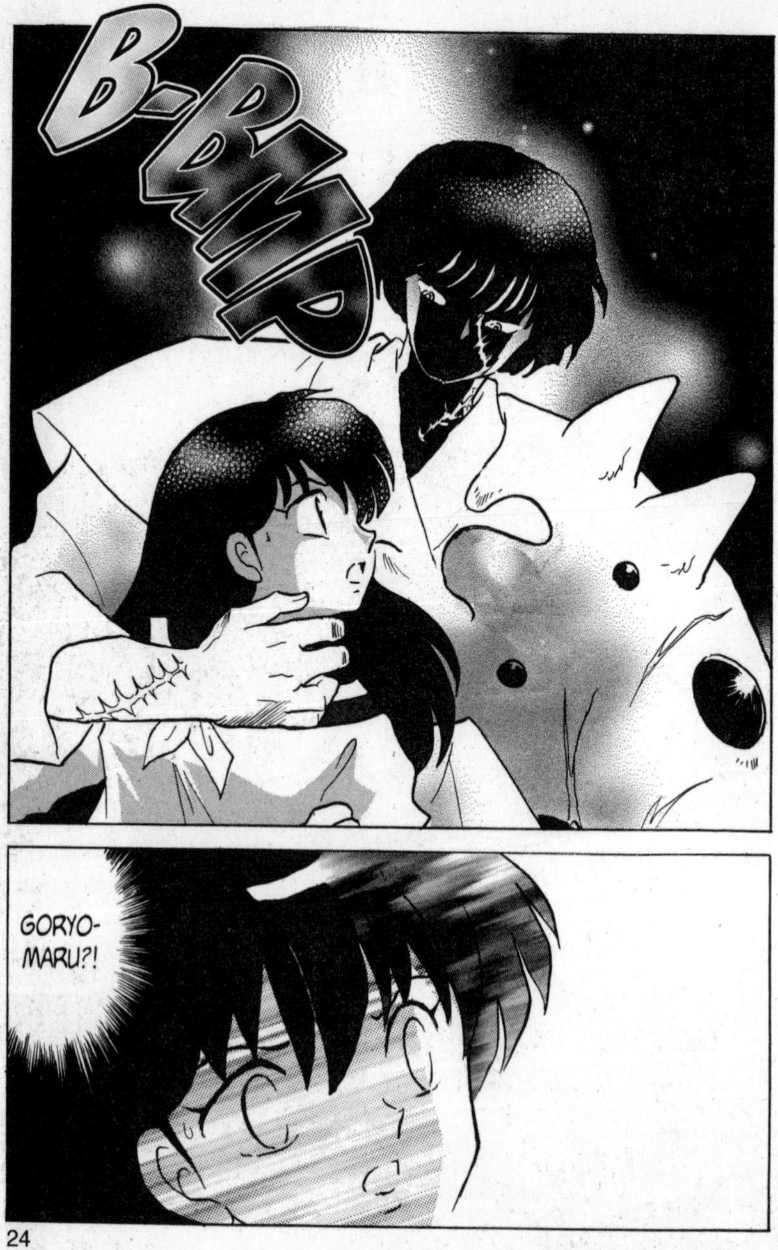
B-BMP
GORYO-
MARU?!

SCROLL 2
KAGURA'S LIFE

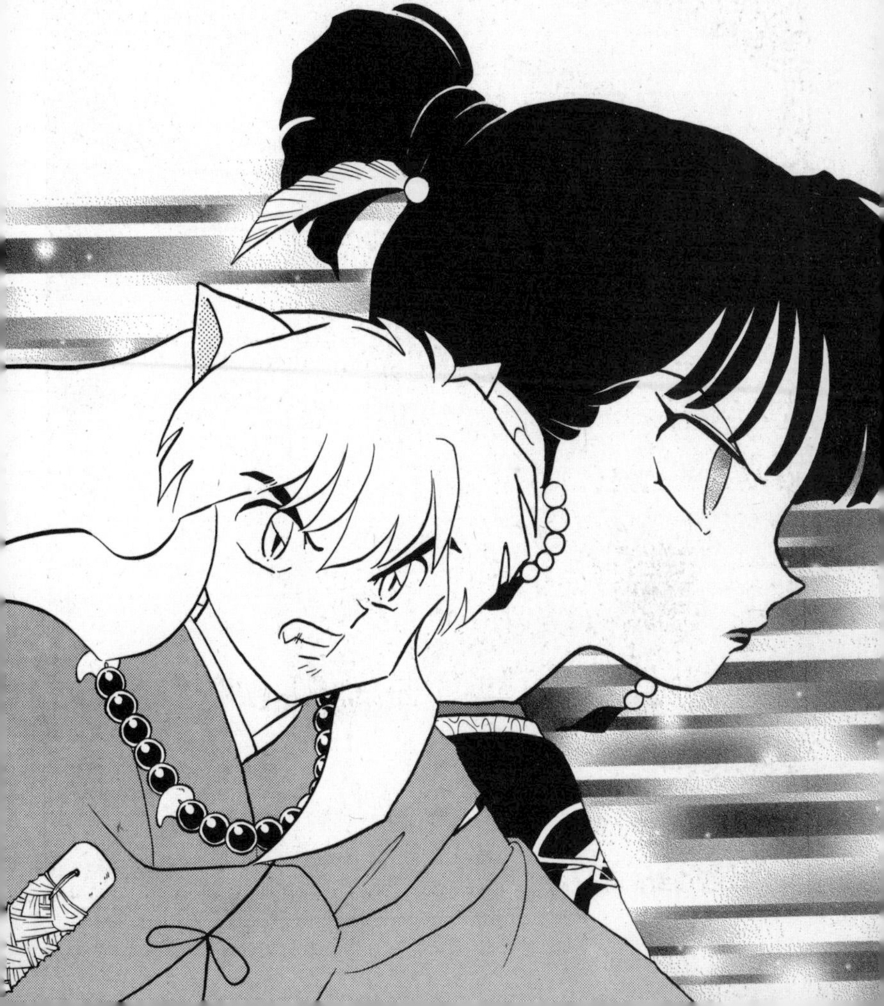

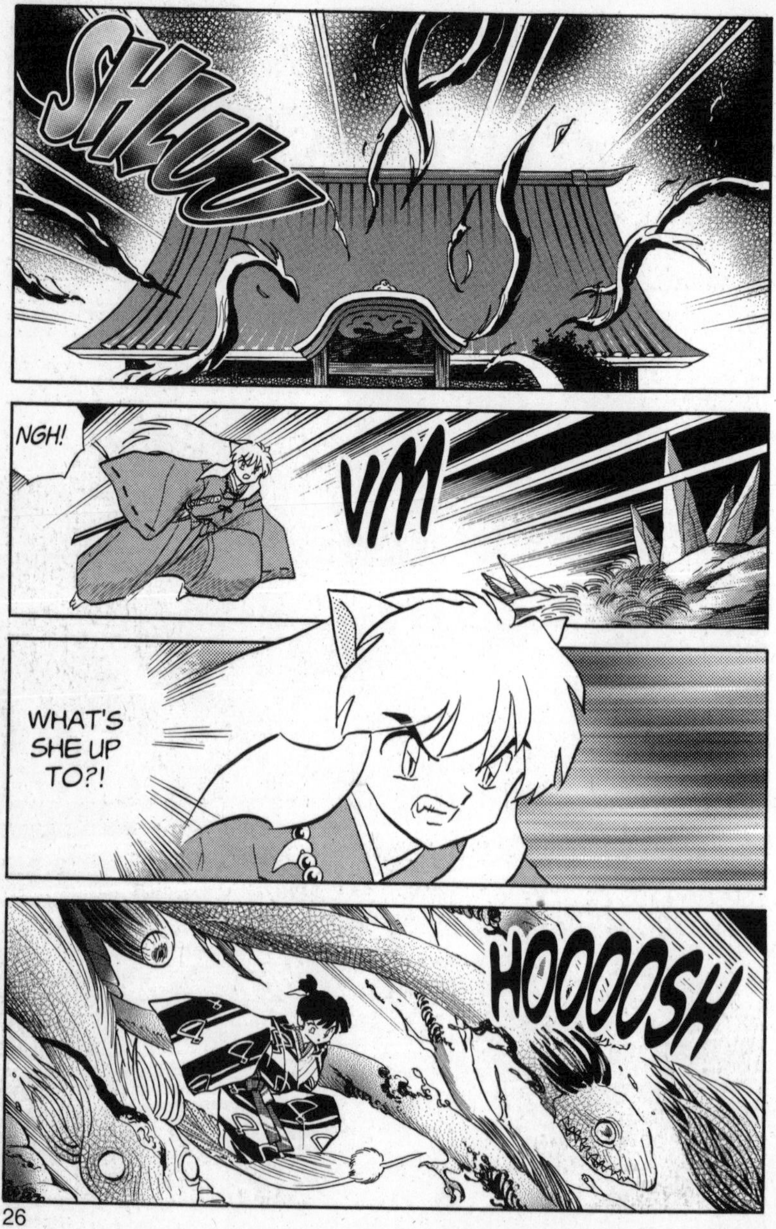
SHUU
NGH!
VM
WHAT'S SHE UP TO?!
HOOOOSH

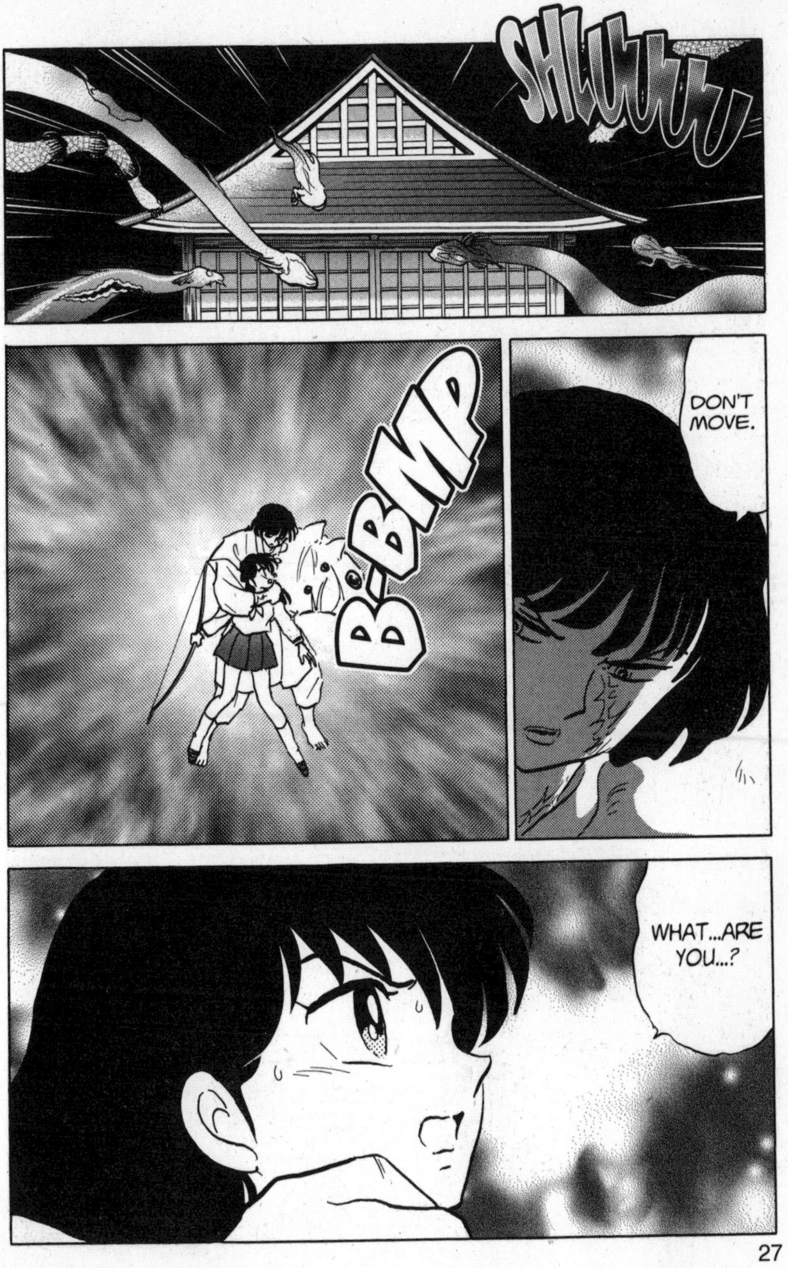
SHLUUUUU
BA-BMP
DON'T MOVE.
WHAT...ARE YOU...?

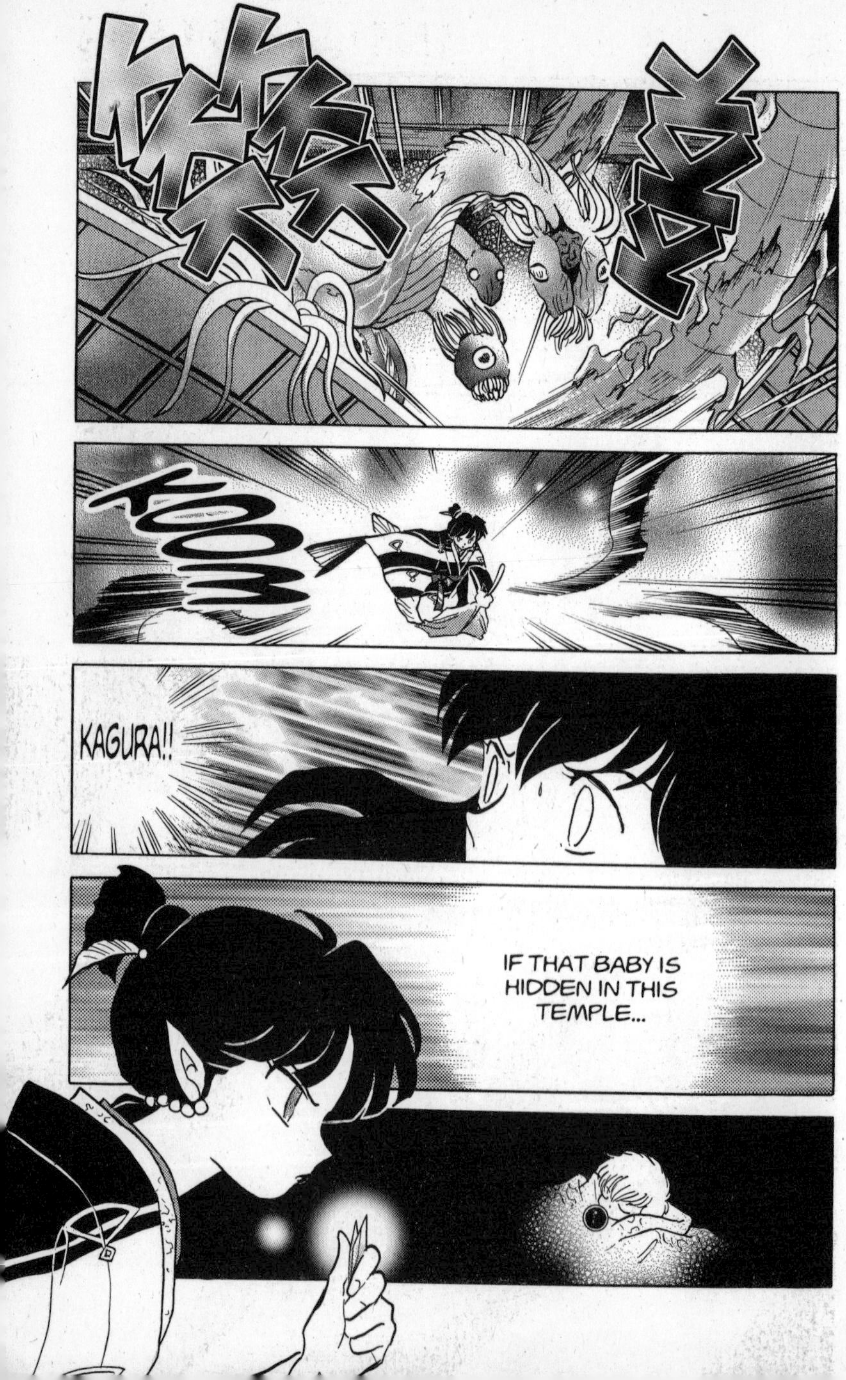
KOOM
KAGURA!!
IF THAT BABY IS HIDDEN IN THIS TEMPLE...

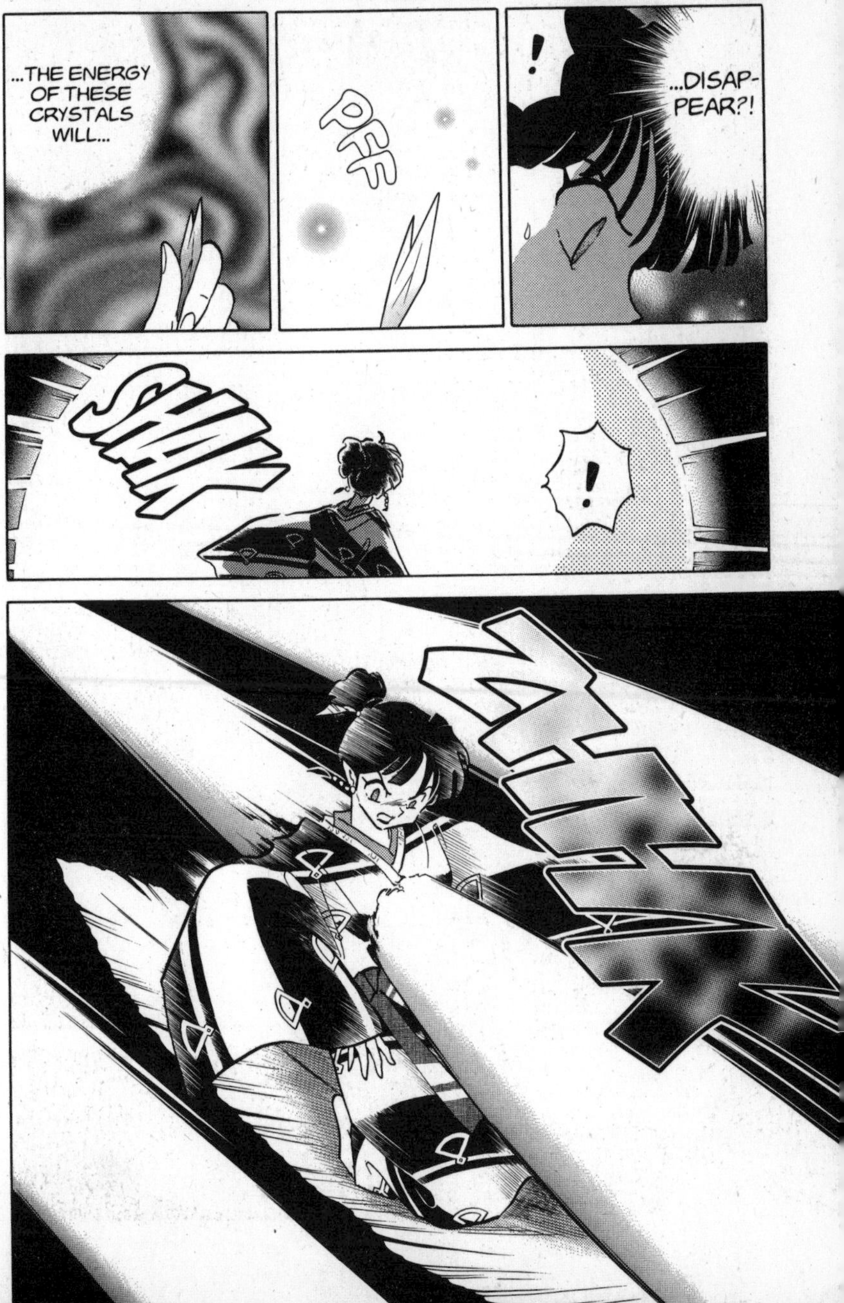
...THE ENERGY OF THESE CRYSTALS WILL...
PFF
!
...DISAP-PEAR?!
SHAK
!

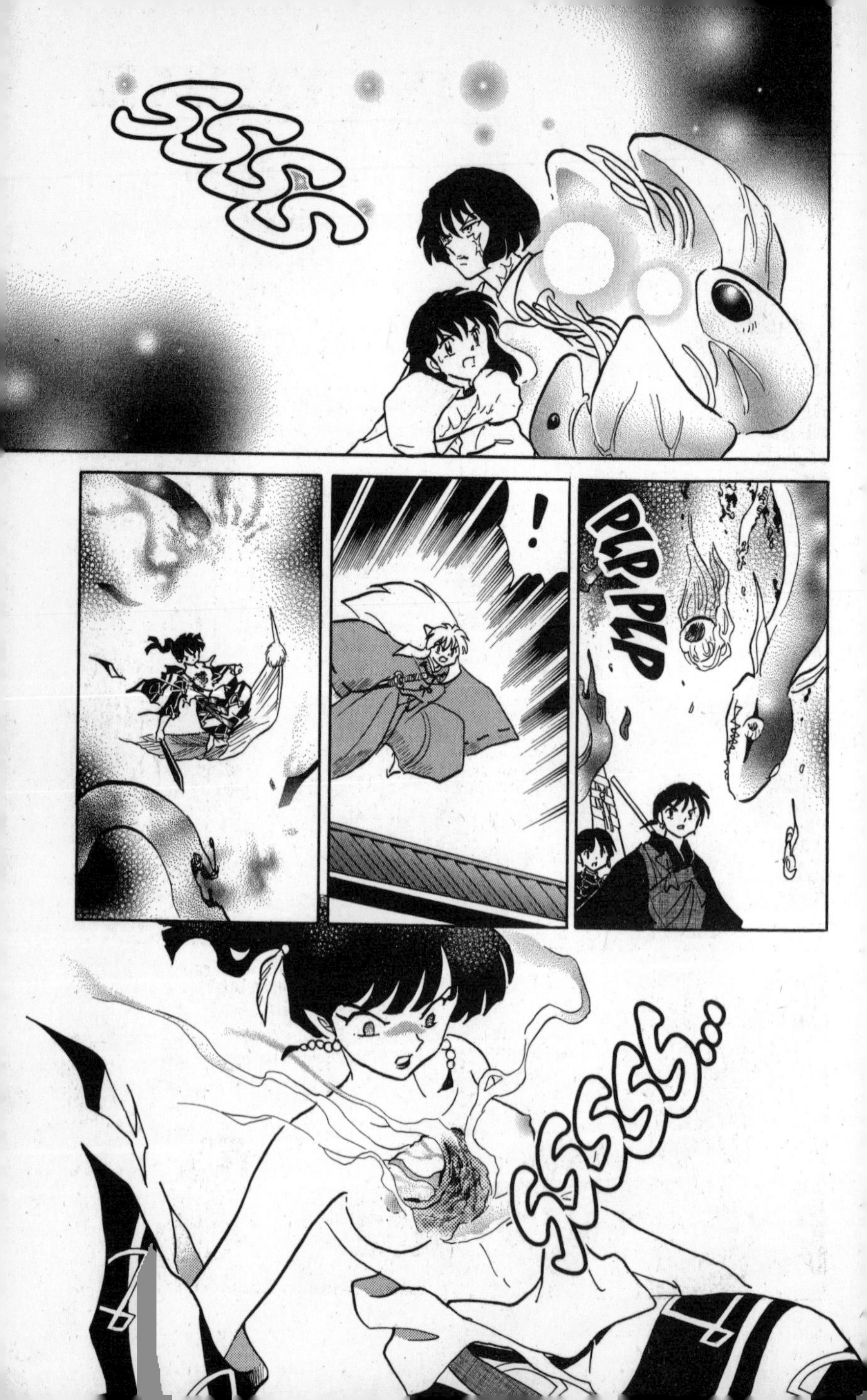
SSSS
!
PLIP PLIP
SSSSS...

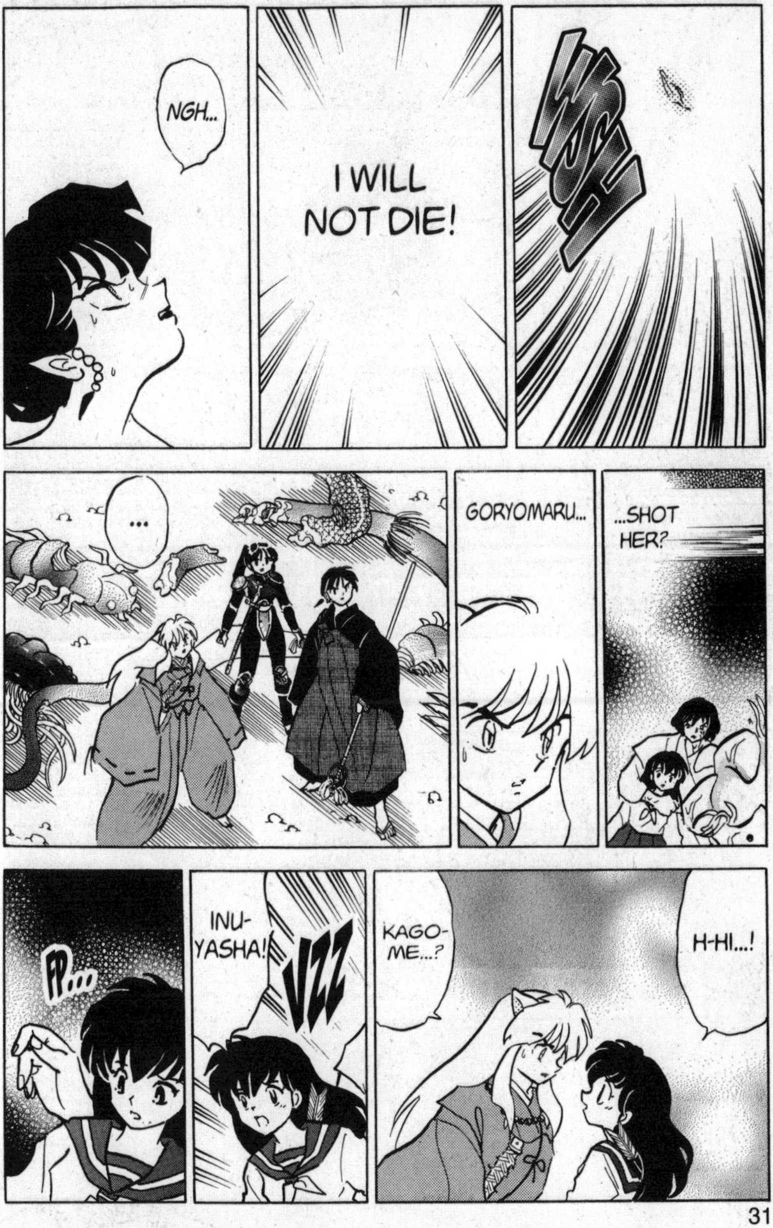
NGH...
I WILL NOT DIE!
...
GORYOMARU...
...SHOT HER?
FP...
INU-YASHA!
VZZ
KAGO-ME...?
H-HI...!

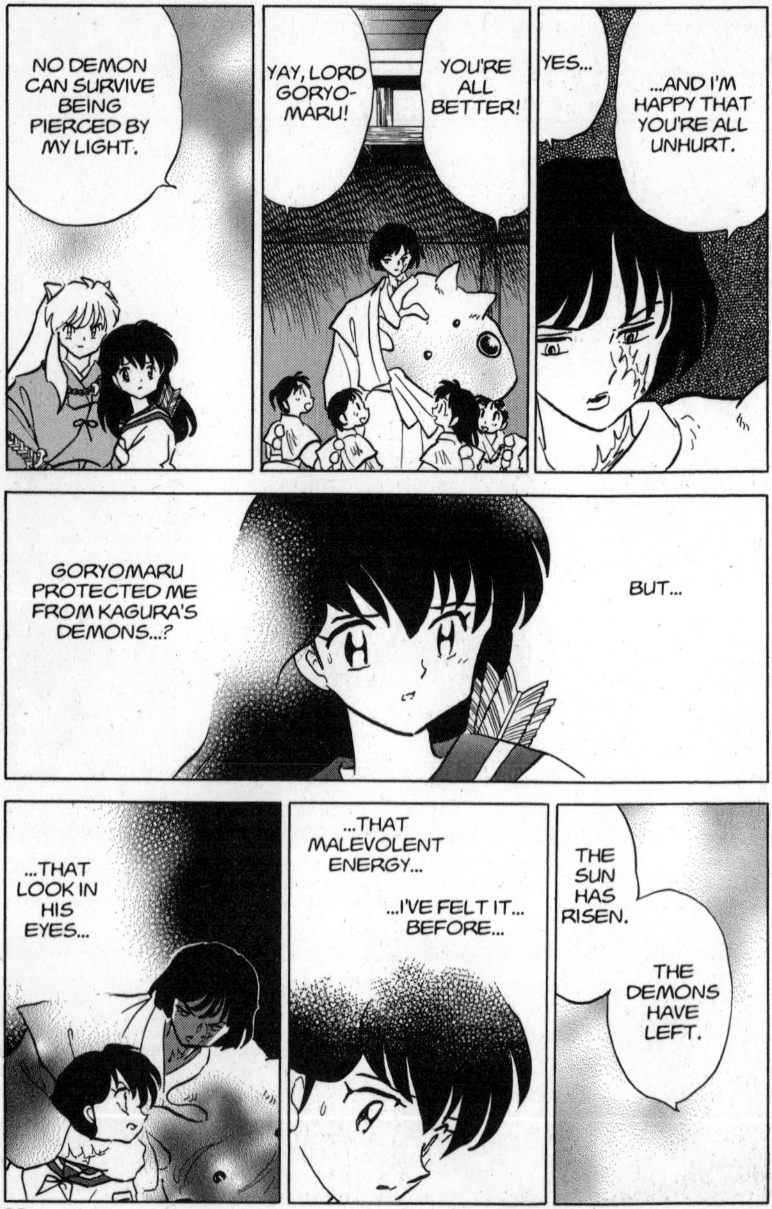
NO DEMON CAN SURVIVE BEING PIERCED BY MY LIGHT.
YAY, LORD GORYO-MARU!
YOU'RE ALL BETTER!
YES...
...AND I'M HAPPY THAT YOU'RE ALL UNHURT.
GORYOMARU PROTECTED ME FROM KAGURA'S DEMONS...?
BUT...
...THAT LOOK IN HIS EYES...
...THAT MALEVOLENT ENERGY...
...I'VE FELT IT... BEFORE...
THE SUN HAS RISEN.
THE DEMONS HAVE LEFT.

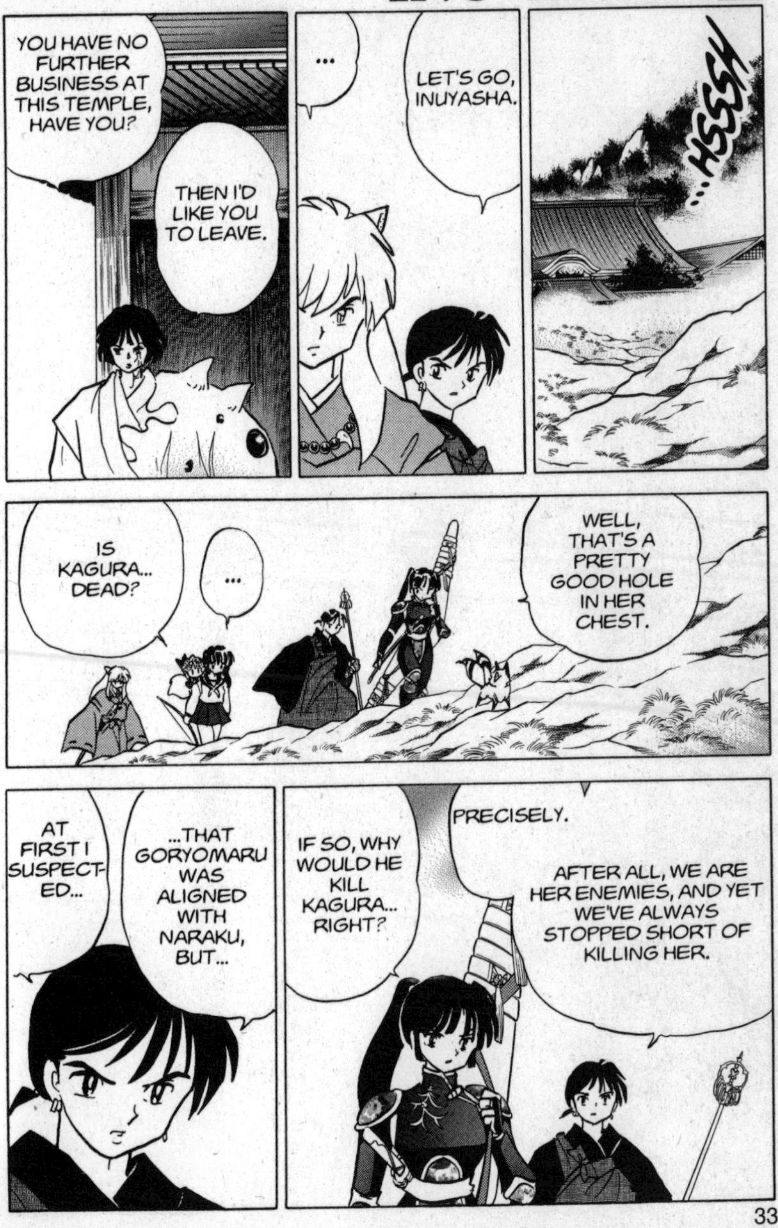
YOU HAVE NO FURTHER BUSINESS AT THIS TEMPLE, HAVE YOU?
THEN I'D LIKE YOU TO LEAVE.
...
LET'S GO, INUYASHA.
HSSSH...
IS KAGURA... DEAD?
...
WELL, THAT'S A PRETTY GOOD HOLE IN HER CHEST.
AT FIRST I SUSPECT-ED...
...THAT GORYOMARU WAS ALIGNED WITH NARAKU, BUT...
IF SO, WHY WOULD HE KILL KAGURA... RIGHT?
PRECISELY.
AFTER ALL, WE ARE HER ENEMIES, AND YET WE'VE ALWAYS STOPPED SHORT OF KILLING HER.

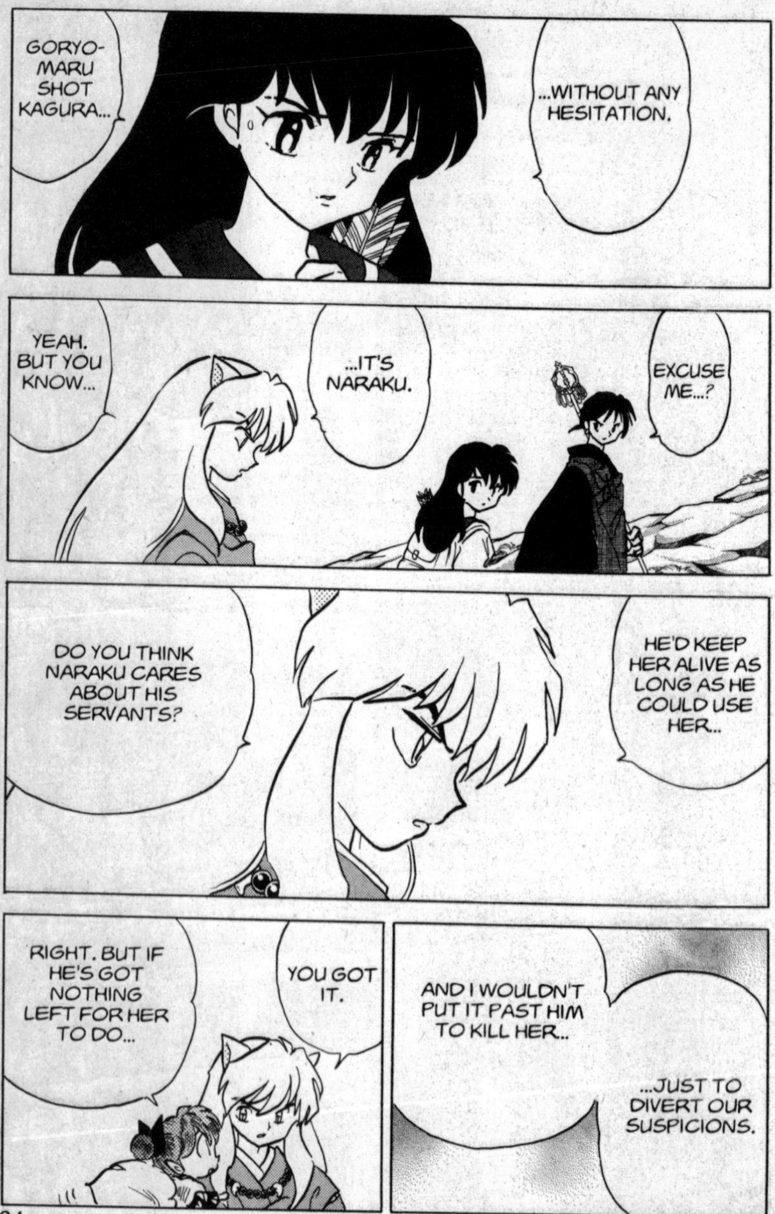
GORYO-MARU SHOT KAGURA...
...WITHOUT ANY HESITATION.
YEAH. BUT YOU KNOW...
...IT'S NARAKU.
EXCUSE ME...?
DO YOU THINK NARAKU CARES ABOUT HIS SERVANTS?
HE'D KEEP HER ALIVE AS LONG AS HE COULD USE HER...
RIGHT. BUT IF HE'S GOT NOTHING LEFT FOR HER TO DO...
YOU GOT IT.
AND I WOULDN'T PUT IT PAST HIM TO KILL HER..
...JUST TO DIVERT OUR SUSPICIONS.

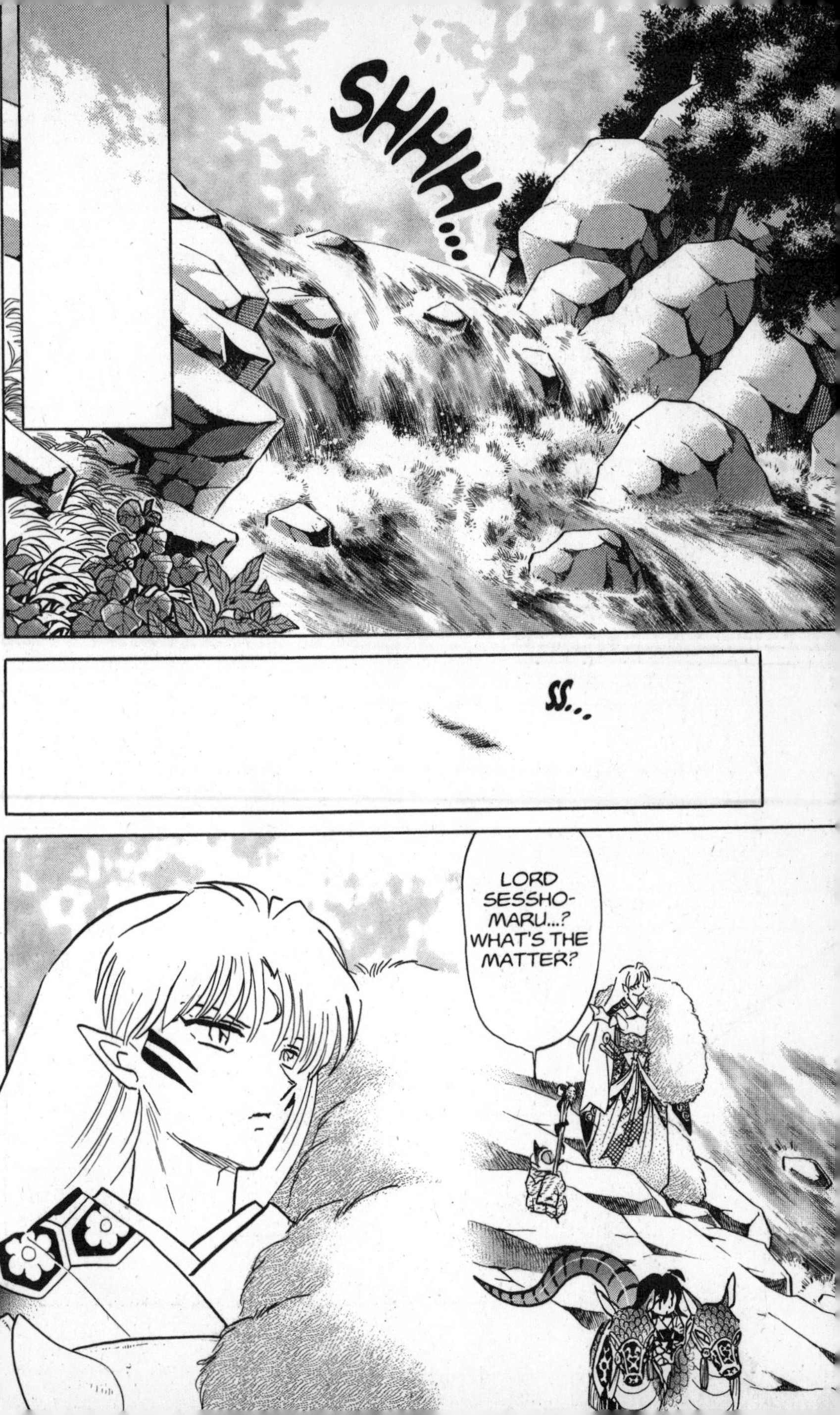
SHHH...
SS...
LORD SESSHO-MARU...? WHAT'S THE MATTER?

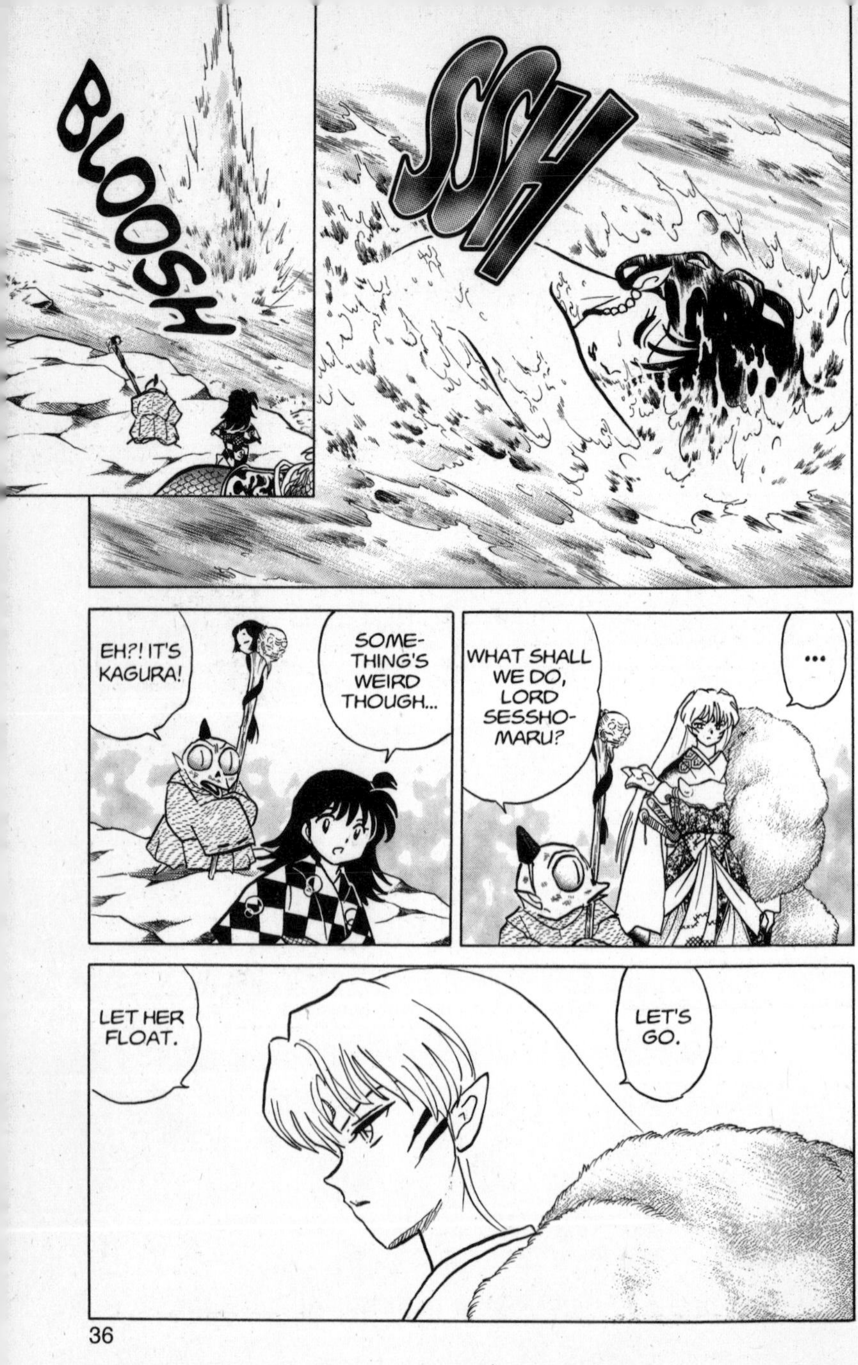
BLOOSH
SSSH
EH?! IT'S KAGURA!
SOME-THING'S WEIRD THOUGH...
WHAT SHALL WE DO, LORD SESSHO-MARU?
...
LET HER FLOAT.
LET'S GO.

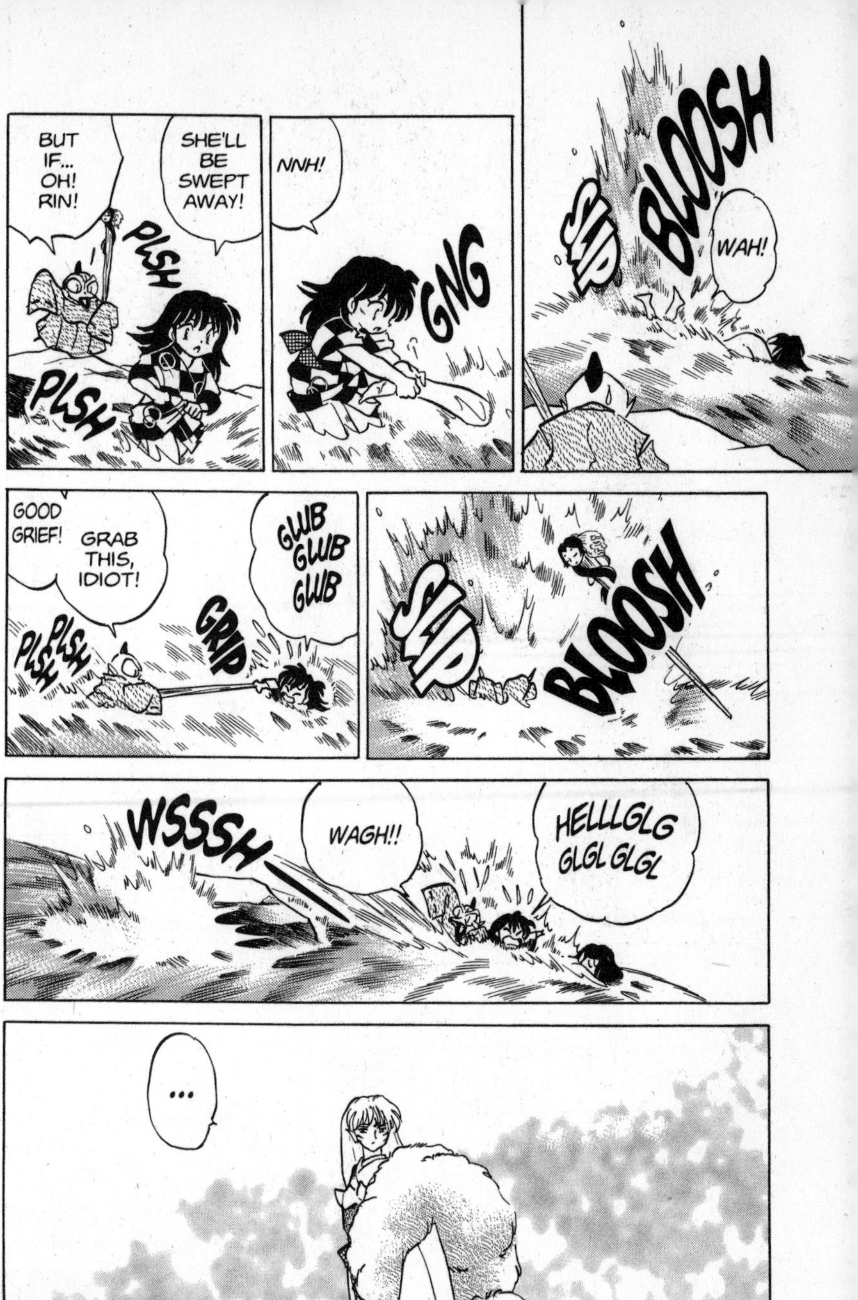

BUT IF... OH! RIN!
SHE'LL BE SWEPT AWAY!
PLSH
PLSH
NNH!
GNG
SLIP
BLOOSH
WAH!
GOOD GRIEF!
GRAB THIS, IDIOT!
PLSH PLSH
GRIP
GLUB GLUB GLUB
SLIP
BLOOSH
WSSSH
WAGH!!
HELLLGLG GLGL GLGL
...

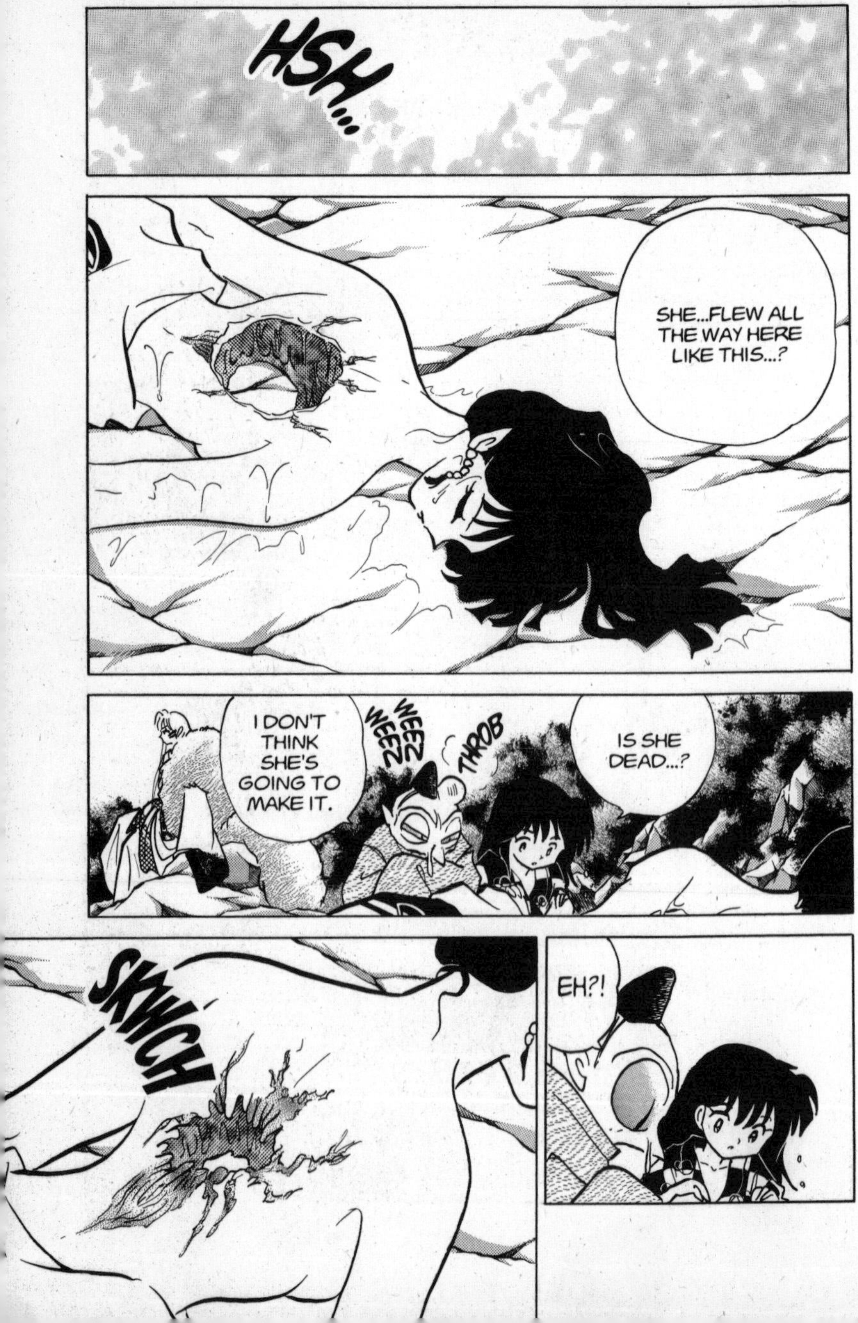
HSH...
SHE...FLEW ALL THE WAY HERE LIKE THIS...?
I DON'T THINK SHE'S GOING TO MAKE IT.
WEEZ WEEZ
THROB
IS SHE DEAD...?
SKWCH
EH?!

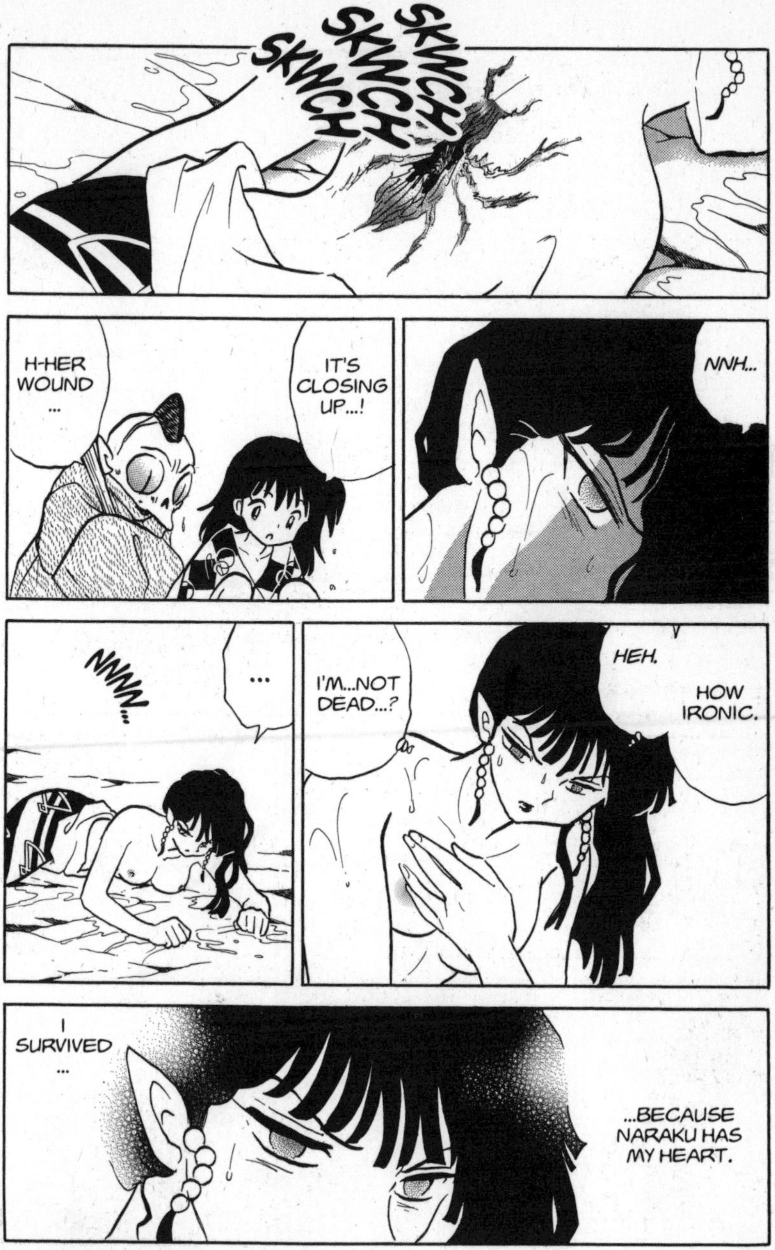
SKWCH SKWCH SKWCH
H-HER WOUND ...
IT'S CLOSING UP...!
NNH...
NNNN...
...
I'M...NOT DEAD...?
HEH.
HOW IRONIC.
I SURVIVED ...
...BECAUSE NARAKU HAS MY HEART.

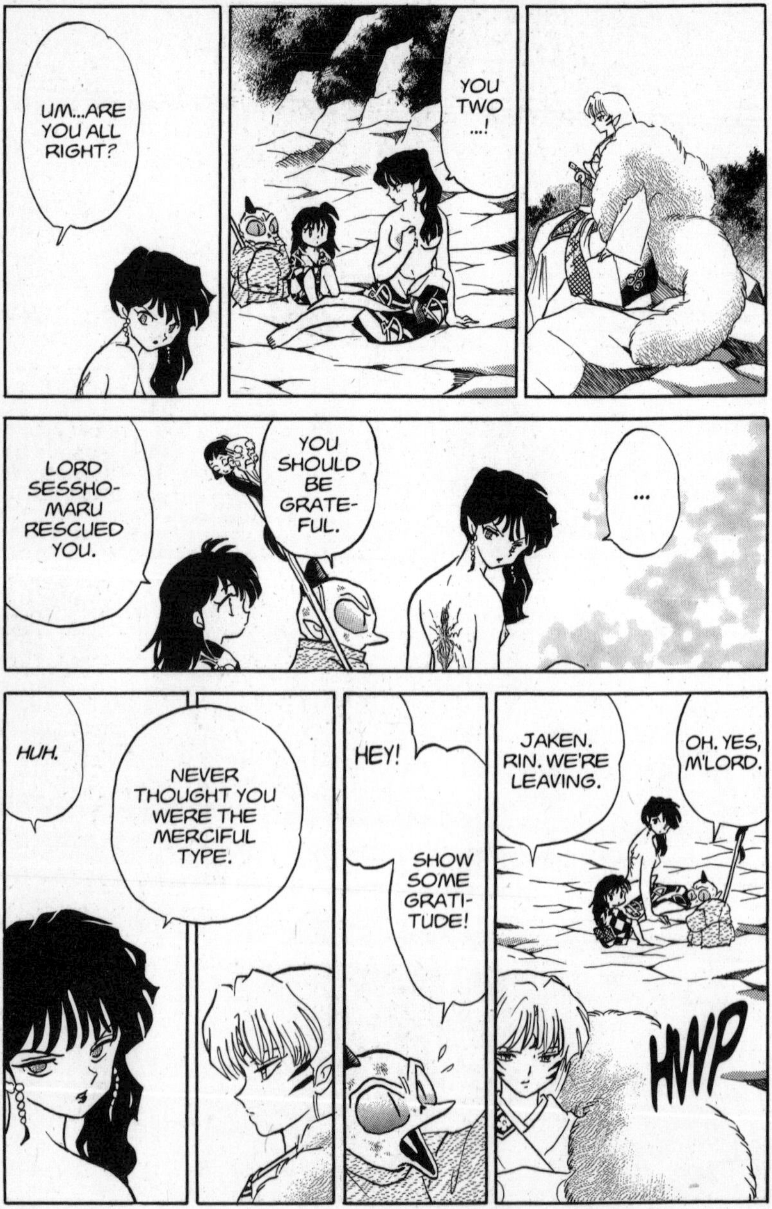
UM...ARE YOU ALL RIGHT?
YOU TWO ...!
LORD SESSHOMARU RESCUED YOU.
YOU SHOULD BE GRATEFUL.
...
HUH.
NEVER THOUGHT YOU WERE THE MERCIFUL TYPE.
HEY!
SHOW SOME GRATITUDE!
JAKEN. RIN. WE'RE LEAVING.
OH. YES, M'LORD.
HWP

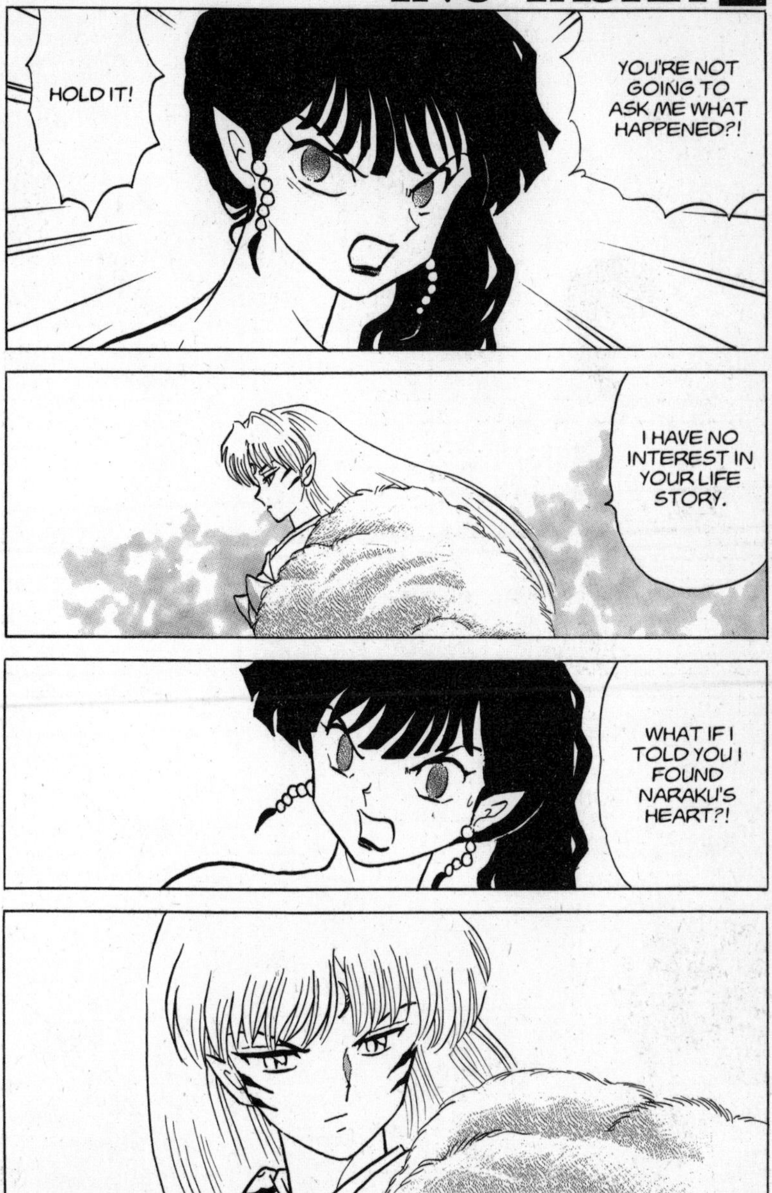
HOLD IT!
YOU'RE NOT GOING TO ASK ME WHAT HAPPENED?!
I HAVE NO INTEREST IN YOUR LIFE STORY.
WHAT IF I TOLD YOU I FOUND NARAKU'S HEART?!

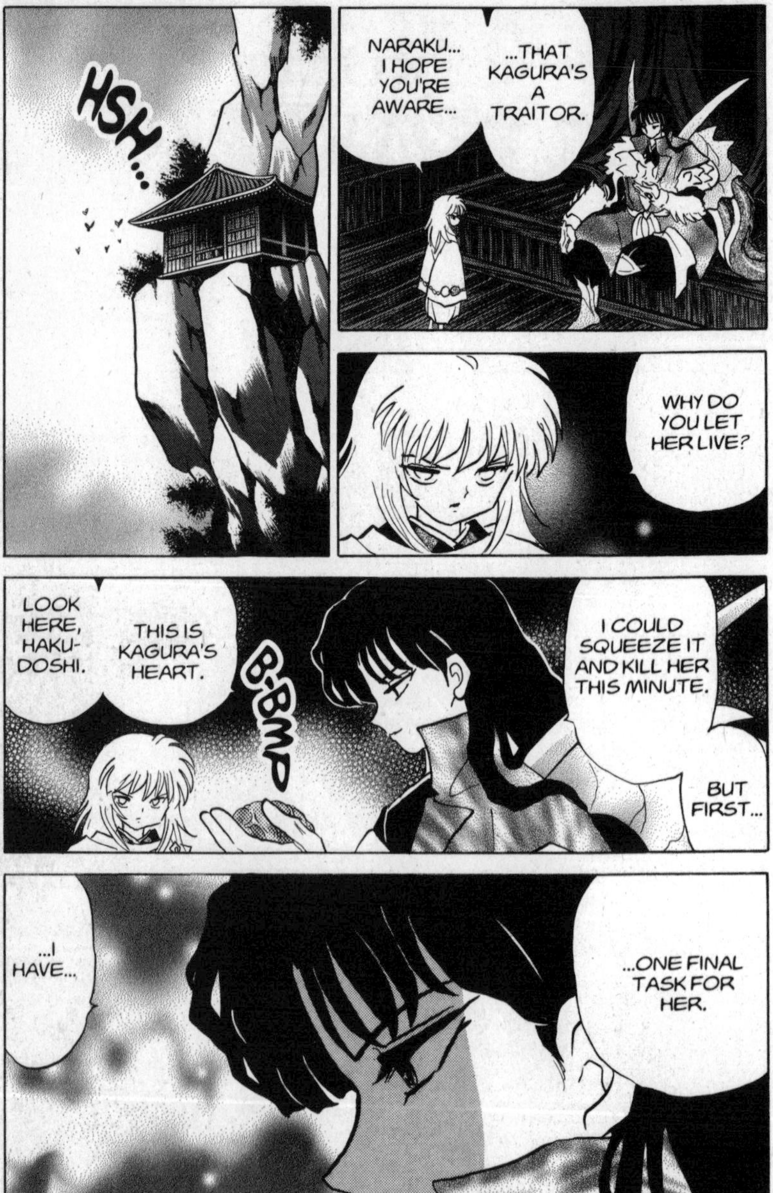
HSH...
NARAKU... I HOPE YOU'RE AWARE...
...THAT KAGURA'S A TRAITOR.
WHY DO YOU LET HER LIVE?
LOOK HERE, HAKU-DOSHI.
THIS IS KAGURA'S HEART.
B-BMP
I COULD SQUEEZE IT AND KILL HER THIS MINUTE.
BUT FIRST...
...I HAVE...
...ONE FINAL TASK FOR HER.

SCROLL 3
THE RAKANZO

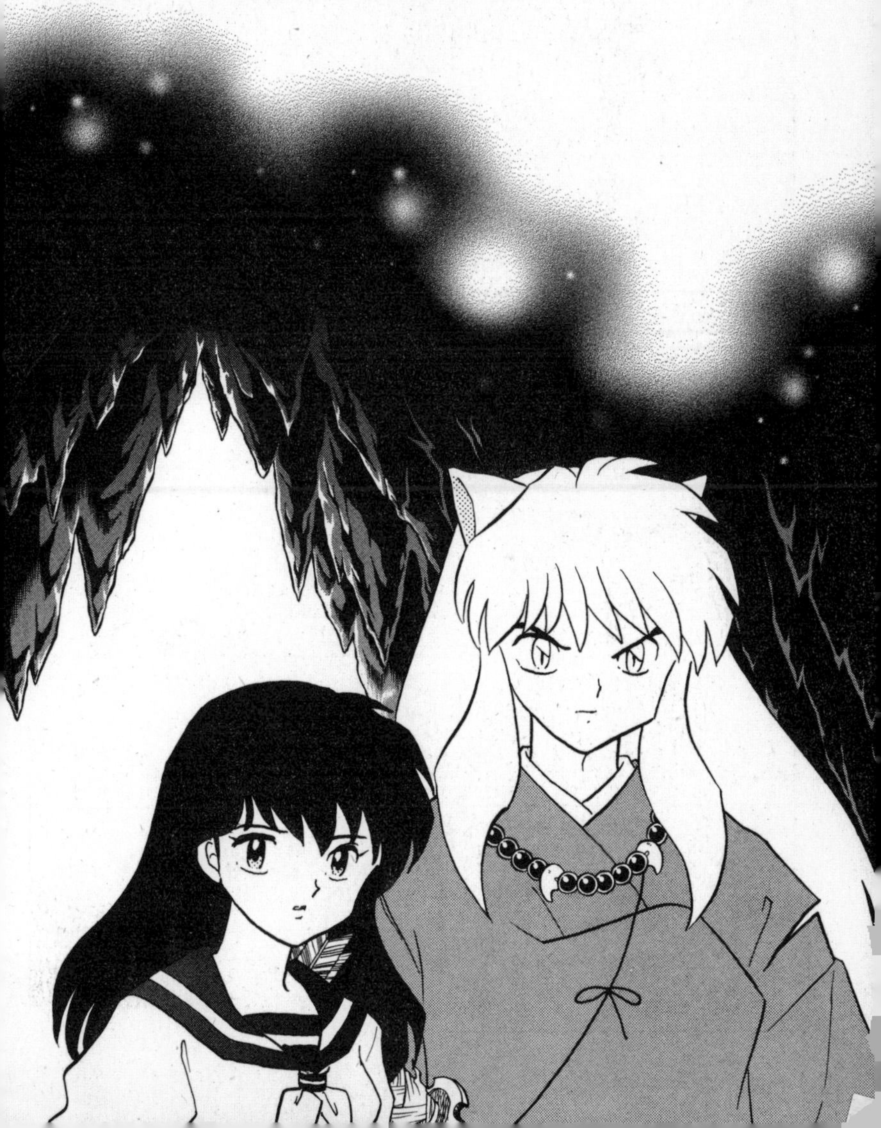

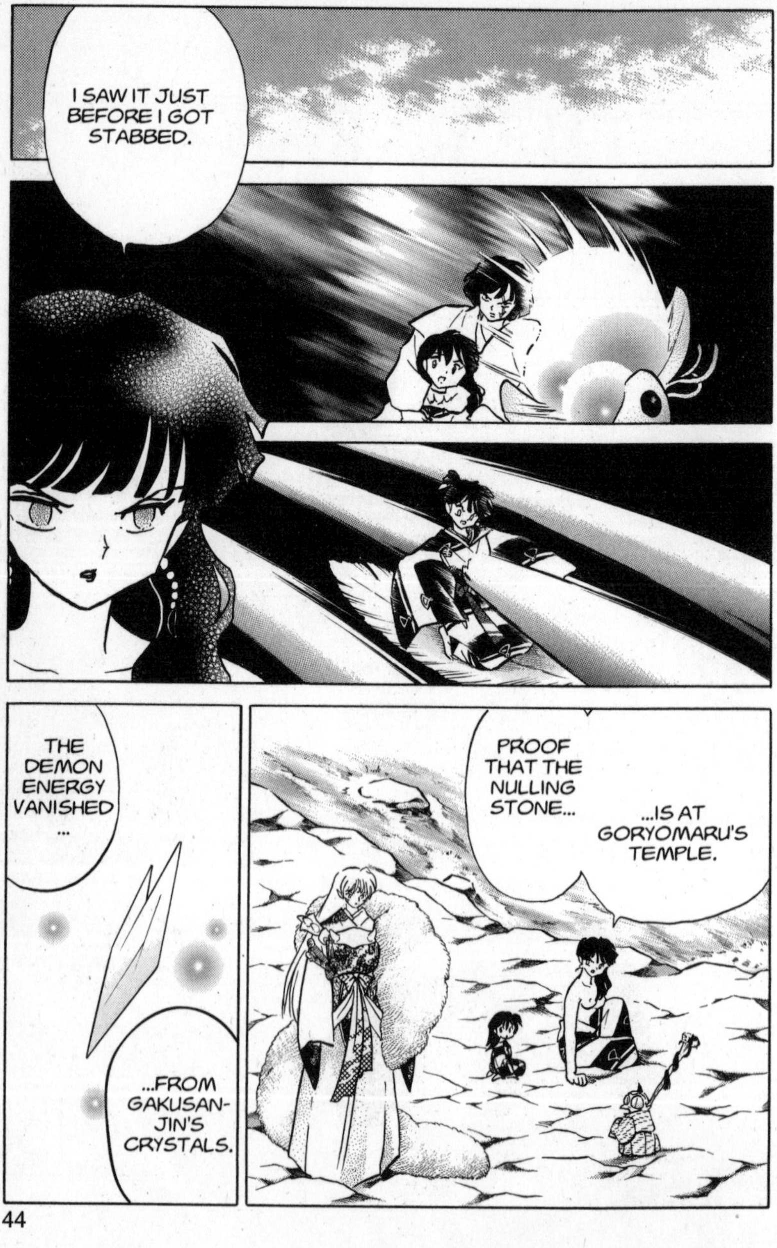
I SAW IT JUST BEFORE I GOT STABBED.
THE DEMON ENERGY VANISHED ...
...FROM GAKUSAN-JIN'S CRYSTALS.
PROOF THAT THE NULLING STONE...
...IS AT GORYOMARU'S TEMPLE.

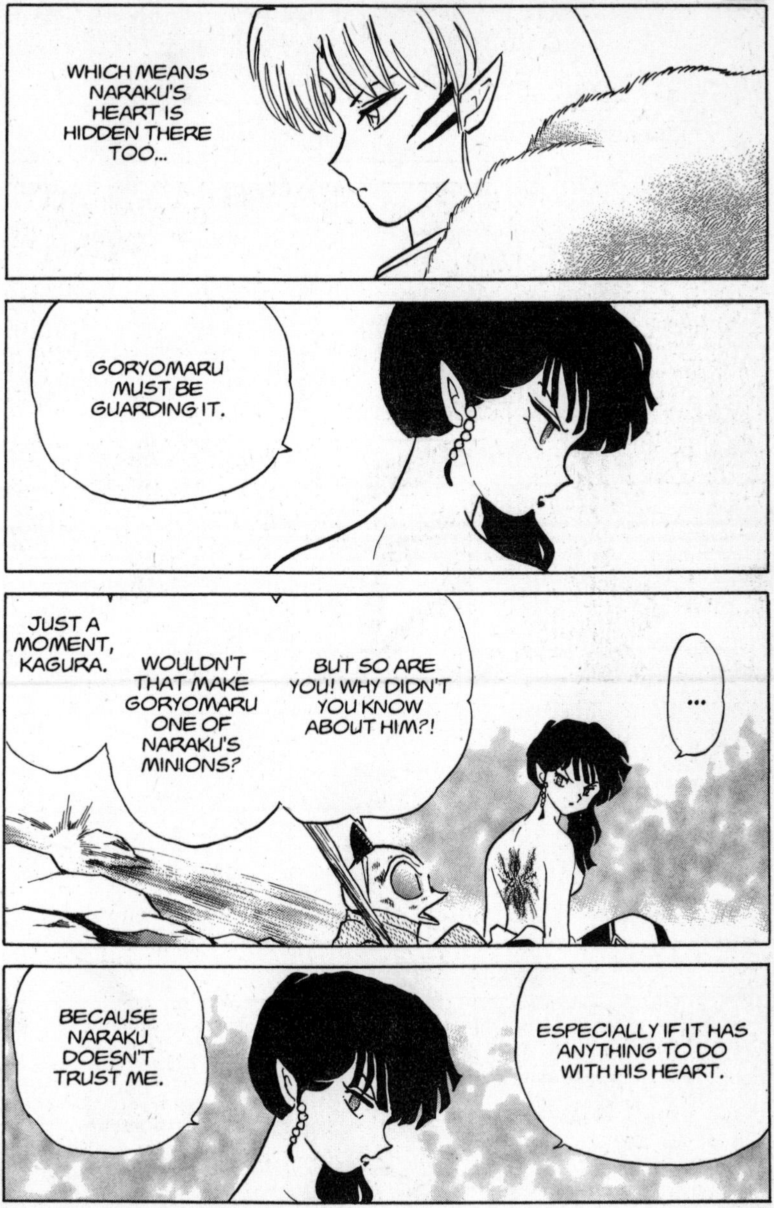
WHICH MEANS NARAKU'S HEART IS HIDDEN THERE TOO...
GORYOMARU MUST BE GUARDING IT.
JUST A MOMENT, KAGURA.
WOULDN'T THAT MAKE GORYOMARU ONE OF NARAKU'S MINIONS?
BUT SO ARE YOU! WHY DIDN'T YOU KNOW ABOUT HIM?!
...
BECAUSE NARAKU DOESN'T TRUST ME.
ESPECIALLY IF IT HAS ANYTHING TO DO WITH HIS HEART.

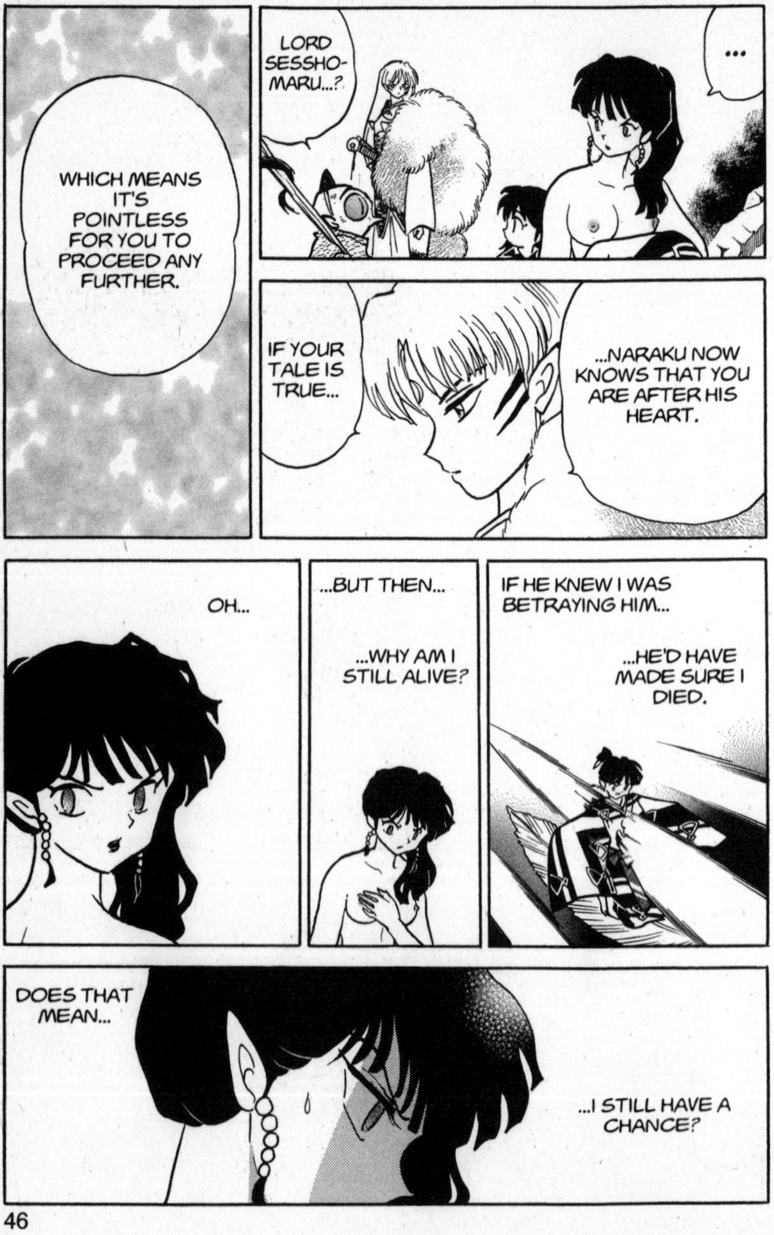
WHICH MEANS IT'S POINTLESS FOR YOU TO PROCEED ANY FURTHER.
LORD SESSHO-MARU...?
...
IF YOUR TALE IS TRUE...
...NARAKU NOW KNOWS THAT YOU ARE AFTER HIS HEART.
OH...
...BUT THEN...
...WHY AM I STILL ALIVE?
IF HE KNEW I WAS BETRAYING HIM...
...HE'D HAVE MADE SURE I DIED.
DOES THAT MEAN...
...I STILL HAVE A CHANCE?

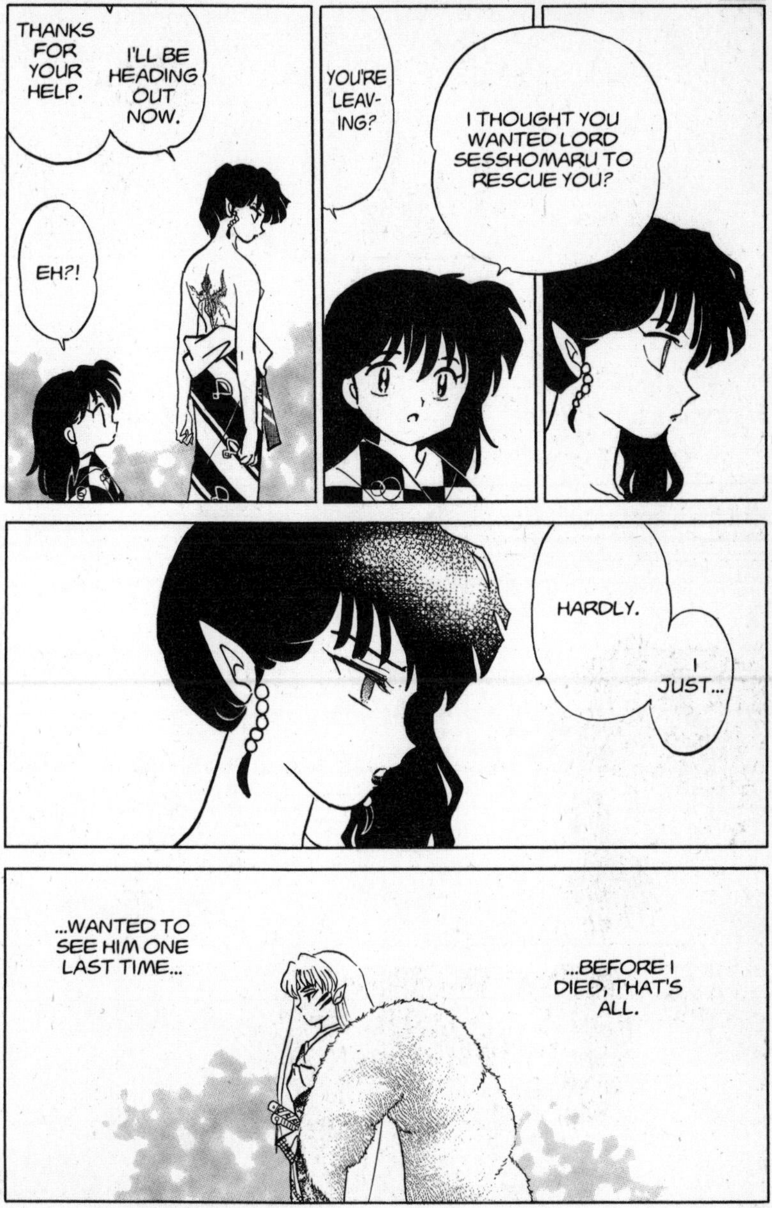
THANKS FOR YOUR HELP.
I'LL BE HEADING OUT NOW.
EH?!
YOU'RE LEAV-ING?
I THOUGHT YOU WANTED LORD SESSHOMARU TO RESCUE YOU?
HARDLY.
I JUST...
...WANTED TO SEE HIM ONE LAST TIME...
...BEFORE I DIED, THAT'S ALL.

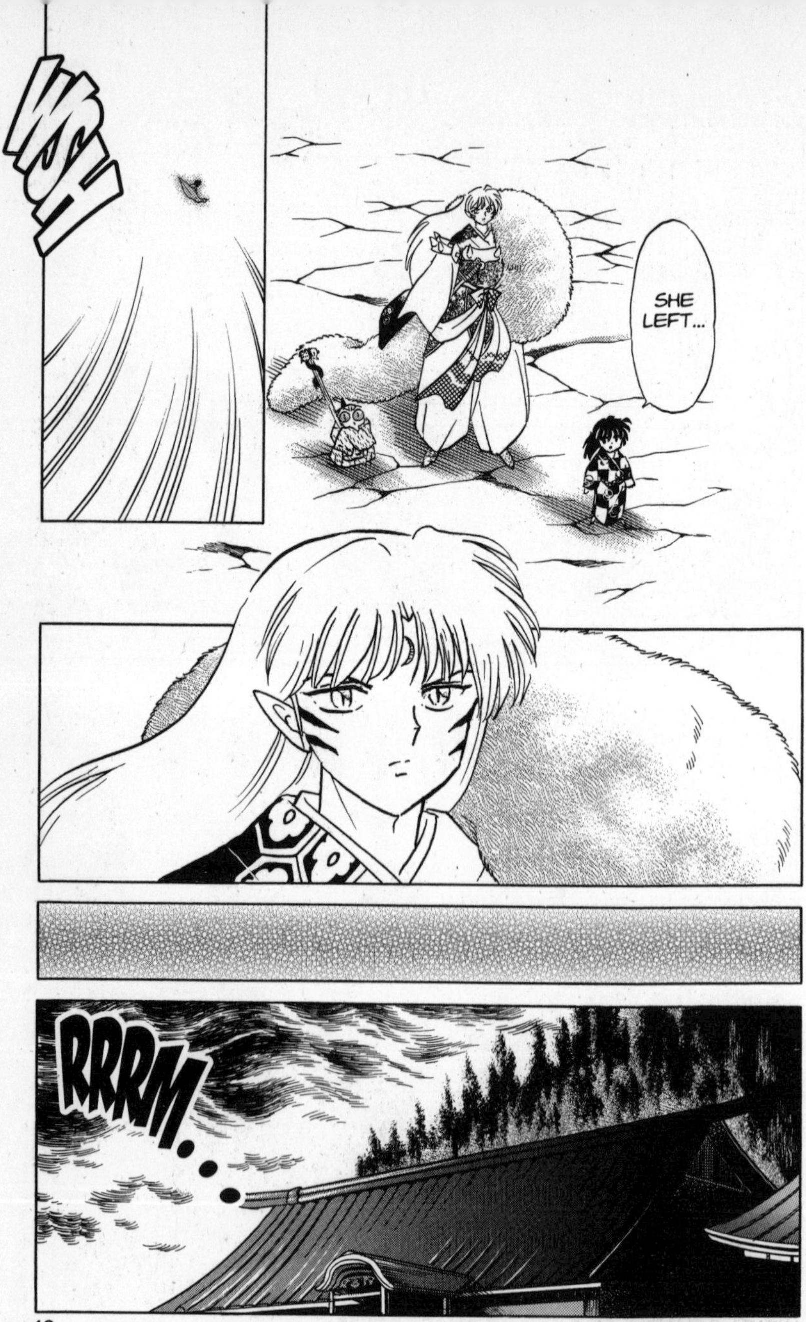
WSH!
SHE LEFT...
RRRM...

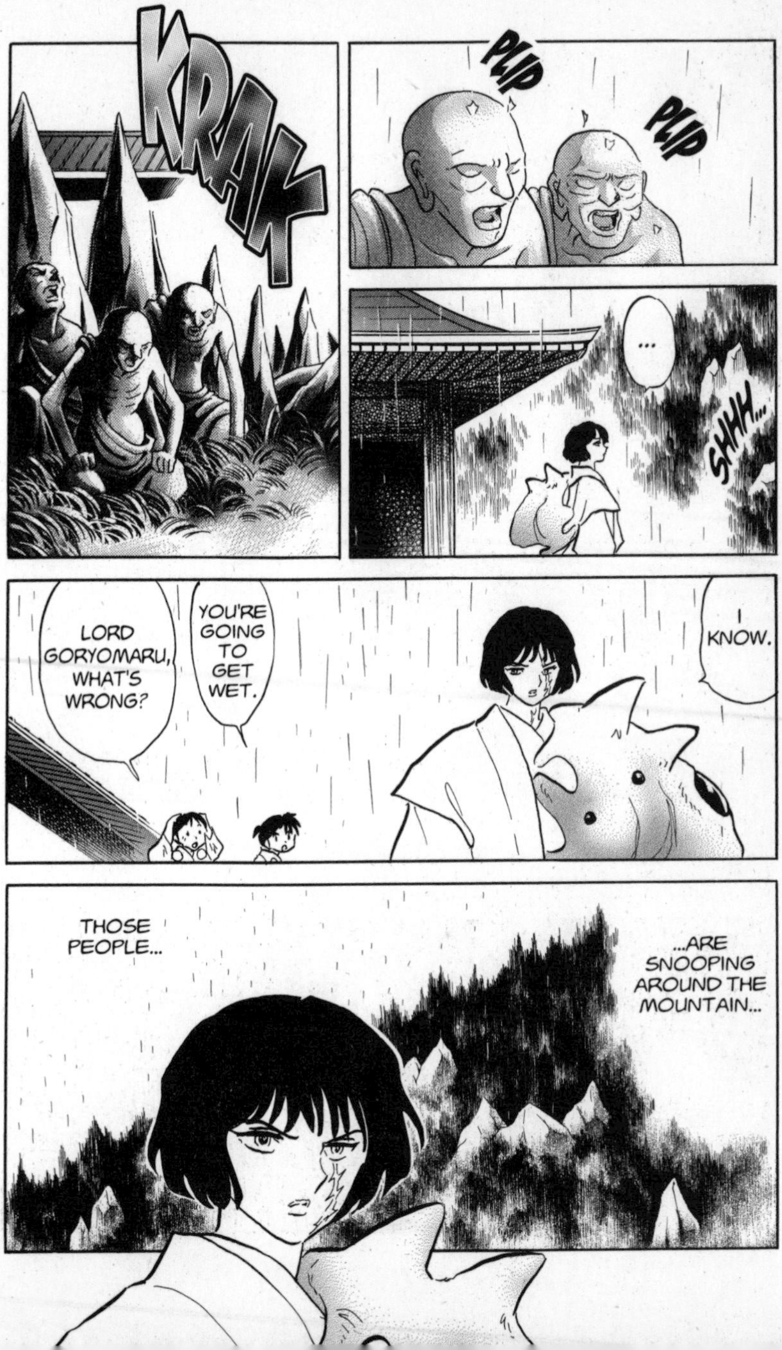
KRAK
PLIP
PLIP
...
SHHH...
LORD GORYOMARU, WHAT'S WRONG?
YOU'RE GOING TO GET WET.
I KNOW.
THOSE PEOPLE...
...ARE SNOOPING AROUND THE MOUNTAIN...

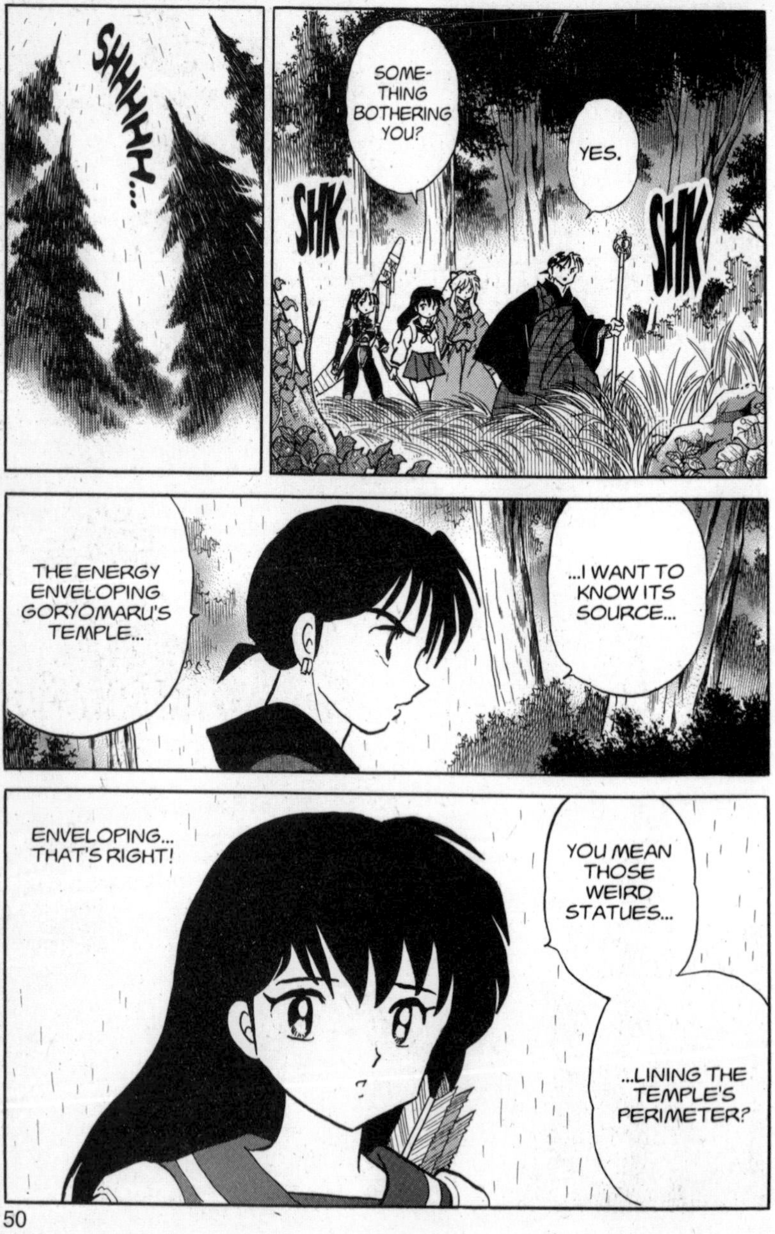
SHHHHH...
SOME-
THING
BOTHERING
YOU?
YES.
SHK
SHK
THE ENERGY ENVELOPING GORYOMARU'S TEMPLE...
...I WANT TO KNOW ITS SOURCE...
ENVELOPING... THAT'S RIGHT!
YOU MEAN THOSE WEIRD STATUES...
...LINING THE TEMPLE'S PERIMETER?

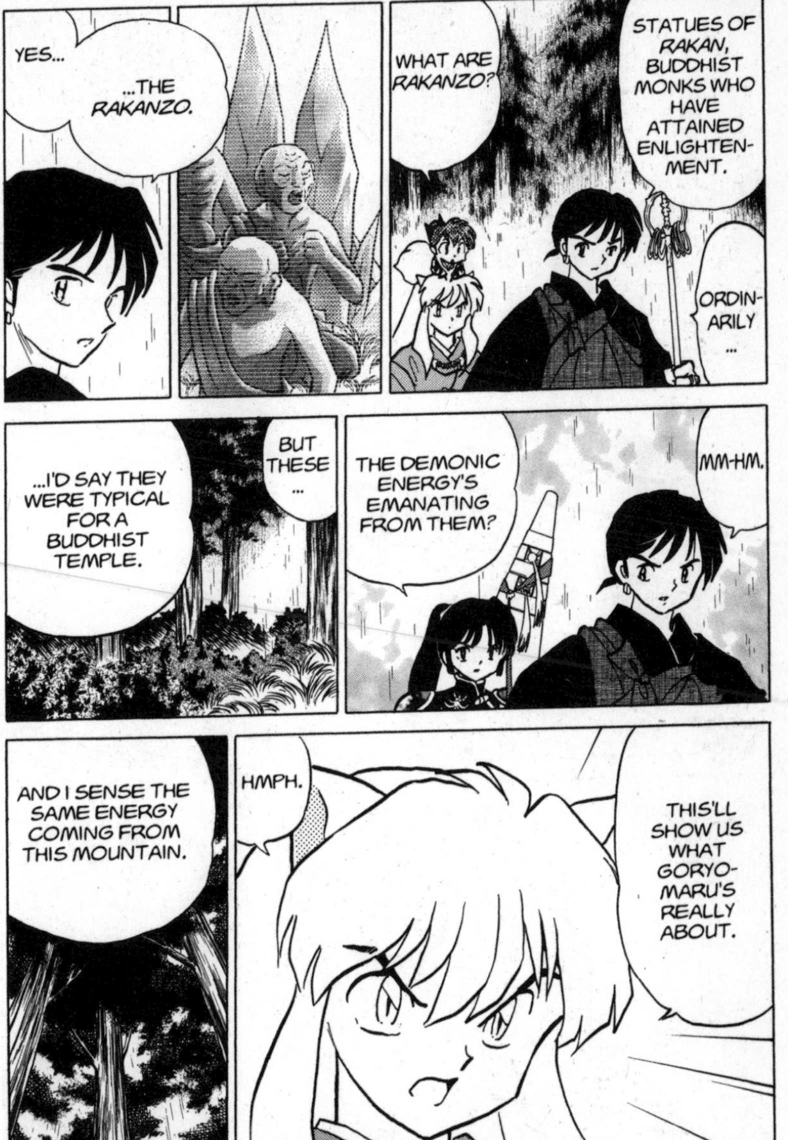
YES...
...THE *RAKANZO.*
WHAT ARE *RAKANZO?*
STATUES OF *RAKAN,* BUDDHIST MONKS WHO HAVE ATTAINED ENLIGHTENMENT.
ORDINARILY...
...I'D SAY THEY WERE TYPICAL FOR A BUDDHIST TEMPLE.
BUT THESE...
THE DEMONIC ENERGY'S EMANATING FROM THEM?
MM-HM.
AND I SENSE THE SAME ENERGY COMING FROM THIS MOUNTAIN.
HMPH.
THIS'LL SHOW US WHAT GORYOMARU'S REALLY ABOUT.

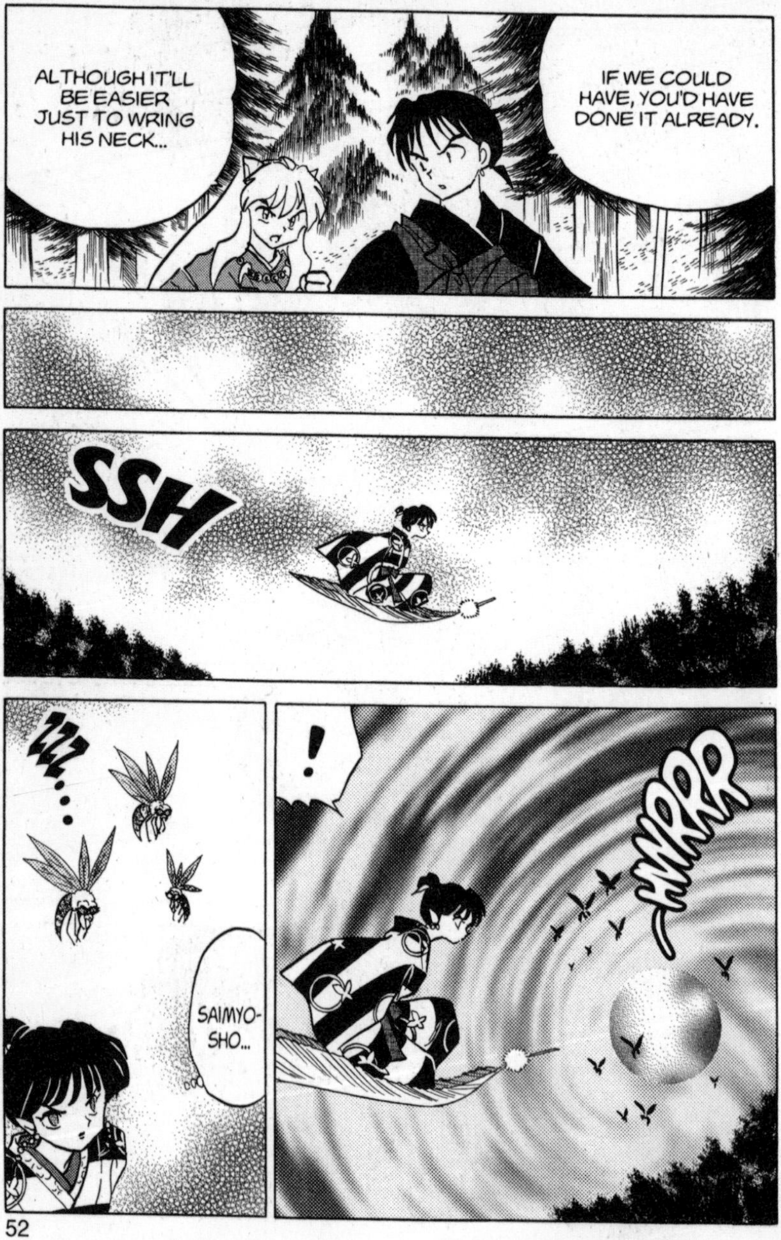

ALTHOUGH IT'LL BE EASIER JUST TO WRING HIS NECK...
IF WE COULD HAVE, YOU'D HAVE DONE IT ALREADY.
SSH
ZZZ...
SAIMYO-SHO...
!
HWRRR

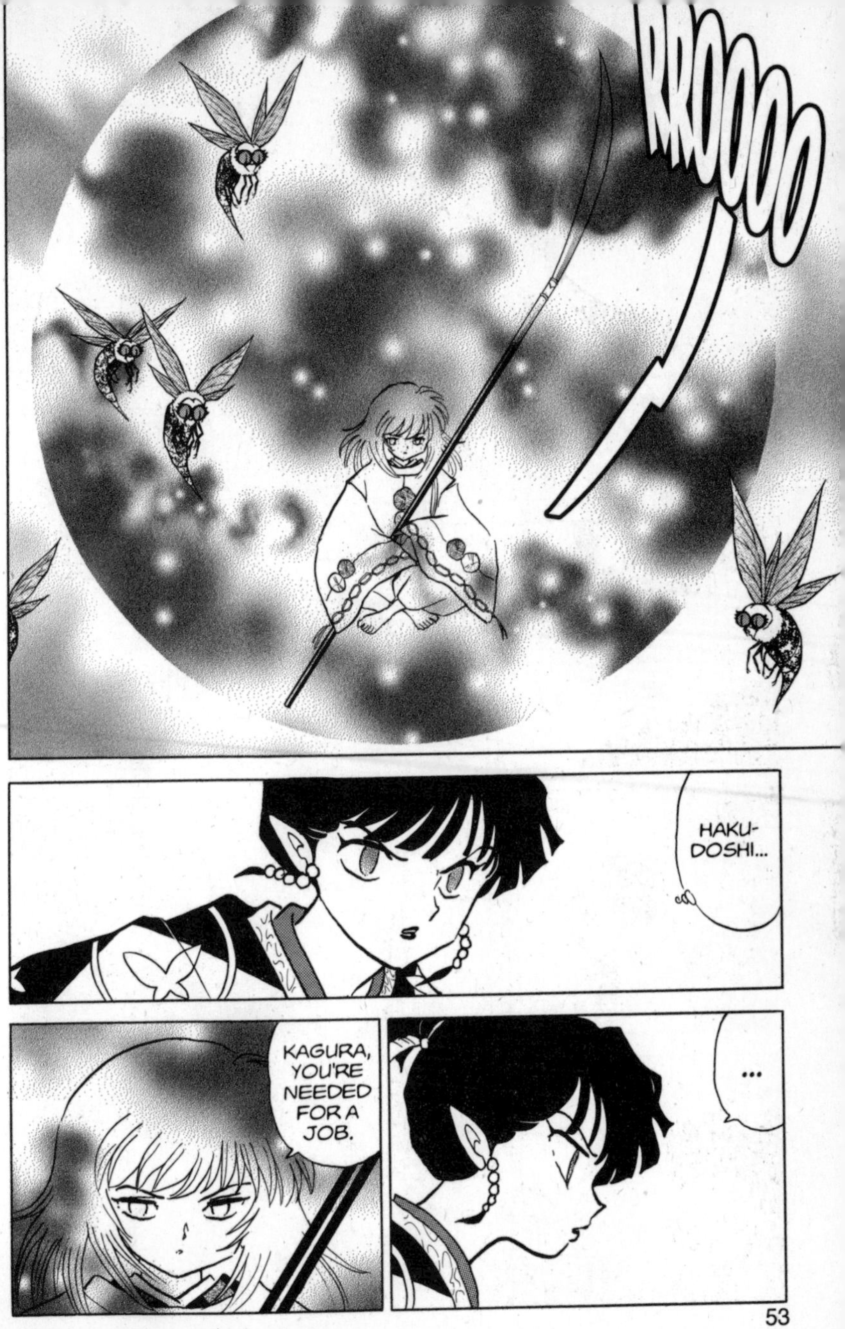
RROOOO
HAKU-DOSHI...
KAGURA, YOU'RE NEEDED FOR A JOB.
...

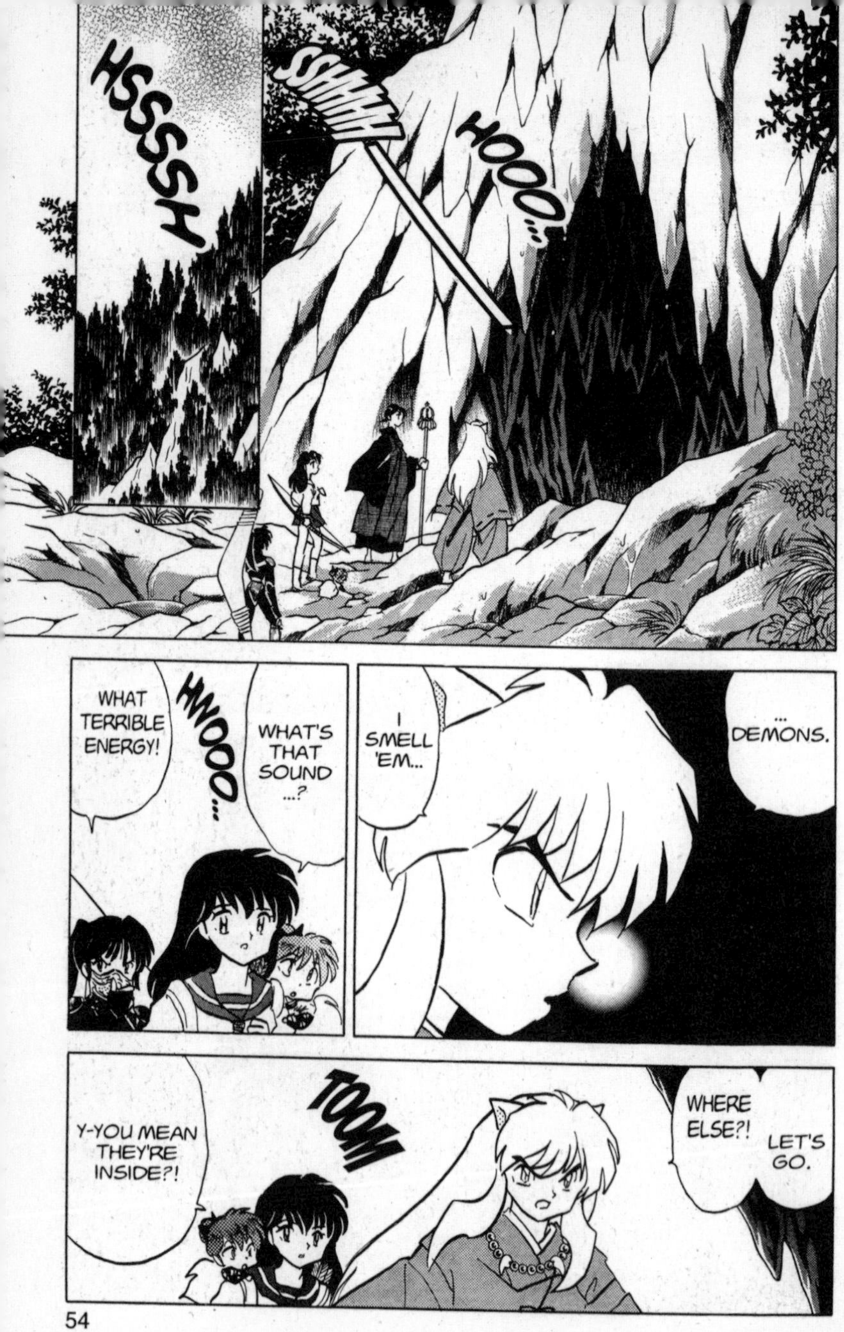
HSSSSH
SSHHH
HOOO...
WHAT TERRIBLE ENERGY!
HWOOOO...
WHAT'S THAT SOUND ...?
I SMELL 'EM...
... DEMONS.
Y-YOU MEAN THEY'RE INSIDE?!
TOOM
WHERE ELSE?!
LET'S GO.

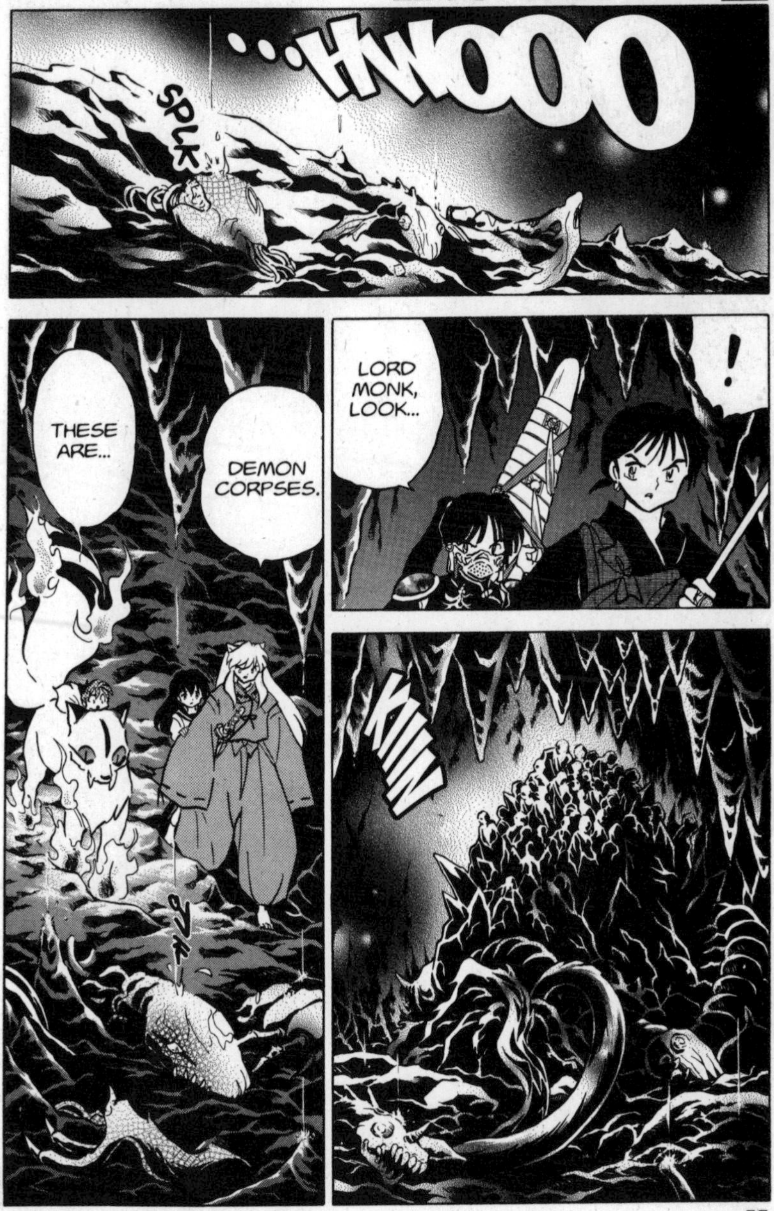
...HWOOO
SPLK
THESE ARE...
DEMON CORPSES.
LORD MONK, LOOK...
!
KWIIN

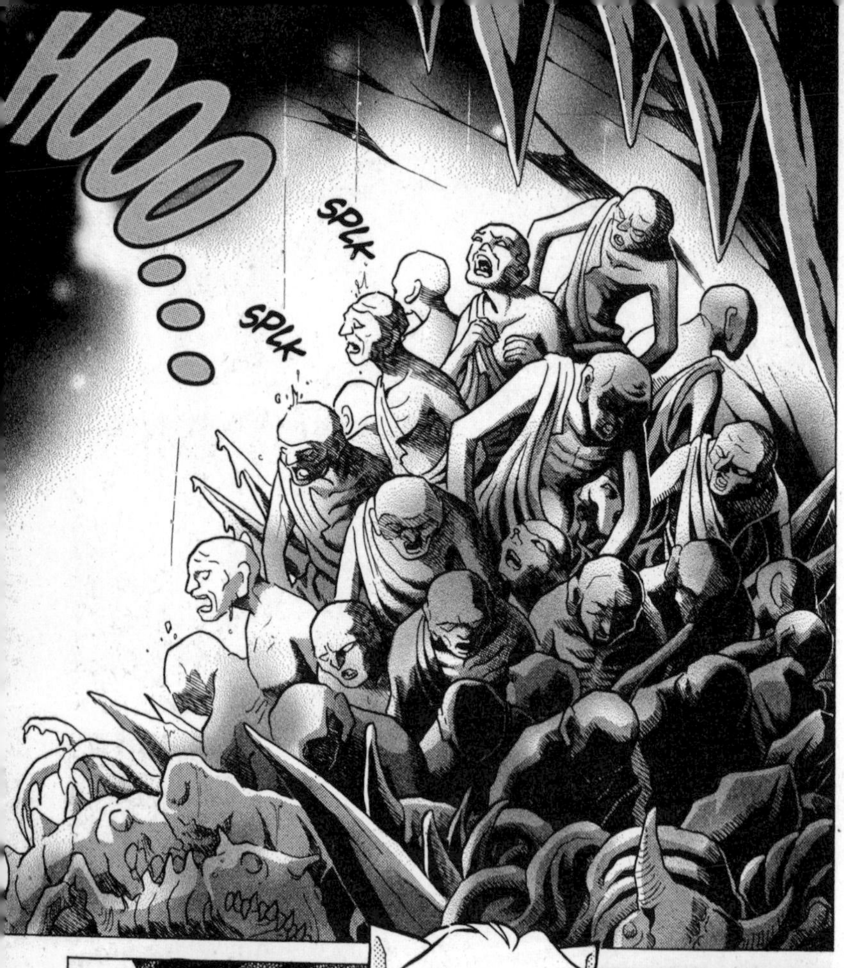
HOOOOOOO
SPLK
SPLK

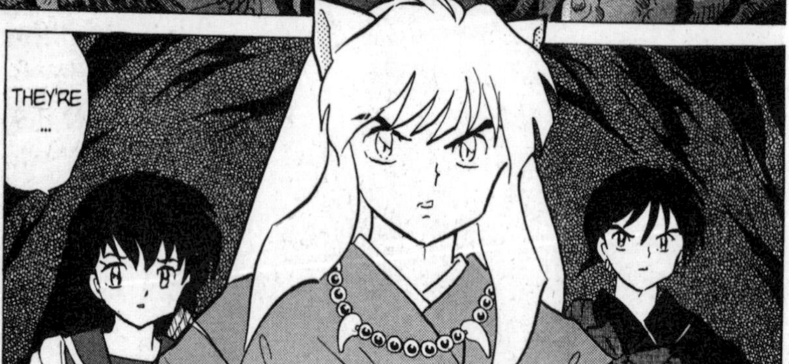
THEY'RE ...

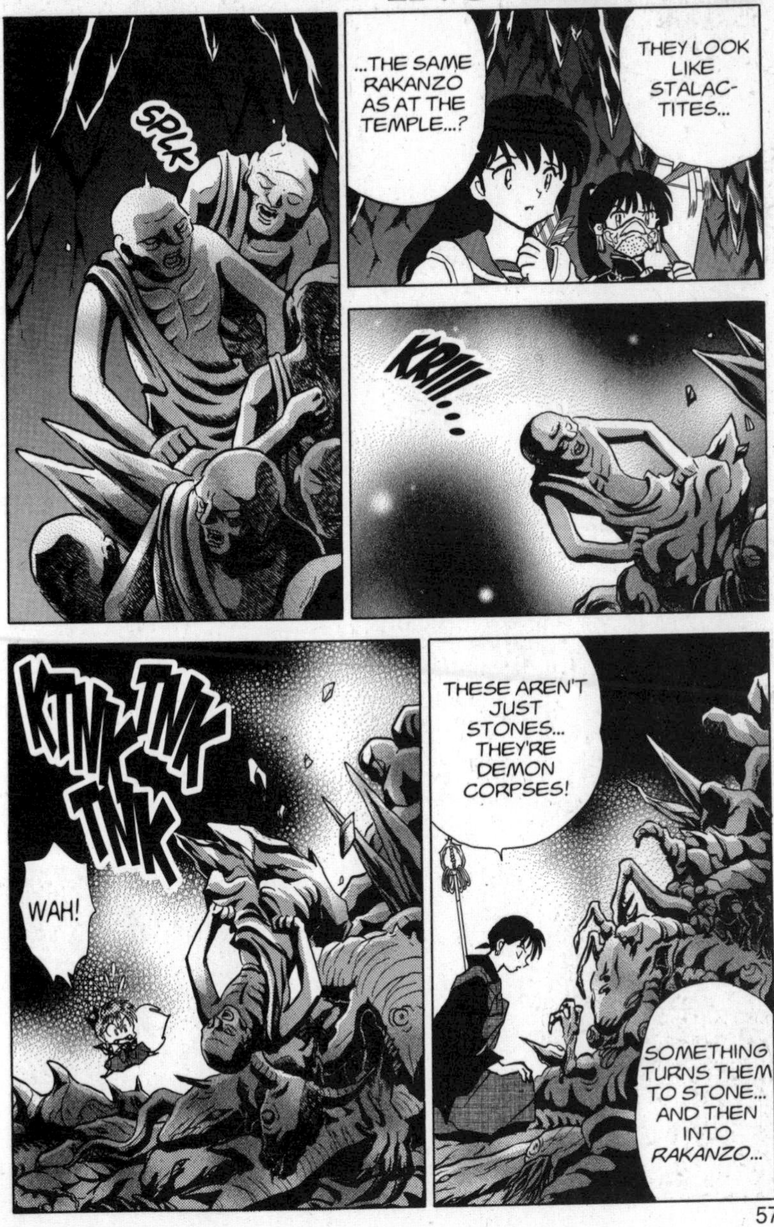
SPLK
...THE SAME RAKANZO AS AT THE TEMPLE...?
THEY LOOK LIKE STALACTITES...
KRIII...
KTINK TINK TINK
WAH!
THESE AREN'T JUST STONES... THEY'RE DEMON CORPSES!
SOMETHING TURNS THEM TO STONE... AND THEN INTO RAKANZO...

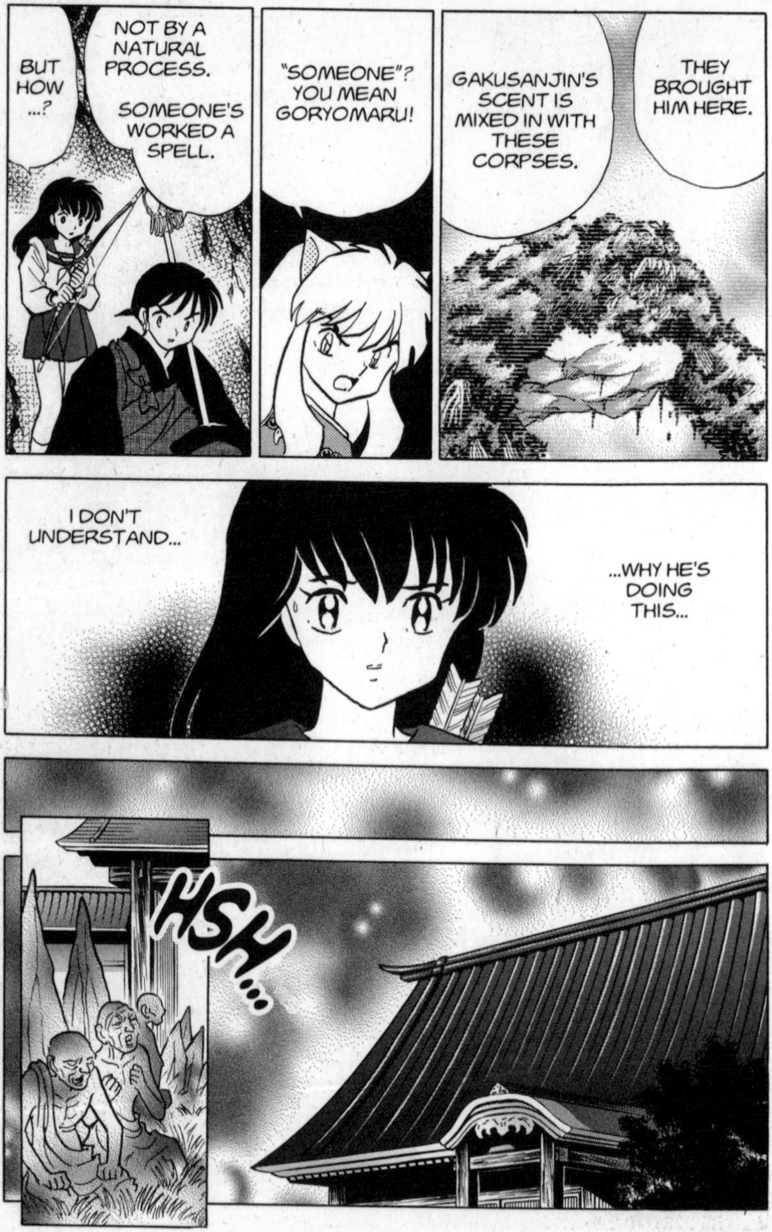
BUT HOW ...?
NOT BY A NATURAL PROCESS.
SOMEONE'S WORKED A SPELL.
"SOMEONE"? YOU MEAN GORYOMARU!
GAKUSANJIN'S SCENT IS MIXED IN WITH THESE CORPSES.
THEY BROUGHT HIM HERE.
I DON'T UNDERSTAND...
...WHY HE'S DOING THIS...
HSH...

THIS IS...

...

WHAT IS IT, KAGURA?

YOU KNOW THIS TEMPLE?

NO...

I GOTTA BE CAREFUL.

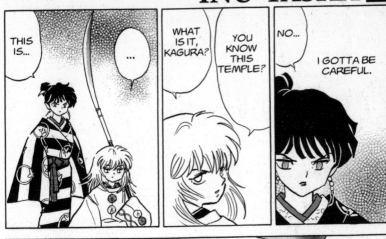

WE ENTRUSTED SOMETHING VALUABLE TO THIS TEMPLE.

BUT IT SEEMS INUYASHA AND THE OTHERS HAVE FERRETED IT OUT.

SOMETHING VALUABLE...?!

THEN HIS HEART *IS* HERE, AFTER ALL?!

FREEZE!

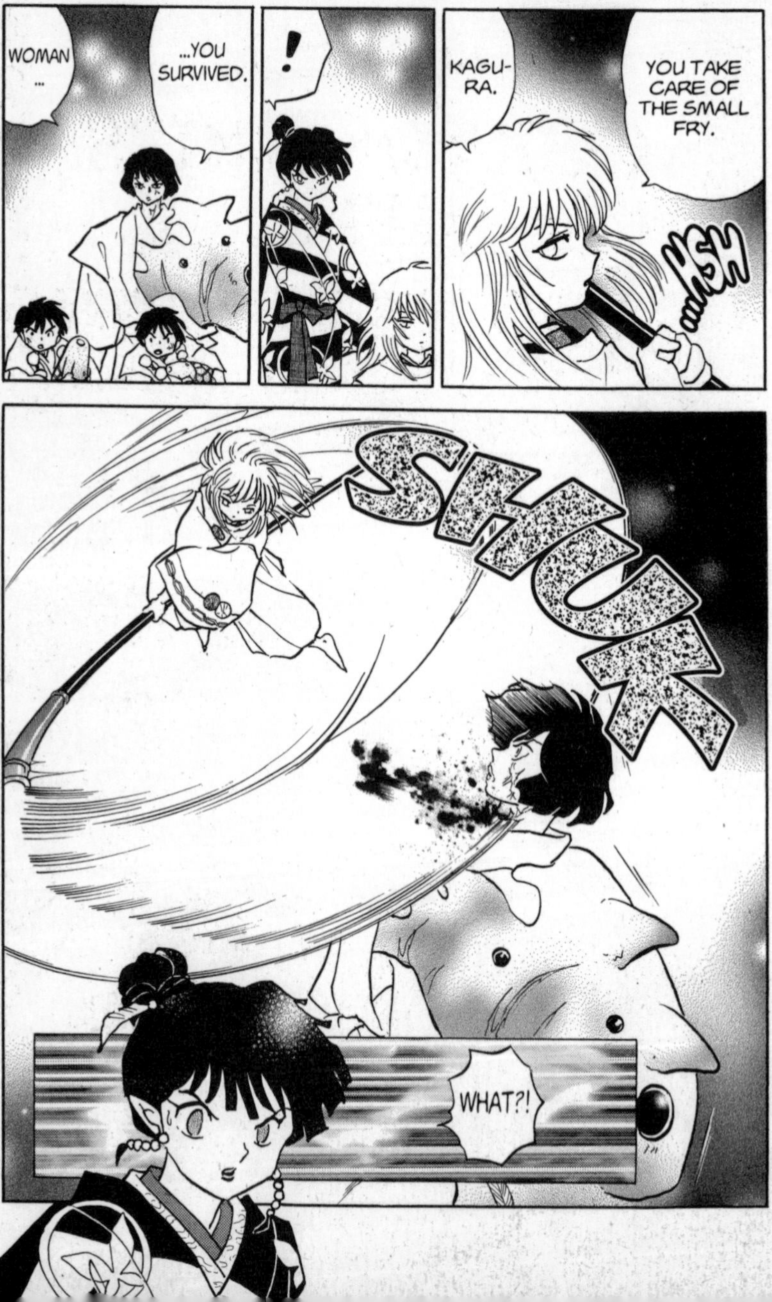

WOMAN ...
...YOU SURVIVED.
!
KAGU-RA.
YOU TAKE CARE OF THE SMALL FRY.
WHOOSH
SHUNK
WHAT?!

SCROLL 4

GORYOMARU'S FATE

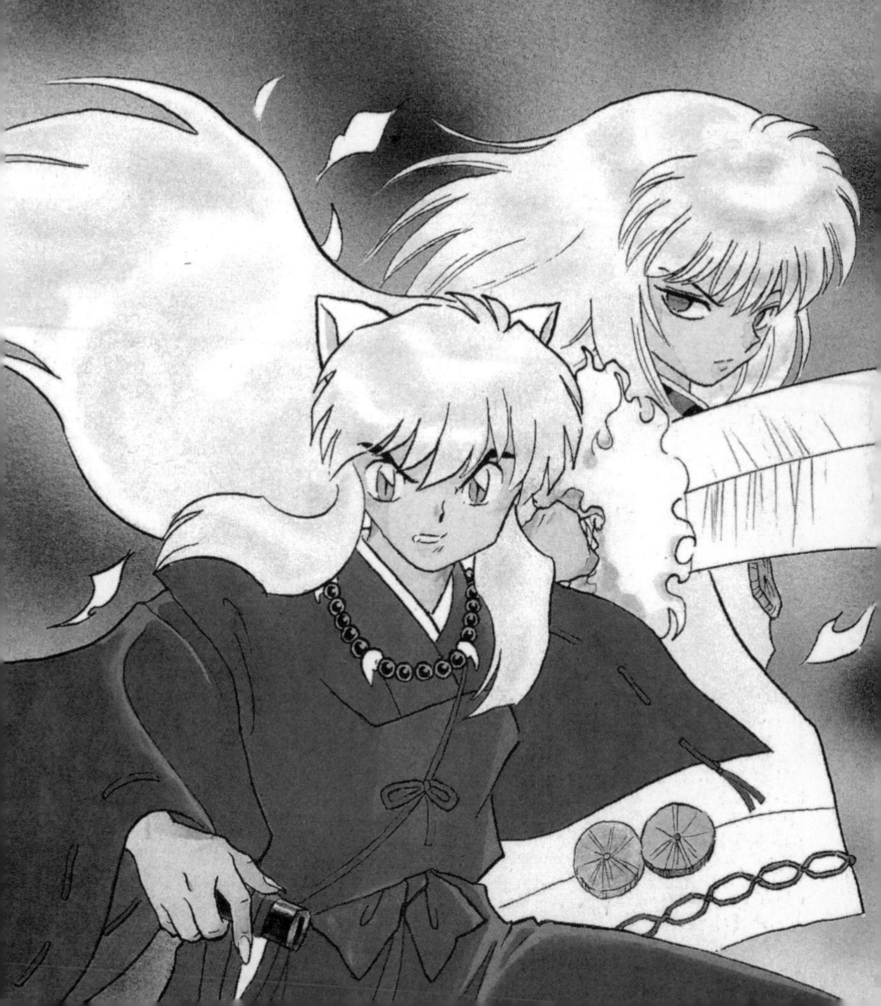

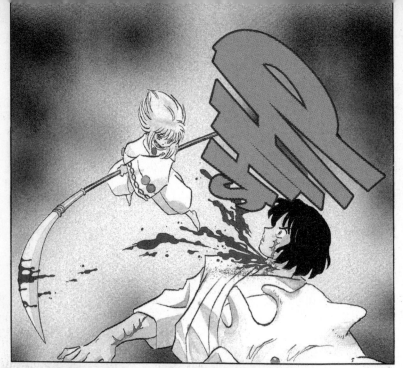

OH...!

...

L-LORD GORYOMARU!

NGH...

MWK MWK

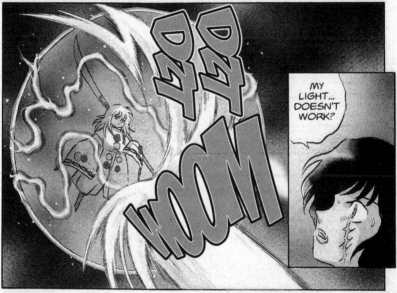

MY LIGHT... DOESN'T WORK?

PEH.

SUCH A PUNY ATTACK.

63

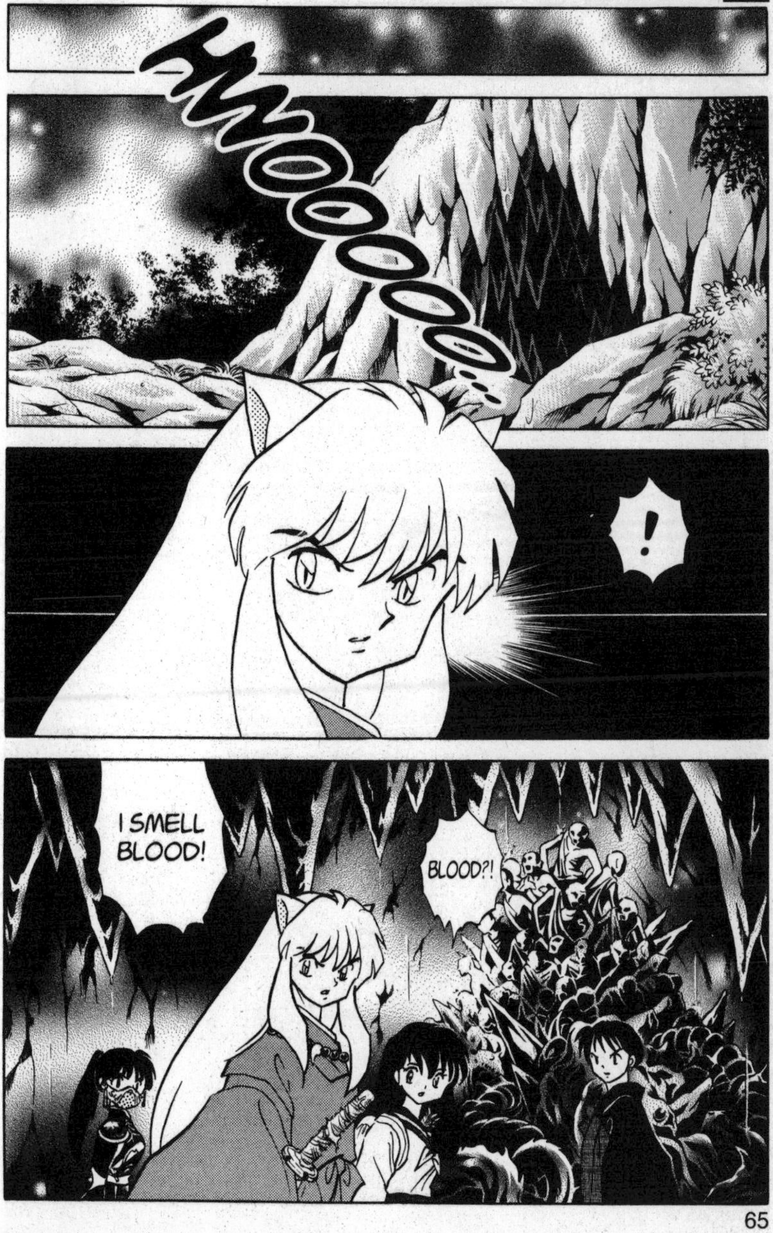
HMMOOOOOO...
!
I SMELL BLOOD!
BLOOD?!

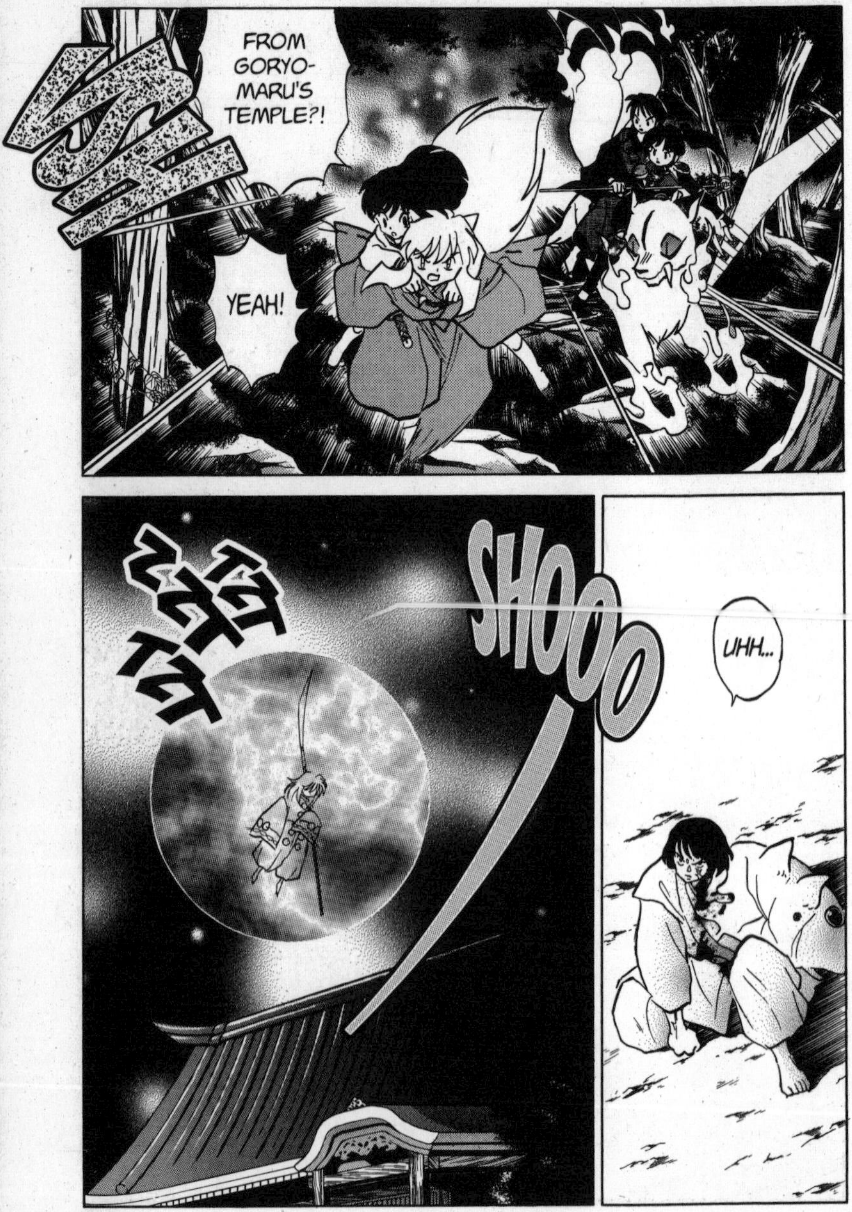
FROM GORYO-MARU'S TEMPLE?!
YEAH!
SHOOO
UHH...

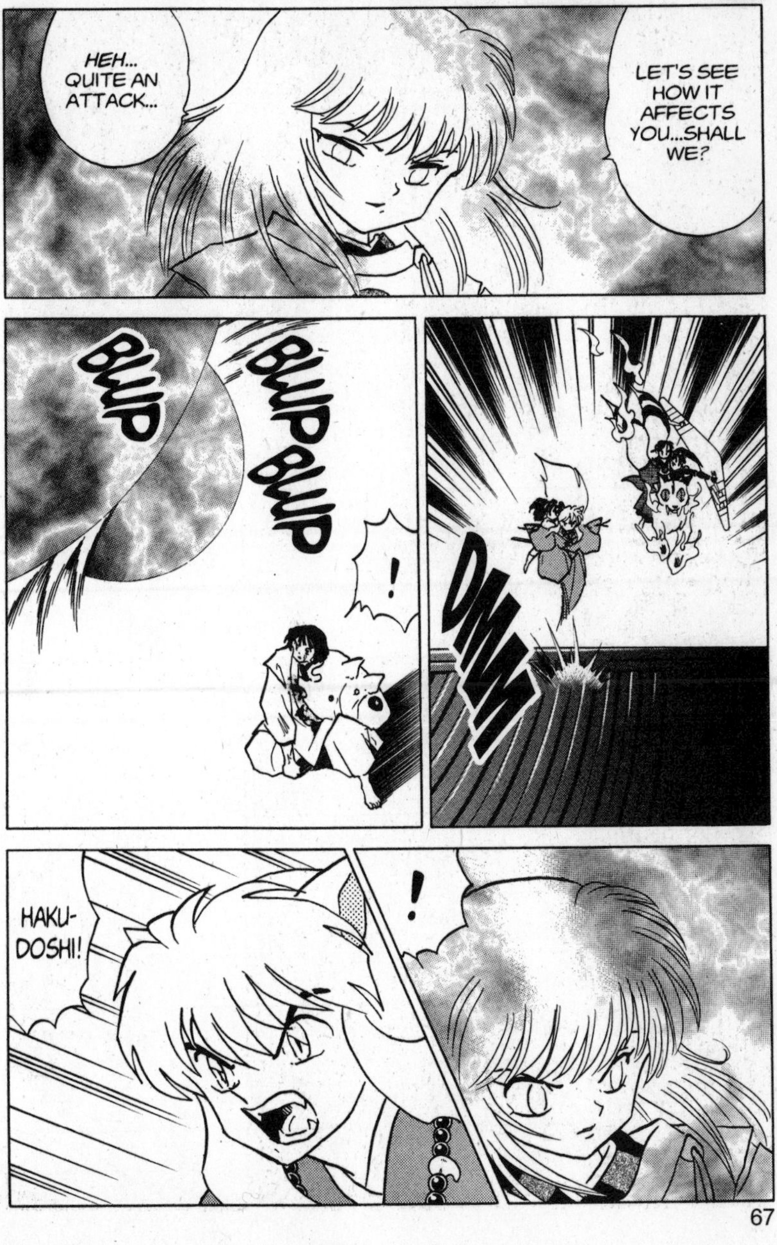
HEH... QUITE AN ATTACK...
LET'S SEE HOW IT AFFECTS YOU...SHALL WE?
BWUP
BWUP BWUP
!
DMM
HAKU-DOSHI!
!

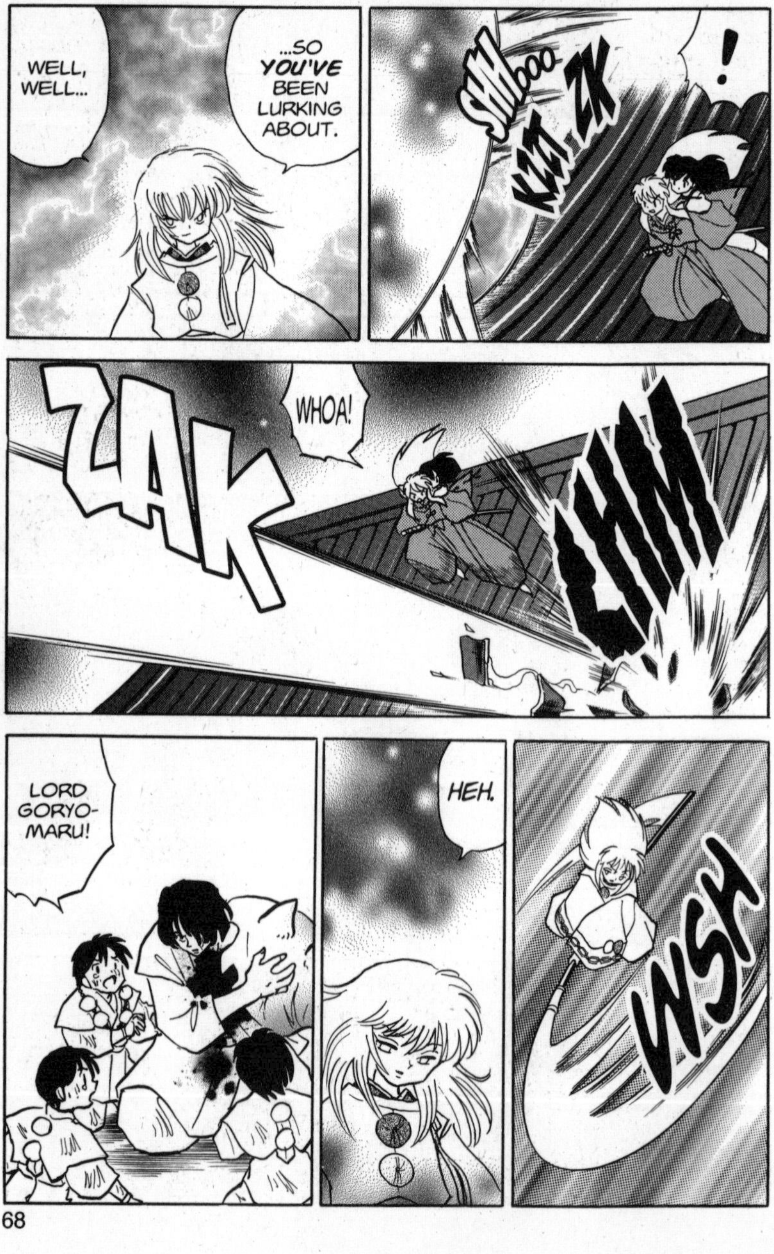
WELL, WELL...
...SO YOU'VE BEEN LURKING ABOUT.
SHOOO
KLIT ZK
!
ZAK
WHOA!
CHM
LORD GORYO-MARU!
HEH.
WSH

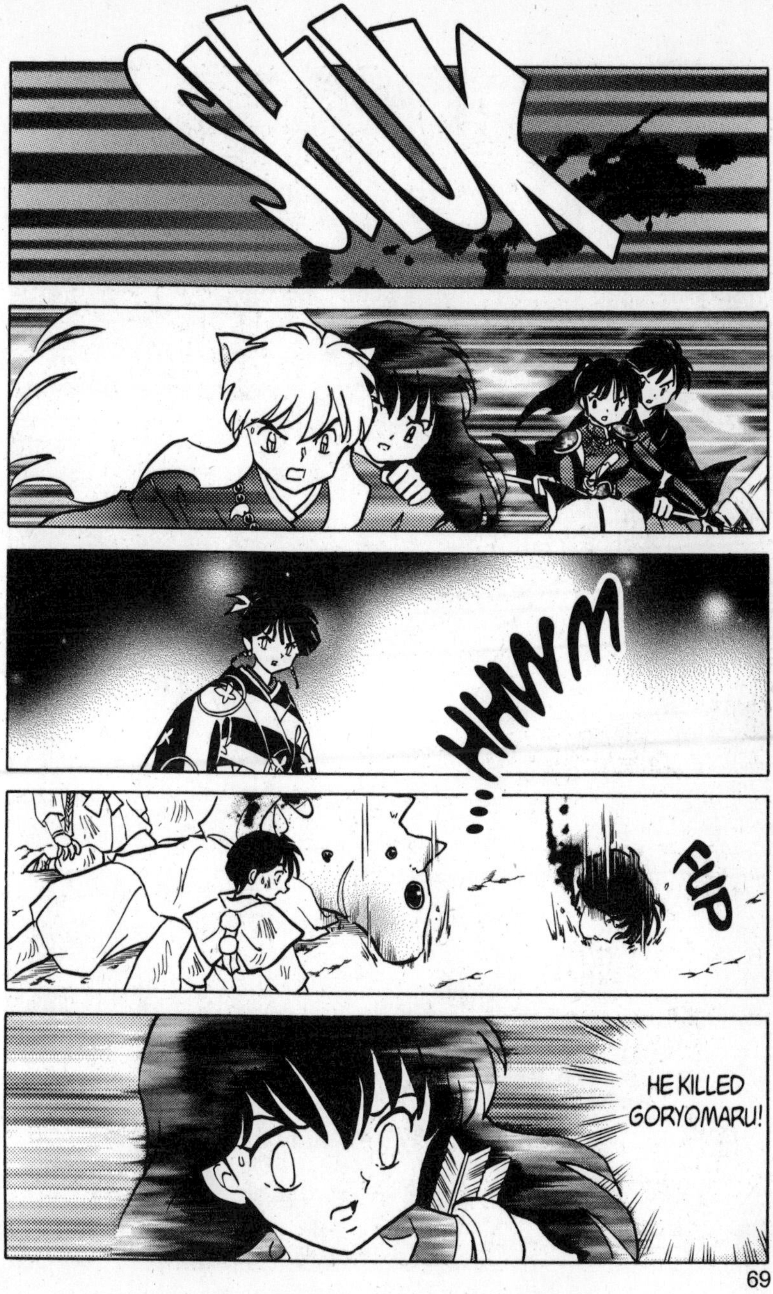
SHUK
FUP
HE KILLED GORYOMARU!

KANNA
...?

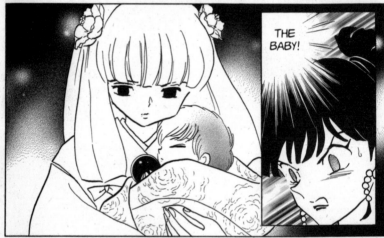

THE BABY!

HE **WAS** HERE, JUST LIKE I THOUGHT!!

DAMN IT!

INUYASHA, LOOK...!

NARAKU'S INFANT?!

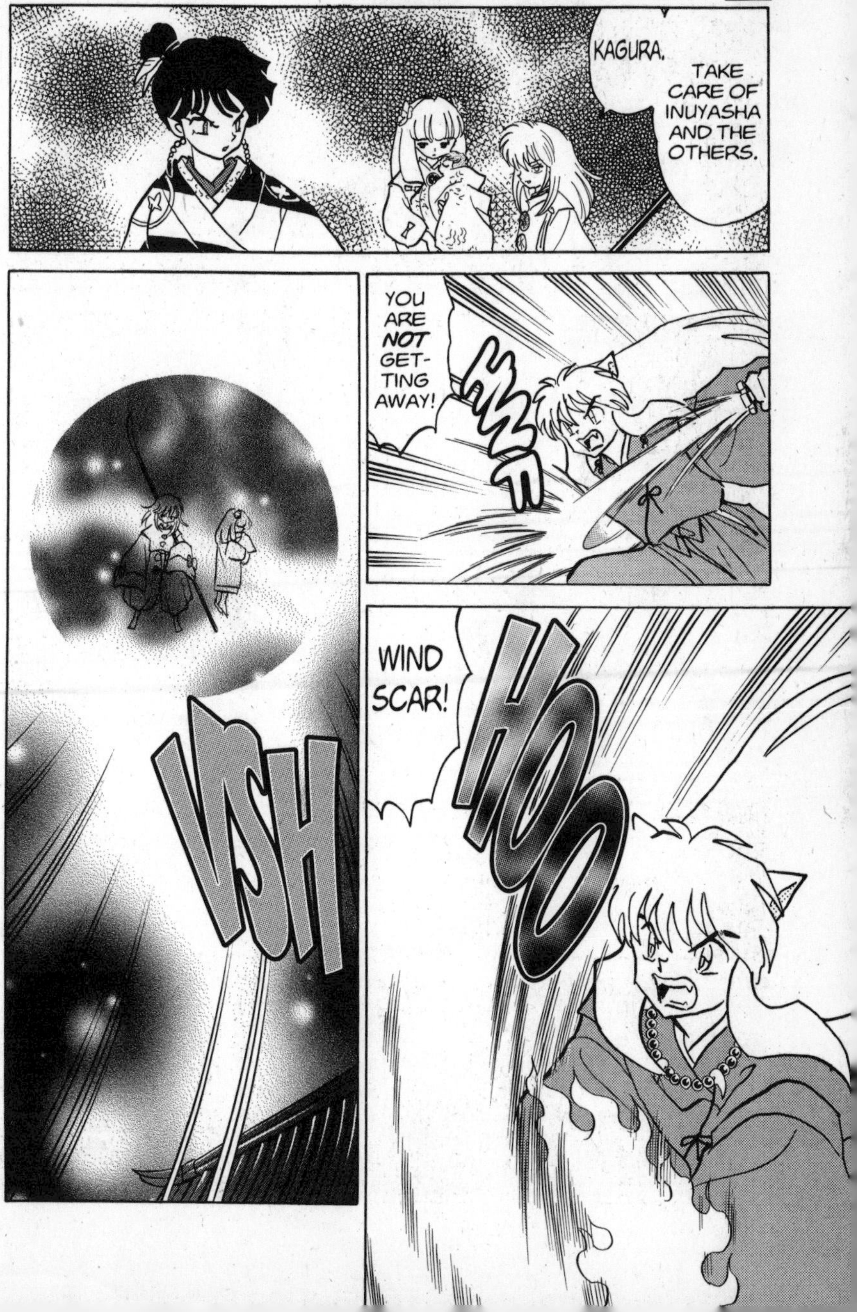
KAGURA.
TAKE CARE OF INUYASHA AND THE OTHERS.
VSH
YOU ARE *NOT* GET-TING AWAY!
FWMF
WIND SCAR!
HOO

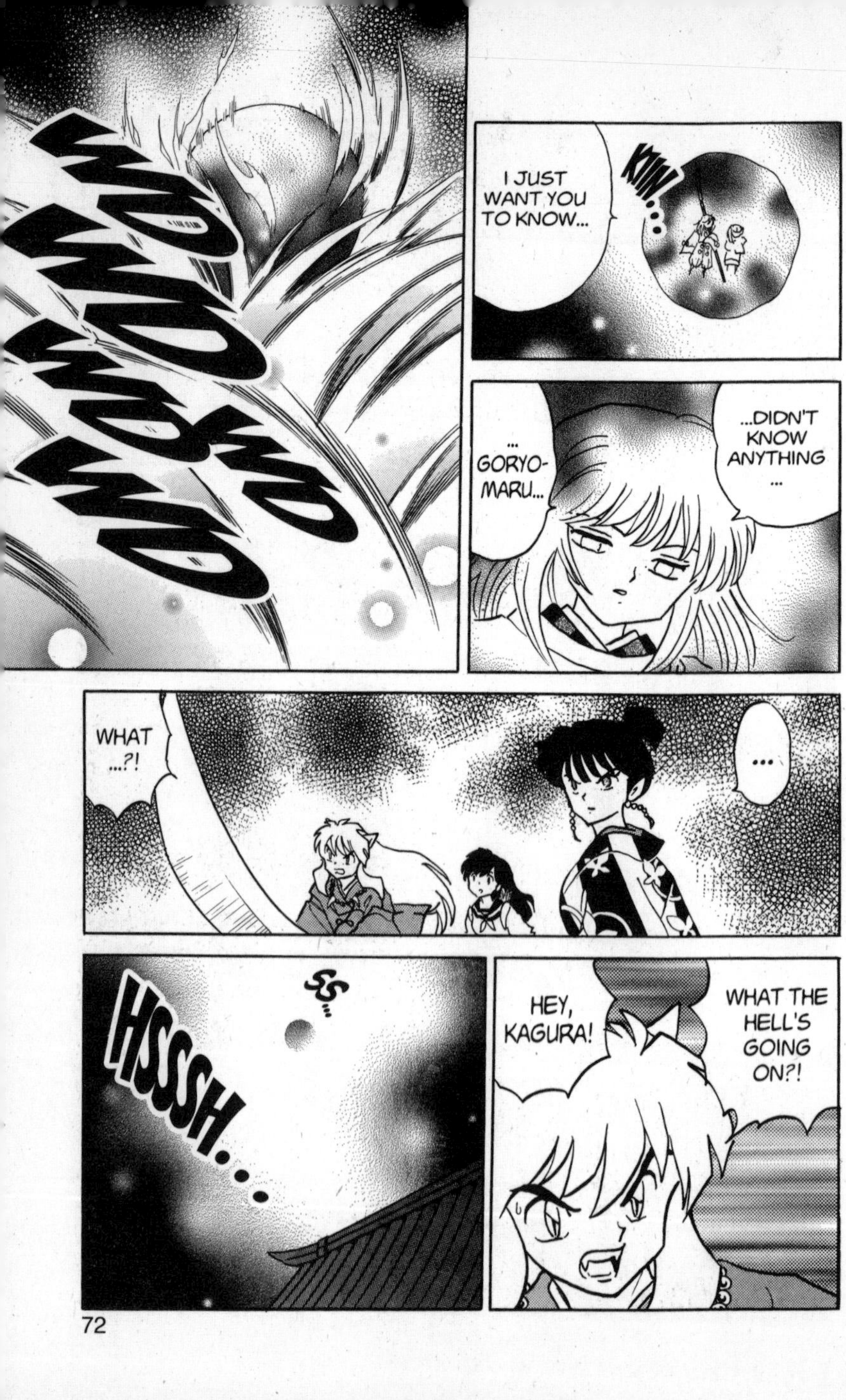
I JUST WANT YOU TO KNOW...
KIN...
... GORYO-MARU...
...DIDN'T KNOW ANYTHING ...
WHAT ...?!
...
HSSSH...
SS...
HEY, KAGURA!
WHAT THE HELL'S GOING ON?!

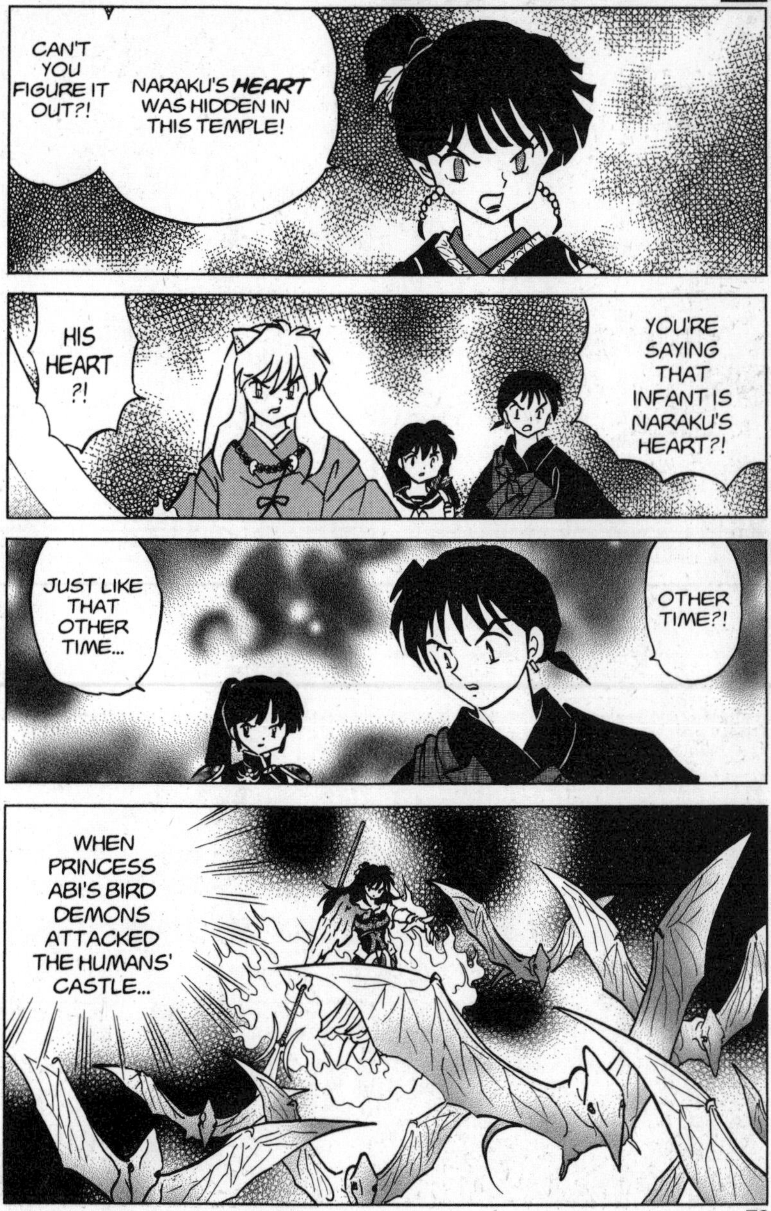
CAN'T YOU FIGURE IT OUT?!
NARAKU'S **HEART** WAS HIDDEN IN THIS TEMPLE!
HIS HEART ?!
YOU'RE SAYING THAT INFANT IS NARAKU'S HEART?!
JUST LIKE THAT OTHER TIME...
OTHER TIME?!
WHEN PRINCESS ABI'S BIRD DEMONS ATTACKED THE HUMANS' CASTLE...

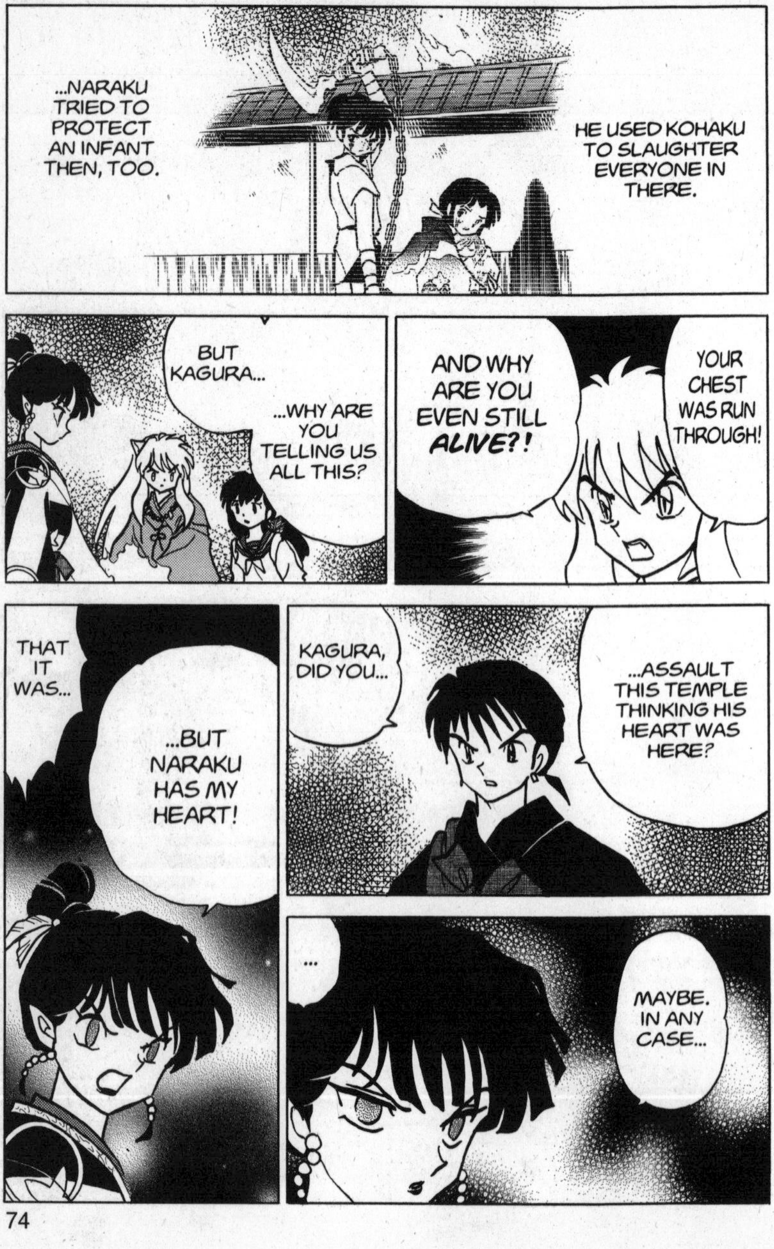
...NARAKU TRIED TO PROTECT AN INFANT THEN, TOO.
HE USED KOHAKU TO SLAUGHTER EVERYONE IN THERE.
BUT KAGURA...
...WHY ARE YOU TELLING US ALL THIS?
AND WHY ARE YOU EVEN STILL ALIVE?!
YOUR CHEST WAS RUN THROUGH!
THAT IT WAS...
...BUT NARAKU HAS MY HEART!
KAGURA, DID YOU...
...ASSAULT THIS TEMPLE THINKING HIS HEART WAS HERE?
...
MAYBE. IN ANY CASE...

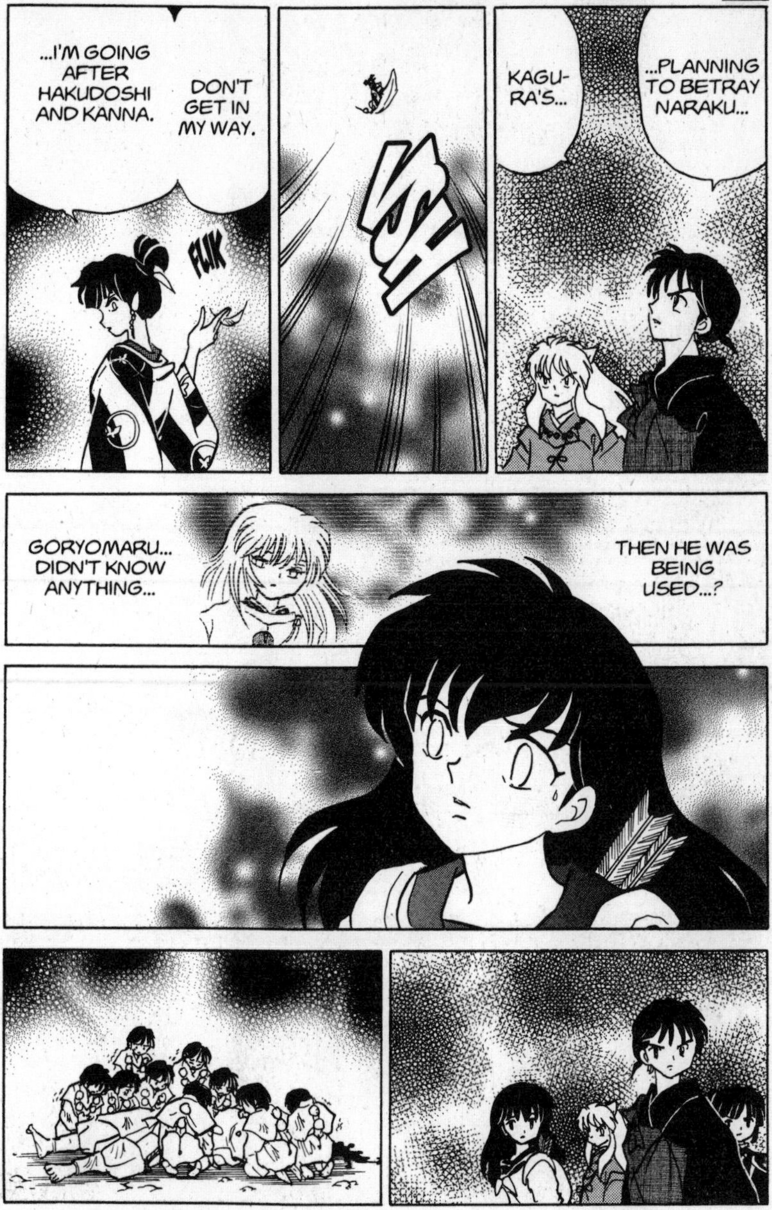
...I'M GOING AFTER HAKUDOSHI AND KANNA.
DON'T GET IN MY WAY.
FLIK
VSSH
KAGU-RA'S...
...PLANNING TO BETRAY NARAKU...
GORYOMARU... DIDN'T KNOW ANYTHING...
THEN HE WAS BEING USED...?

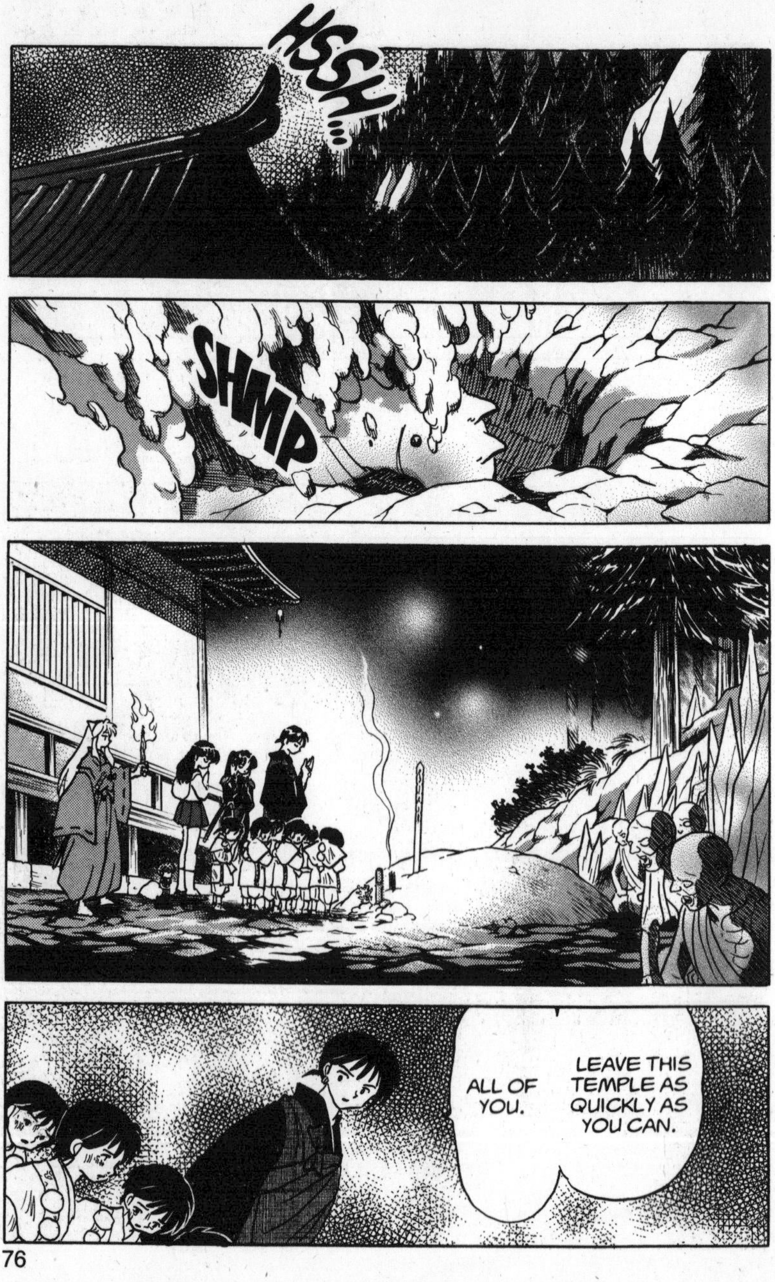
HSSH...
SHMP
ALL OF YOU.
LEAVE THIS TEMPLE AS QUICKLY AS YOU CAN.

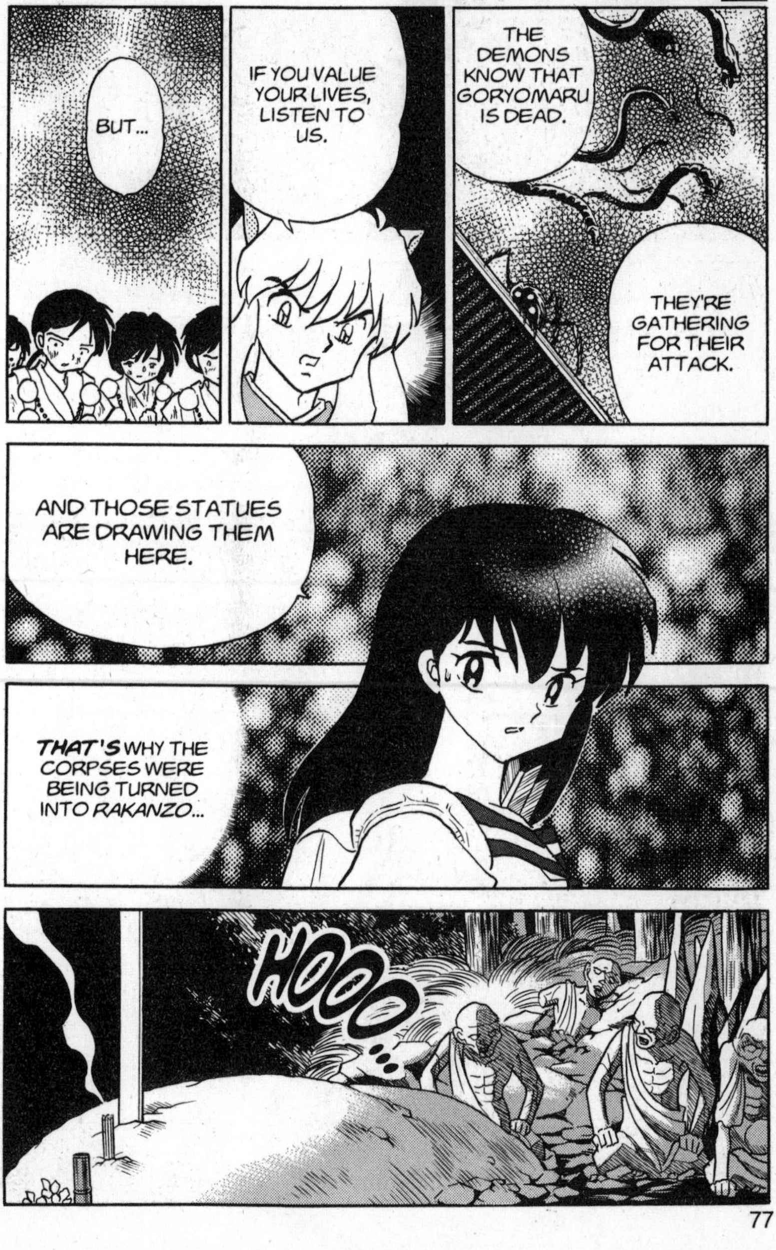
BUT...
IF YOU VALUE YOUR LIVES, LISTEN TO US.
THE DEMONS KNOW THAT GORYOMARU IS DEAD.
THEY'RE GATHERING FOR THEIR ATTACK.
AND THOSE STATUES ARE DRAWING THEM HERE.
THAT'S WHY THE CORPSES WERE BEING TURNED INTO RAKANZO...
HOOO...

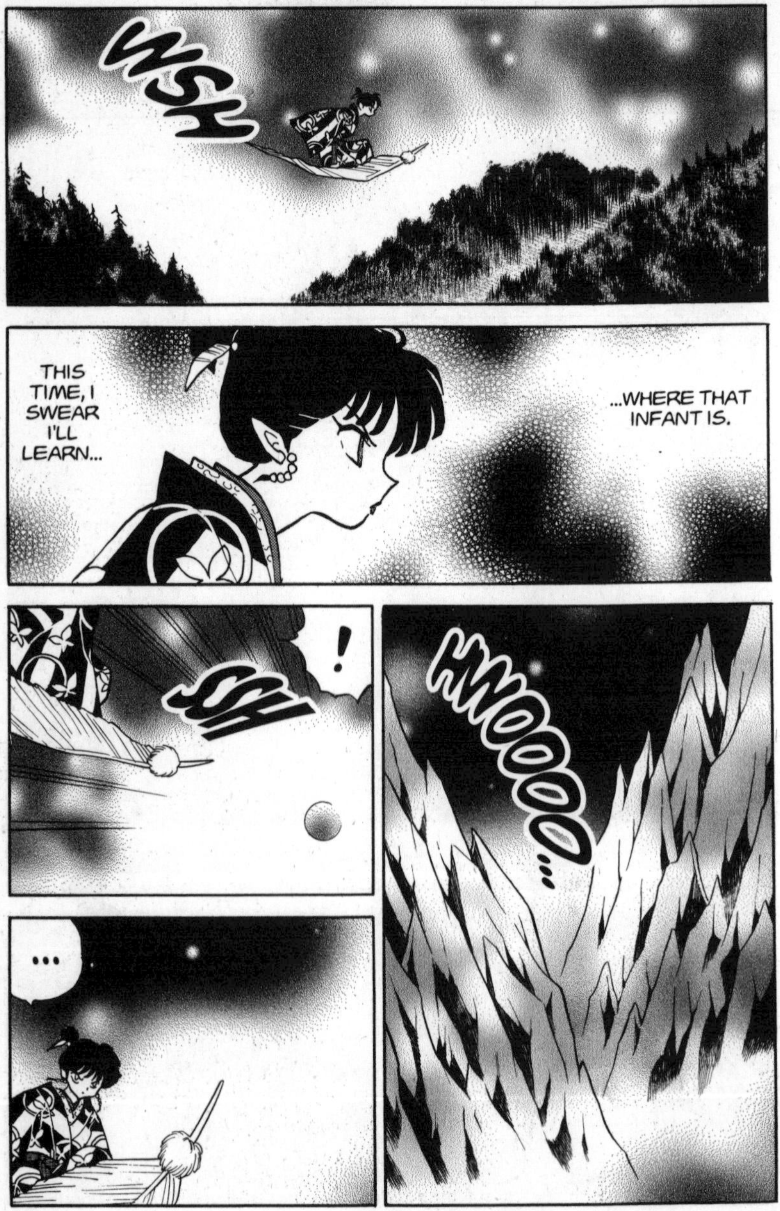
WSH
THIS TIME, I SWEAR I'LL LEARN...
...WHERE THAT INFANT IS.
SSH
!
...
HWOOOOO...

HOOOOO...

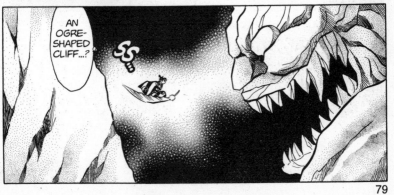

AN OGRE-SHAPED CLIFF...?

SS

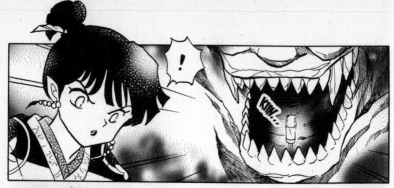

!

KIN...

SHHHH...

B-BMP

WHAT NOW?

DO I JUST FOLLOW THEM IN?!

SCROLL 5
THE OGRE CLIFF

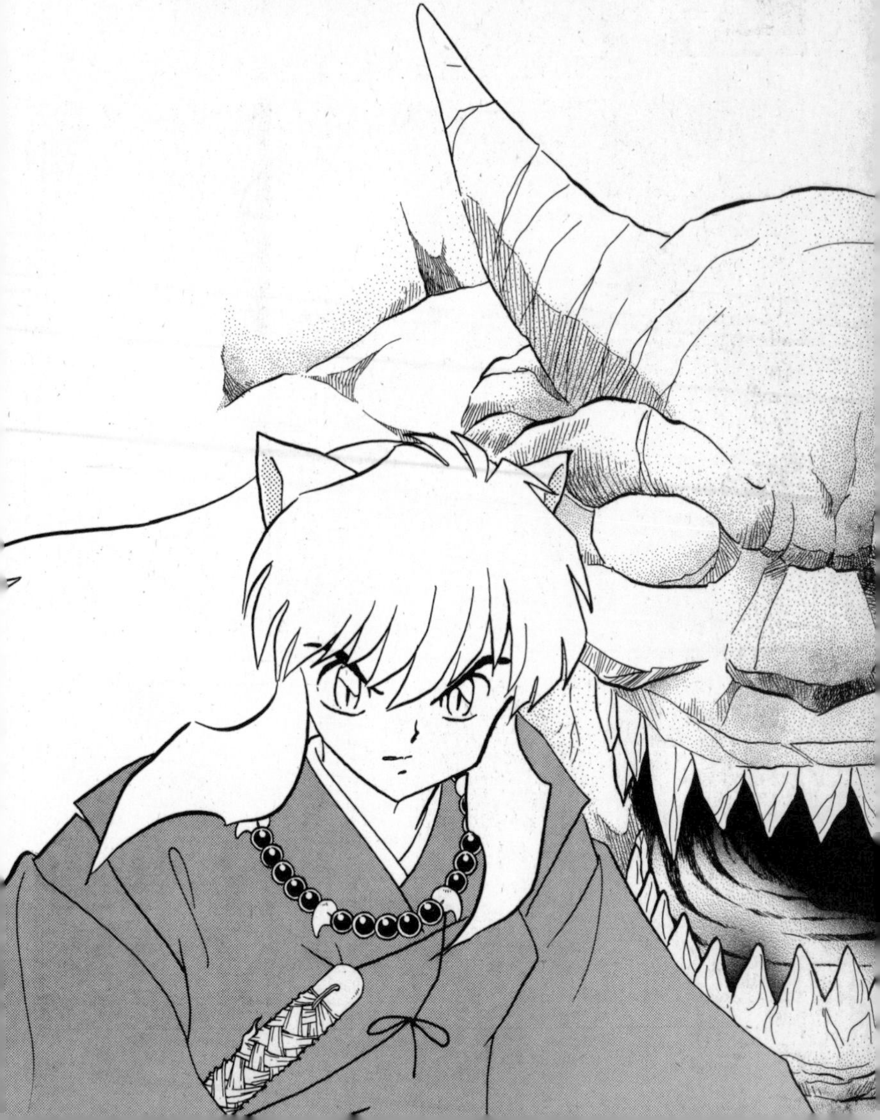

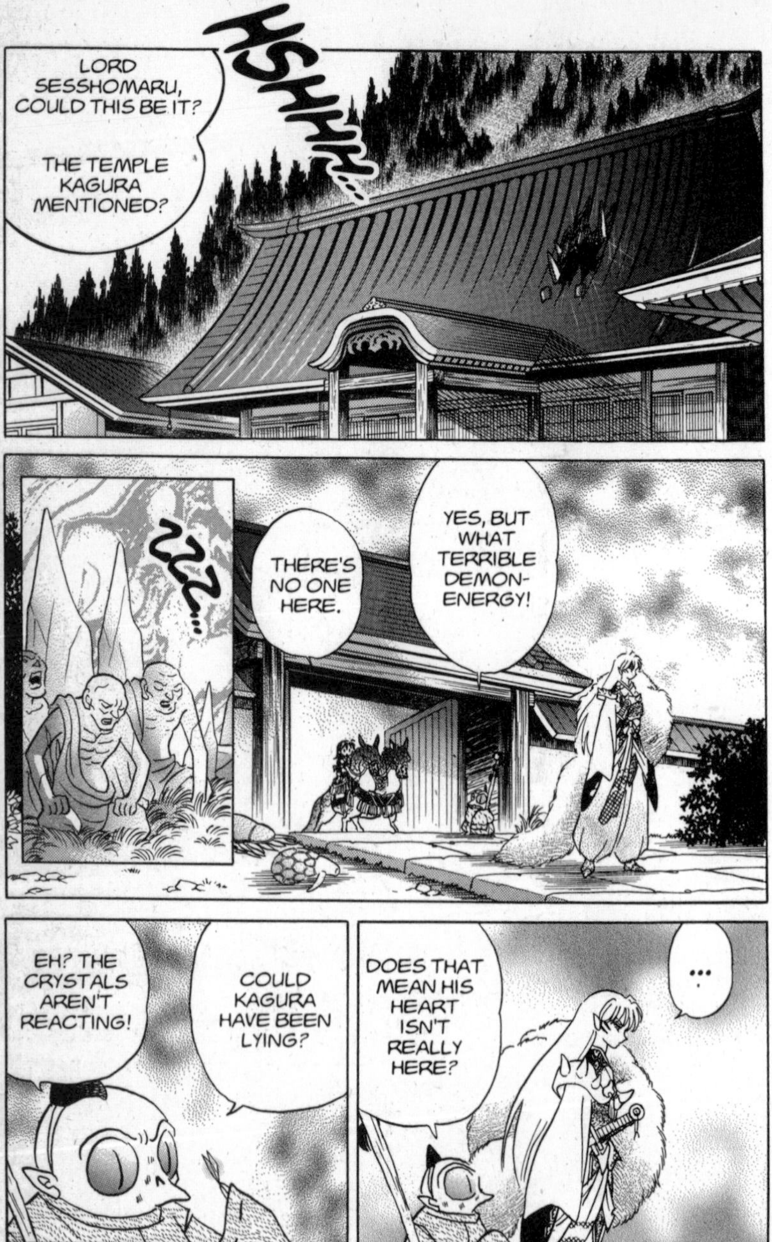
LORD SESSHOMARU, COULD THIS BE IT?
THE TEMPLE KAGURA MENTIONED?
HSHHH...
ZZZ...
THERE'S NO ONE HERE.
YES, BUT WHAT TERRIBLE DEMON-ENERGY!
EH? THE CRYSTALS AREN'T REACTING!
COULD KAGURA HAVE BEEN LYING?
DOES THAT MEAN HIS HEART ISN'T REALLY HERE?
...

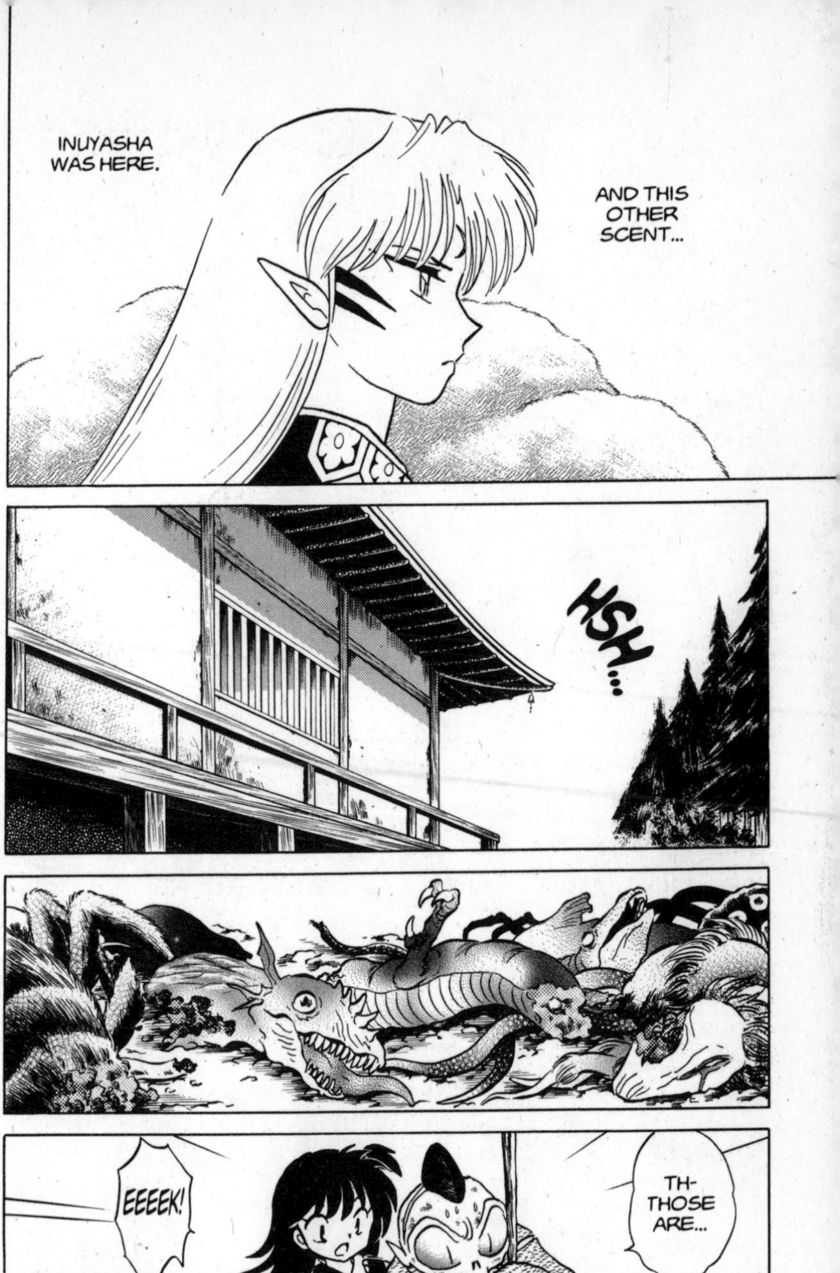
INUYASHA WAS HERE.
AND THIS OTHER SCENT...
HSH...
EEEEK!
TH- THOSE ARE...

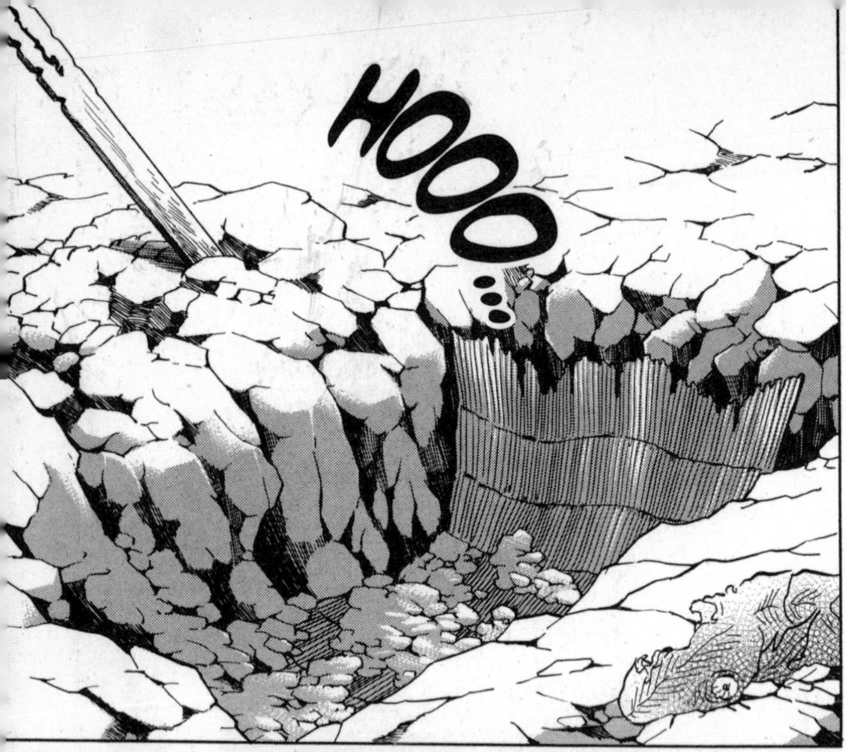
HOOO...

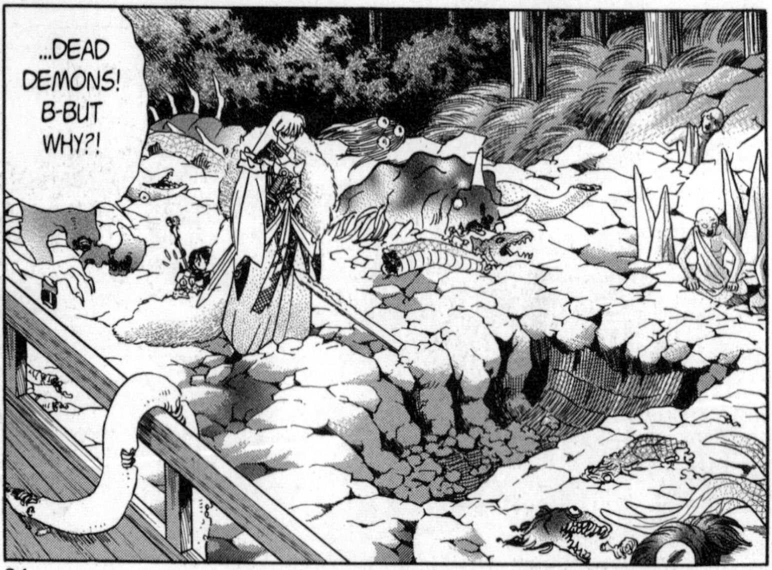
...DEAD DEMONS! B-BUT WHY?!

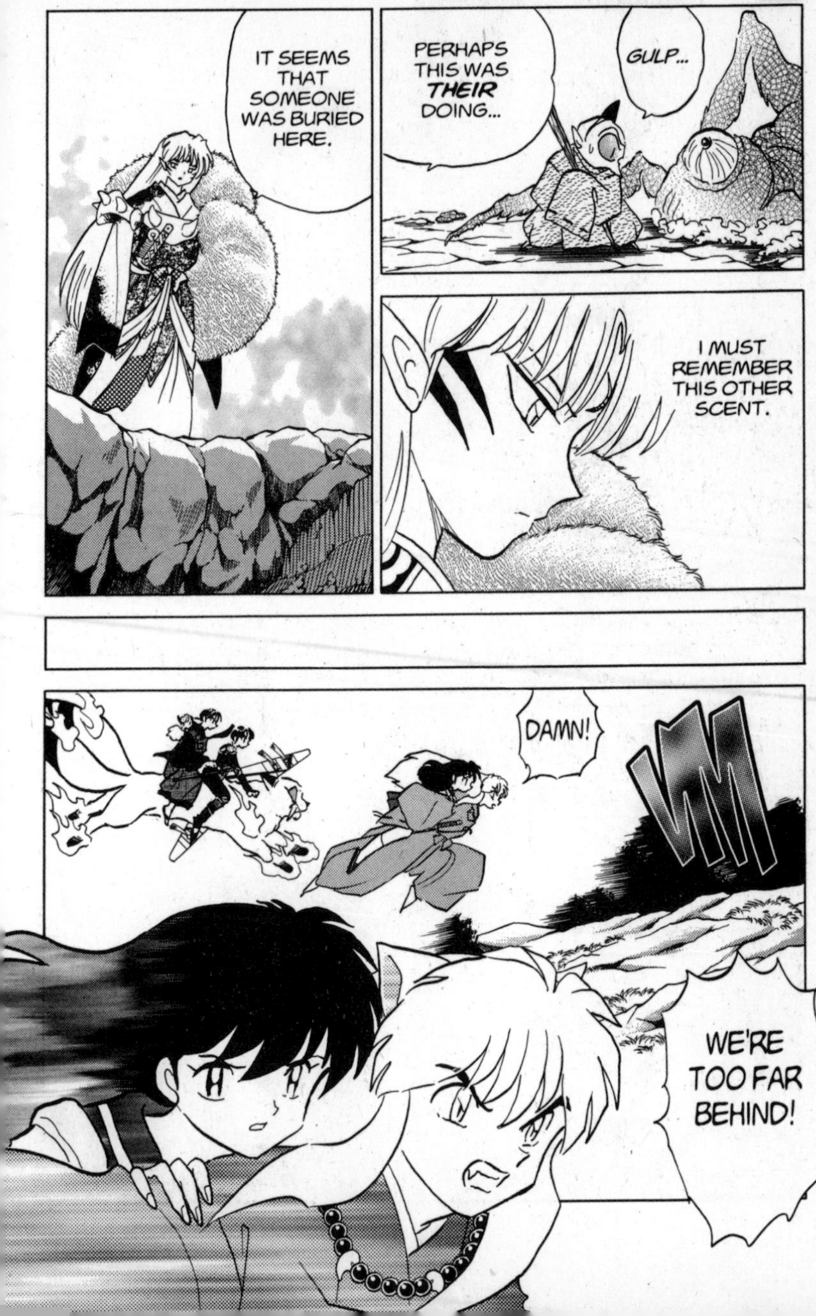
IT SEEMS THAT SOMEONE WAS BURIED HERE.
PERHAPS THIS WAS **THEIR** DOING...
GULP...
I MUST REMEMBER THIS OTHER SCENT.
DAMN!
WE'RE TOO FAR BEHIND!

IT COULDN'T BE HELPED. WE COULDN'T SIMPLY LEAVE GORYOMARU'S BODY LYING THERE.

I KNOW, I KNOW!

AND NOW WE KNOW THAT THAT INFANT IS NARAKU'S HEART...

SO IT WAS WORTH IT TO...

BUT IT'S NOT ENOUGH!

WE'VE GOT TO FIND NARAKU...

...BEFORE HE HIDES HIS HEART SOMEWHERE ELSE!

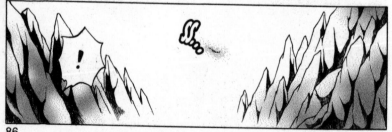

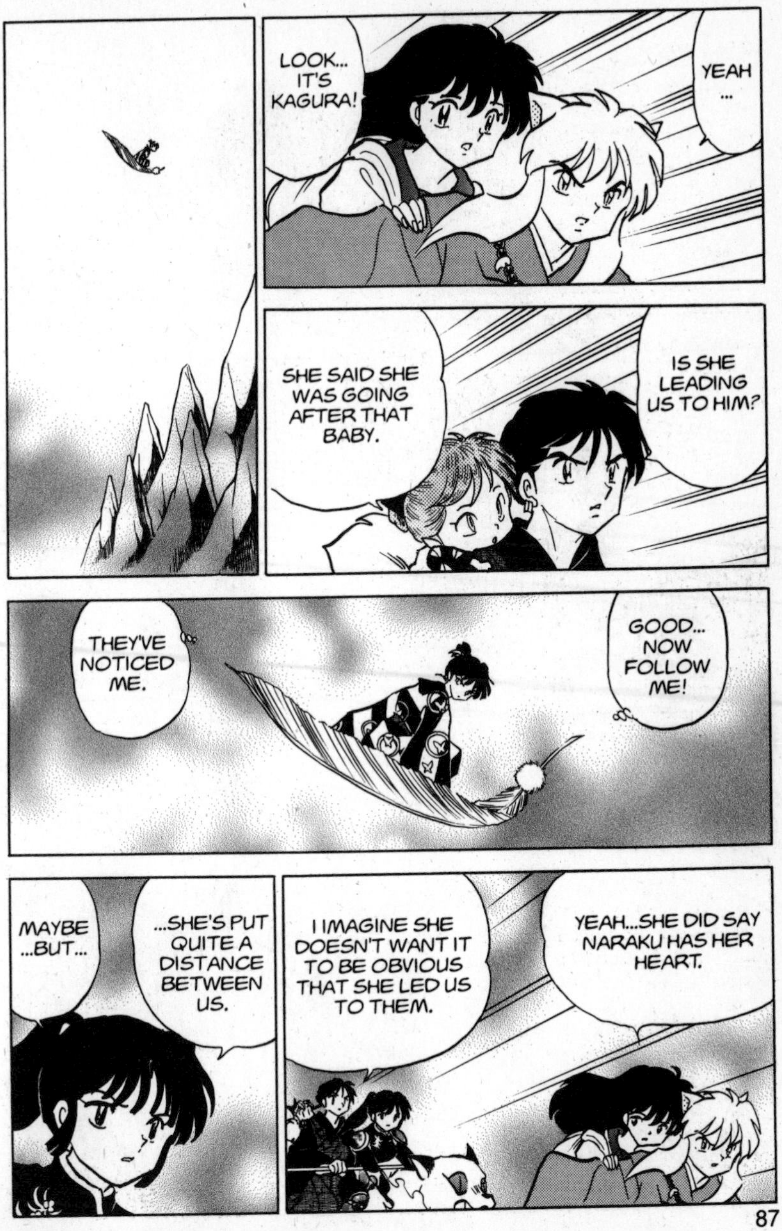
LOOK... IT'S KAGURA!
YEAH ...
SHE SAID SHE WAS GOING AFTER THAT BABY.
IS SHE LEADING US TO HIM?
THEY'VE NOTICED ME.
GOOD... NOW FOLLOW ME!
MAYBE ...BUT...
...SHE'S PUT QUITE A DISTANCE BETWEEN US.
I IMAGINE SHE DOESN'T WANT IT TO BE OBVIOUS THAT SHE LED US TO THEM.
YEAH...SHE DID SAY NARAKU HAS HER HEART.

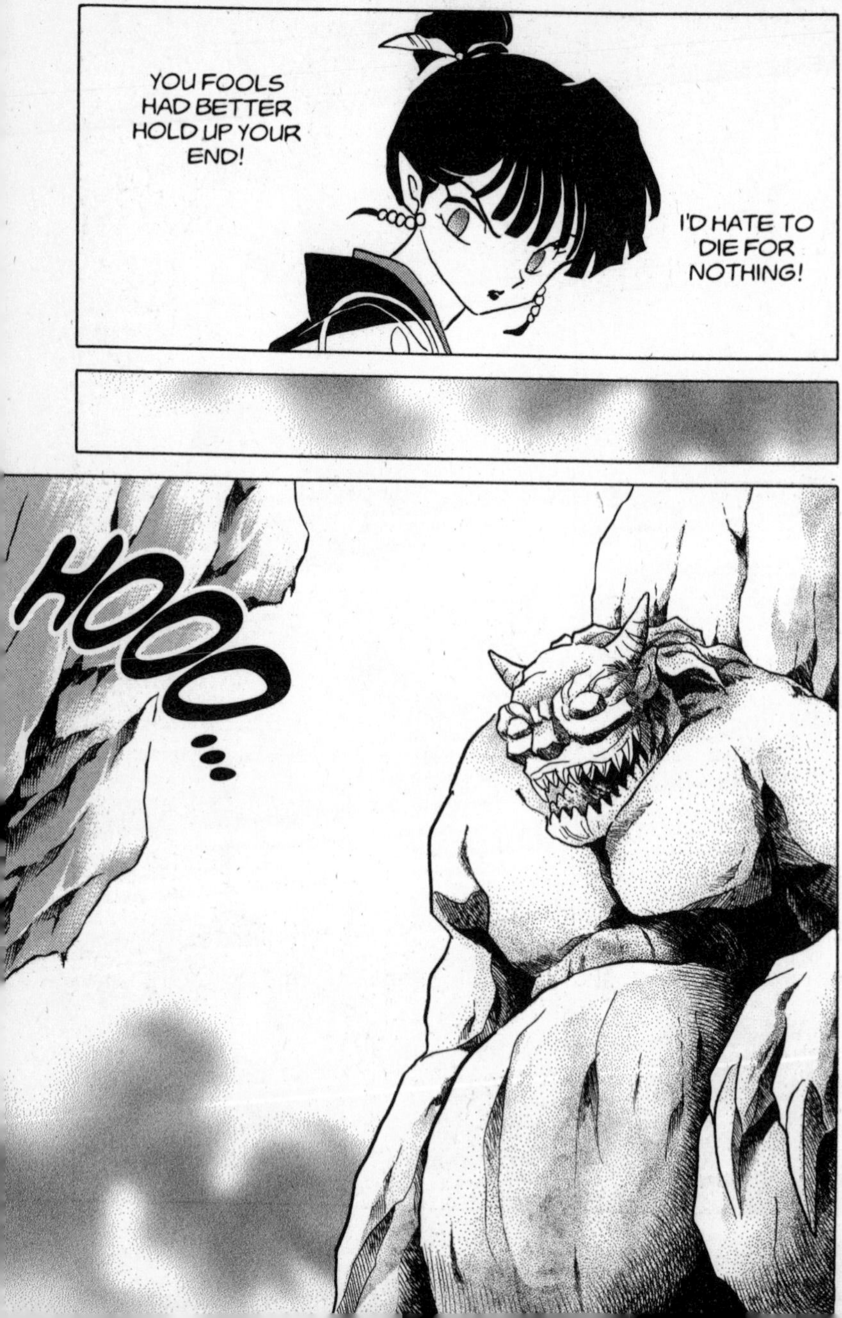
YOU FOOLS HAD BETTER HOLD UP YOUR END!
I'D HATE TO DIE FOR NOTHING!
HOOO...

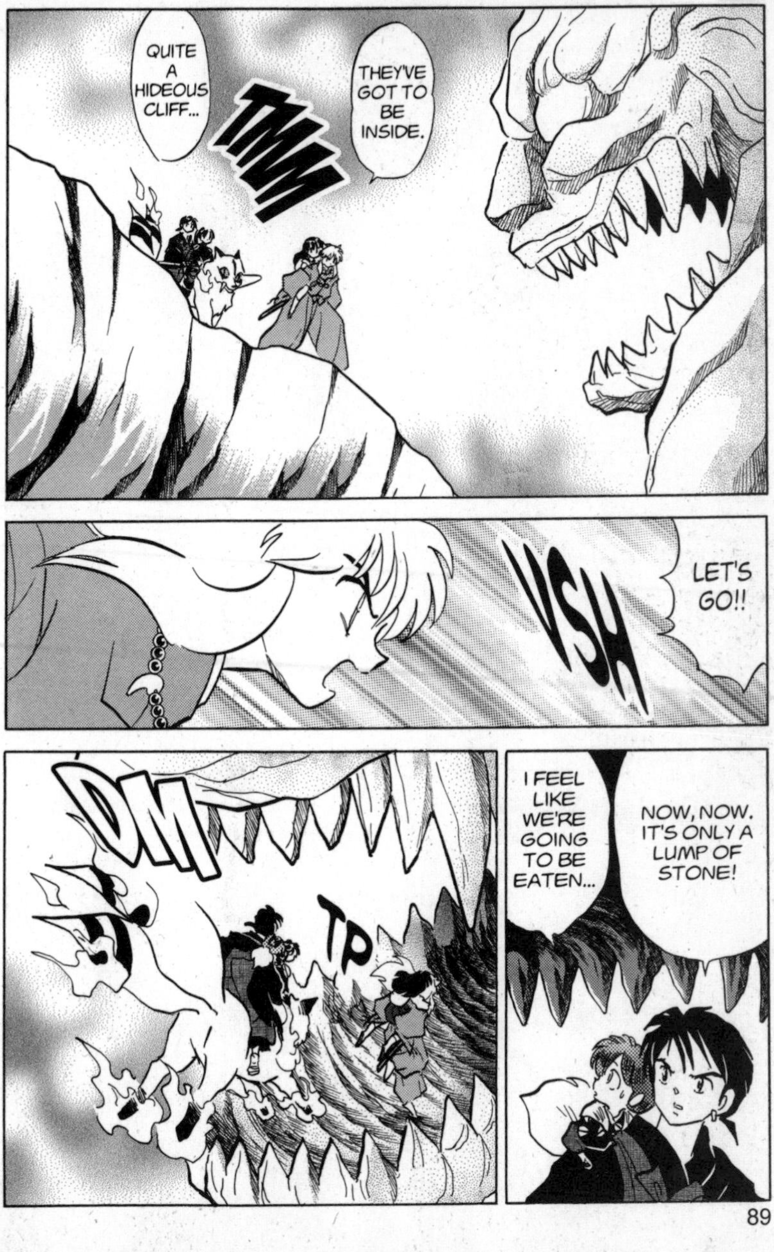
QUITE A HIDEOUS CLIFF...
TMM
THEY'VE GOT TO BE INSIDE.
VSH
LET'S GO!!
DM
TP
I FEEL LIKE WE'RE GOING TO BE EATEN...
NOW, NOW. IT'S ONLY A LUMP OF STONE!

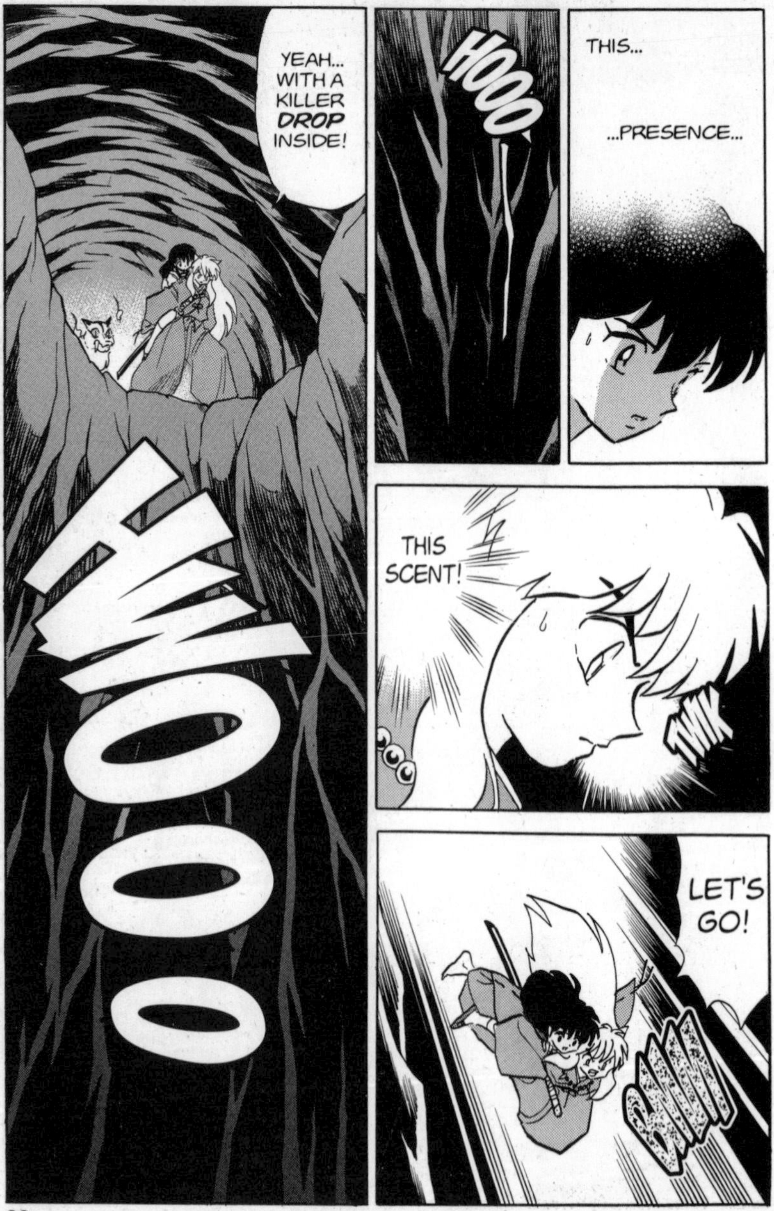
YEAH... WITH A KILLER **DROP** INSIDE!
HOOO
THIS...
...PRESENCE...
THIS SCENT!
LET'S GO!

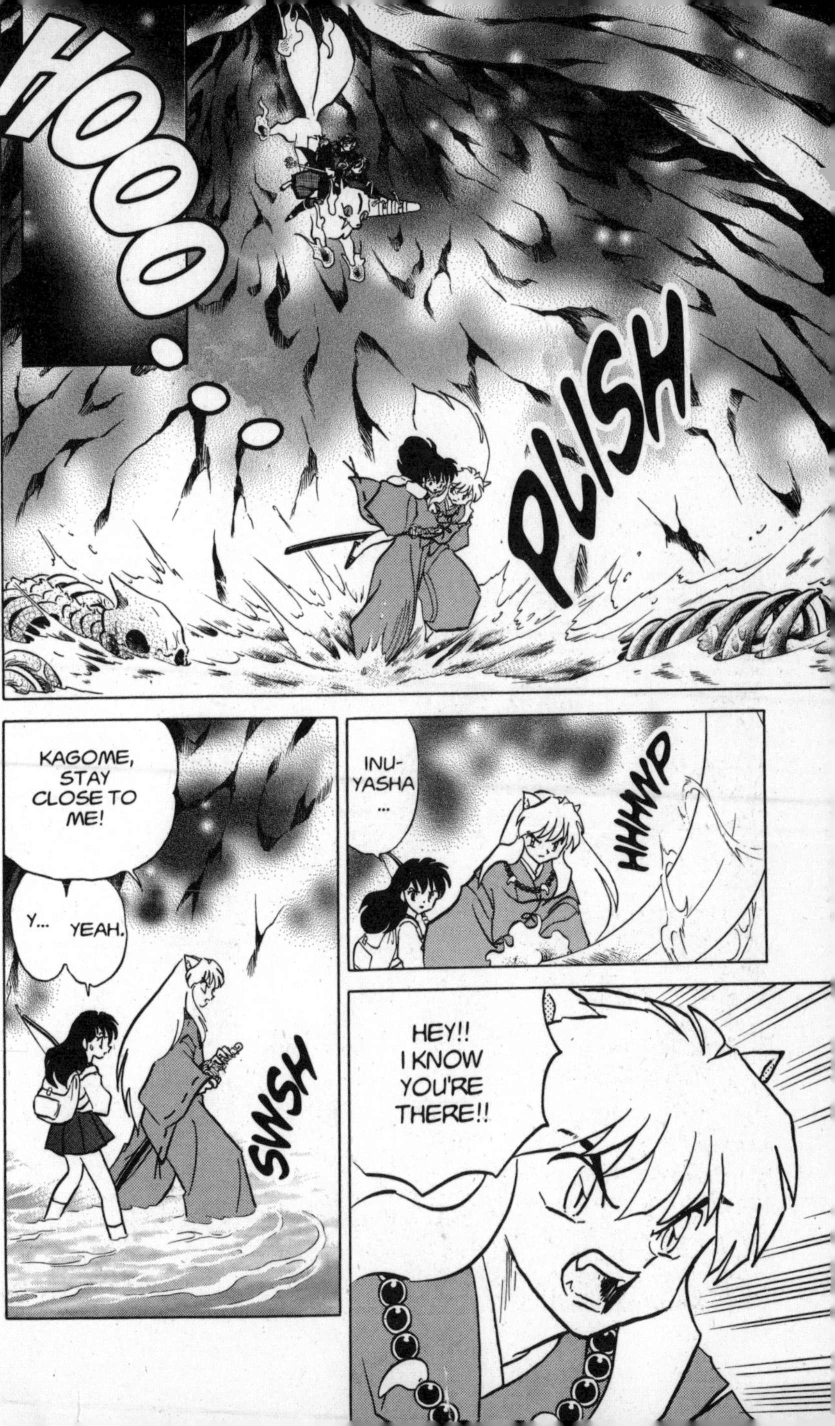
HOOO...
PLISH
KAGOME, STAY CLOSE TO ME!
Y... YEAH.
SWSH
INU-YASHA...
HHHWP
HEY!! I KNOW YOU'RE THERE!!

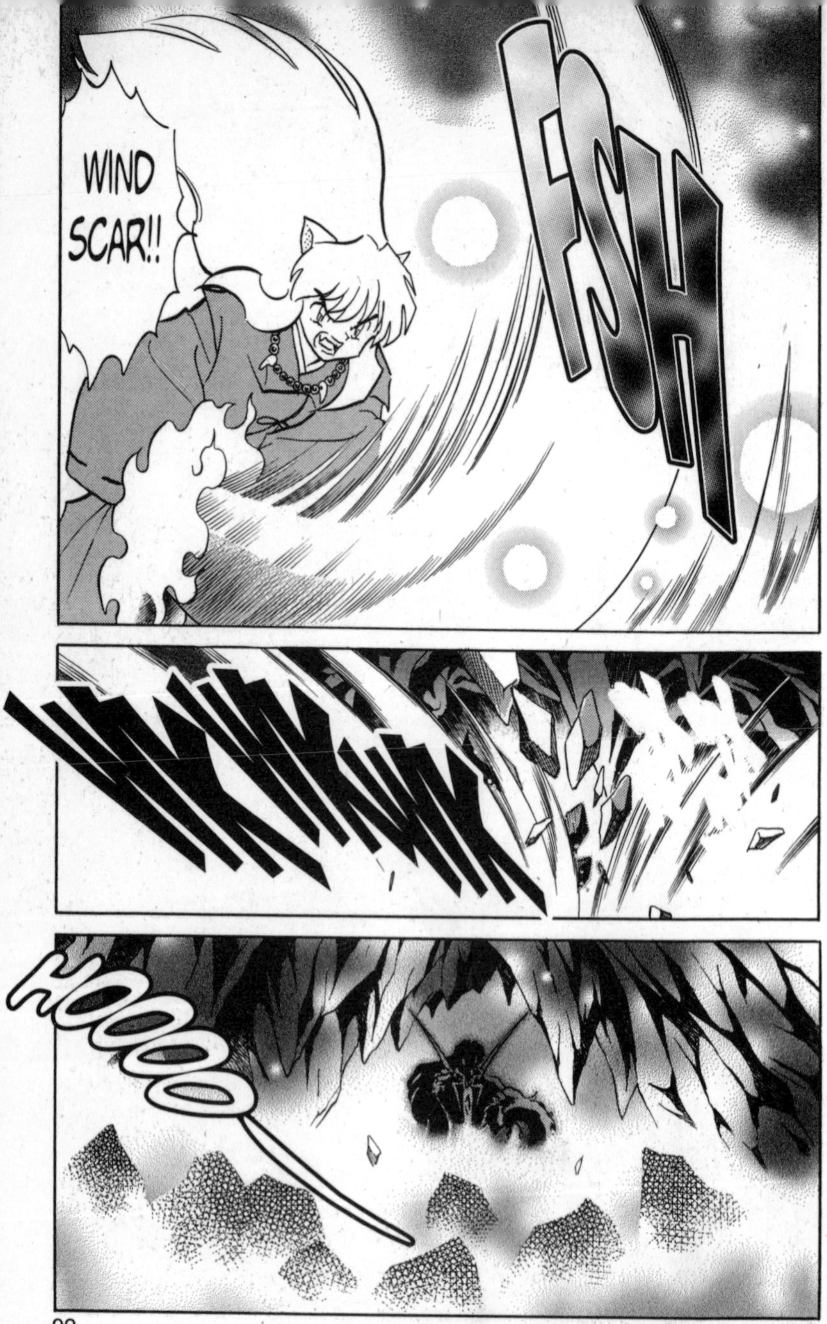
WIND SCAR!!
FSSH
VRRRRRMMM
HOOOO

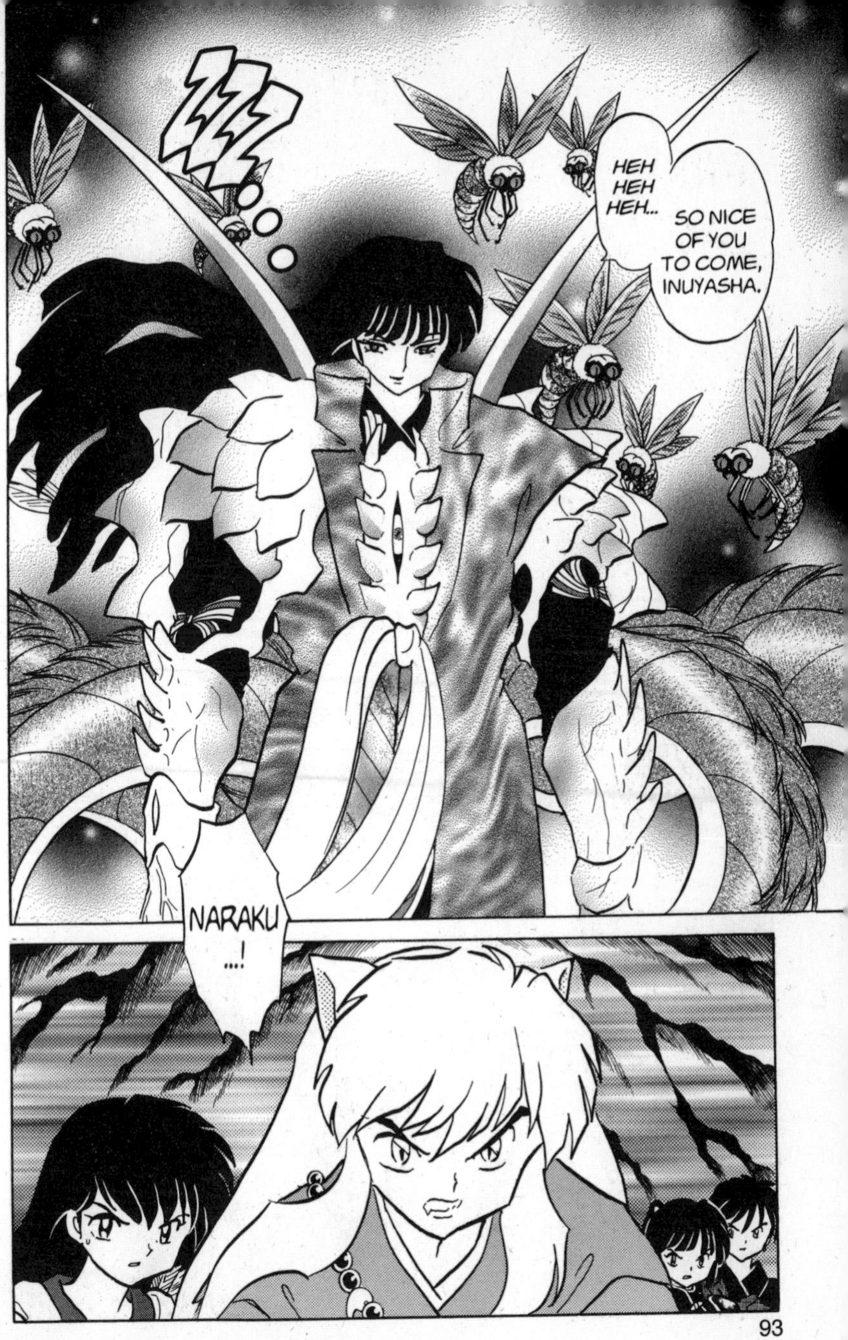
HEH HEH HEH...
SO NICE OF YOU TO COME, INUYASHA.
NARAKU ...!

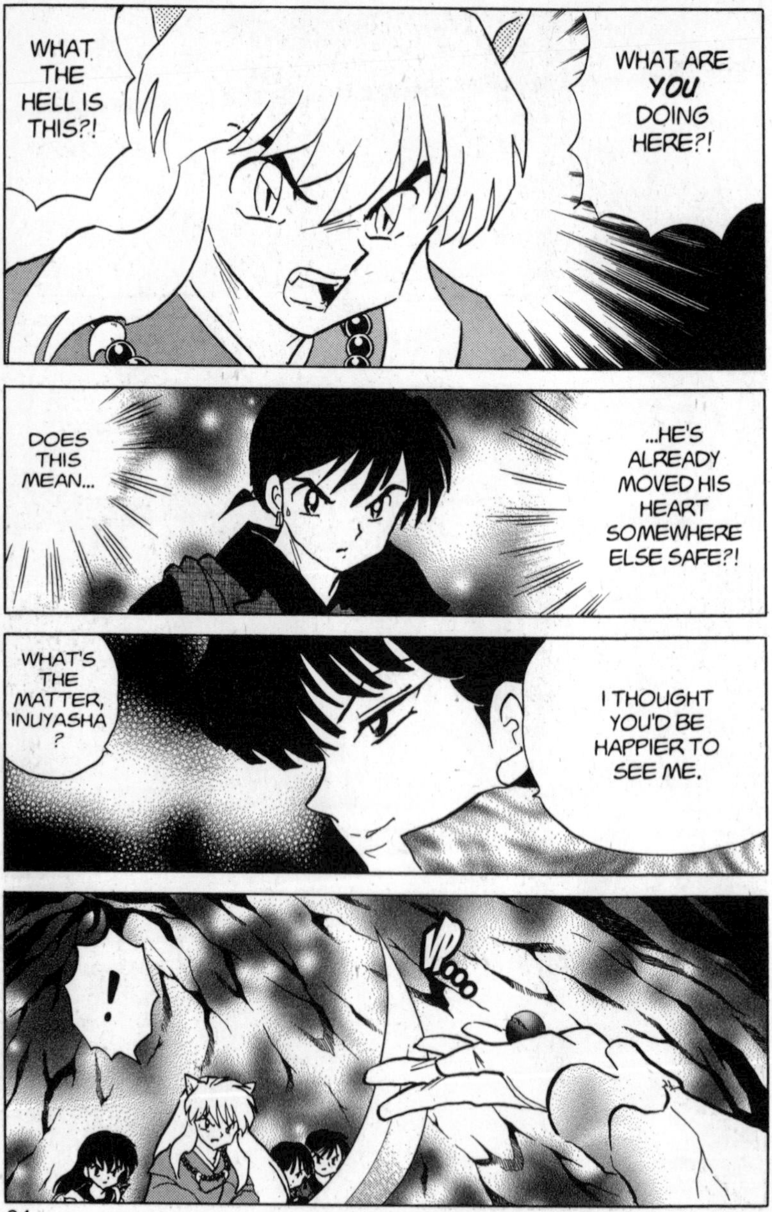
WHAT THE HELL IS THIS?!
WHAT ARE YOU DOING HERE?!
DOES THIS MEAN...
...HE'S ALREADY MOVED HIS HEART SOMEWHERE ELSE SAFE?!
WHAT'S THE MATTER, INUYASHA?
I THOUGHT YOU'D BE HAPPIER TO SEE ME.
!

THE SHIKON JEWEL...!

ITS EVIL AURA'S GOTTEN EVEN STRONGER!

HEH...DO LEAVE ME A GIFT BEFORE YOU HEAD TO THE AFTERLIFE, HM?

I MEAN...

...THE SHIKON SHARD THE WOMAN HAS.

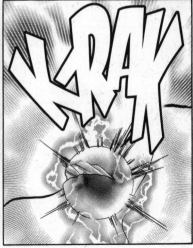

K-RAK

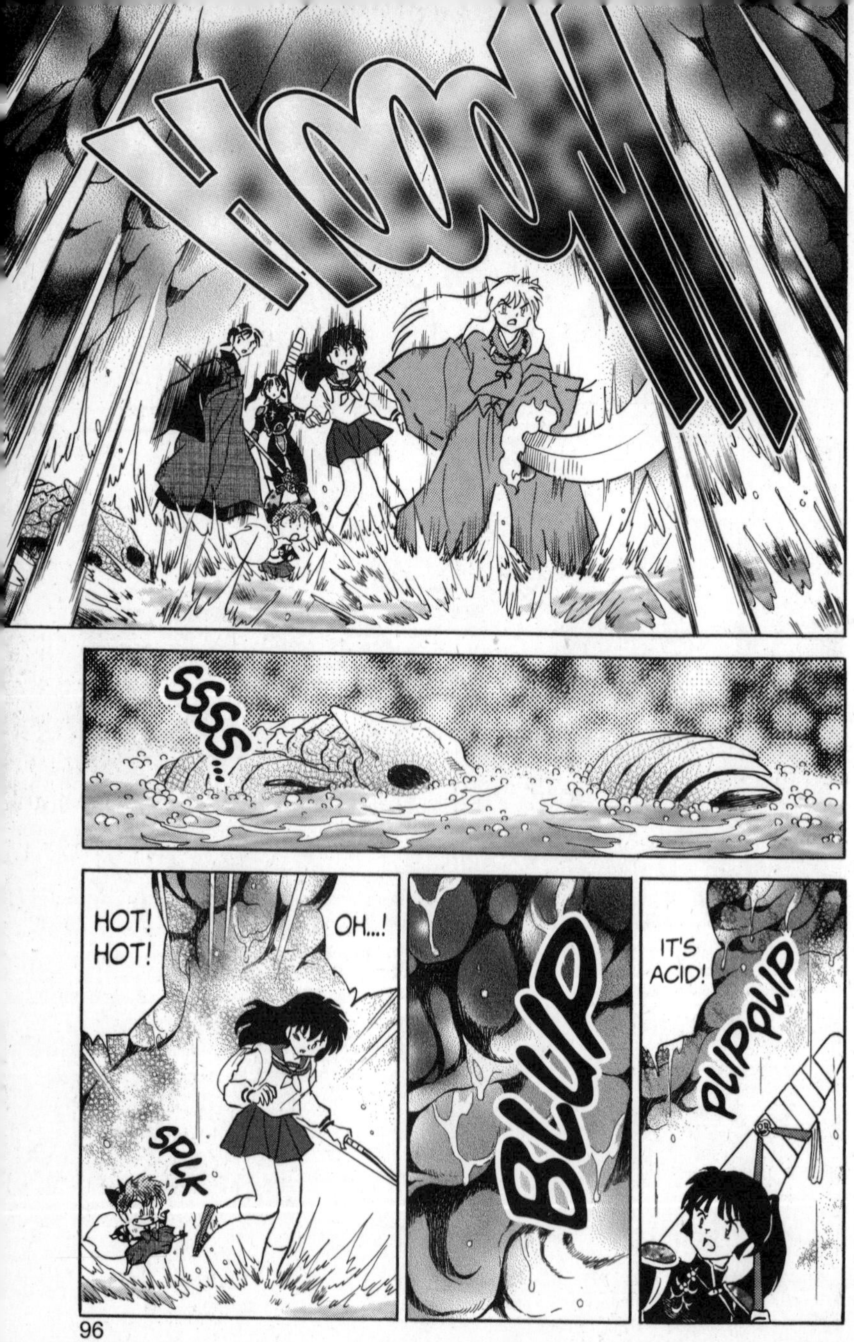
HOOOM
SSSS...
HOT! HOT!
OH...!
SPLK
BLUP
IT'S ACID!
PLIPPLIP

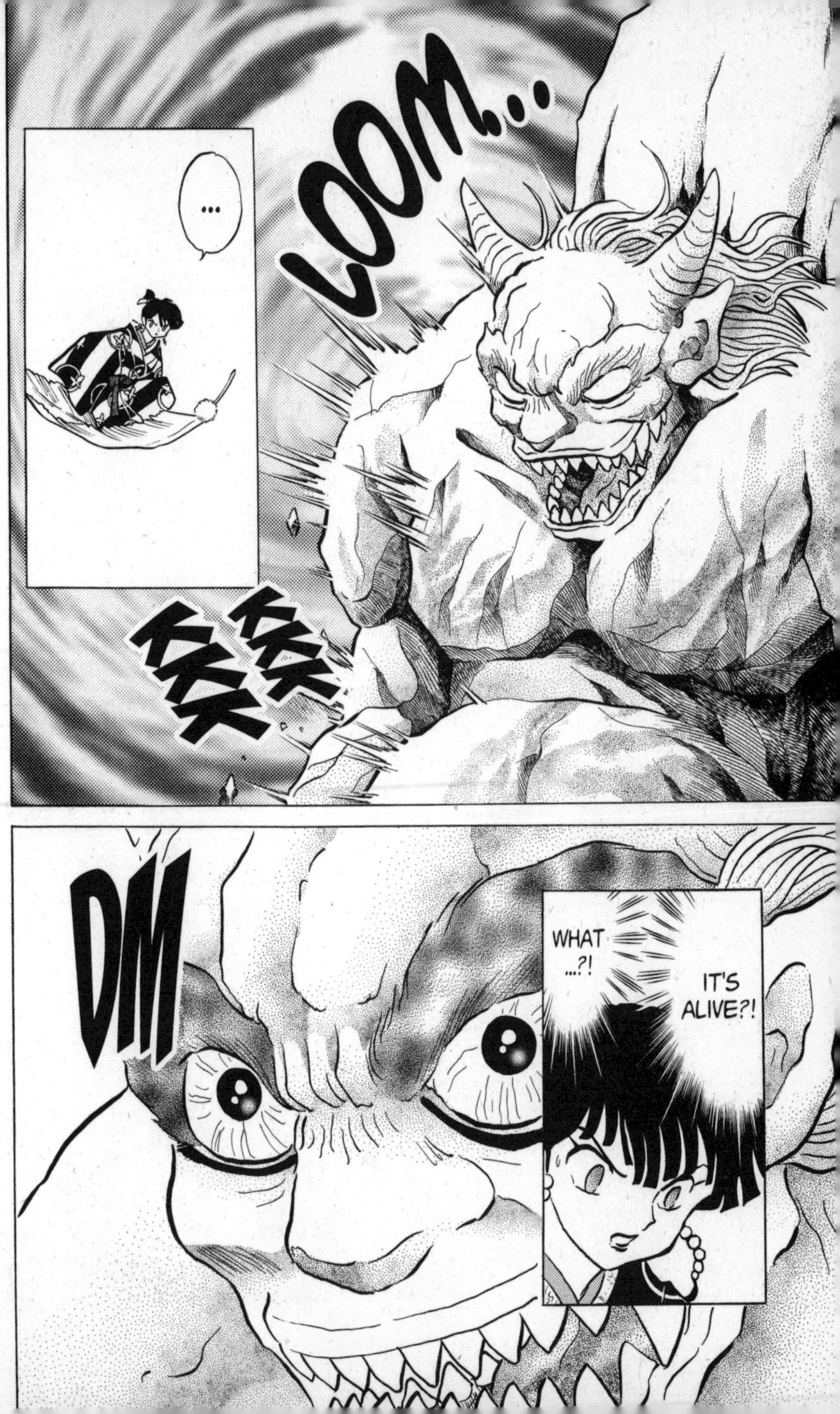
LOOM...
...
KKKK
KKKK
WHAT ...?!
IT'S ALIVE?!
DIM

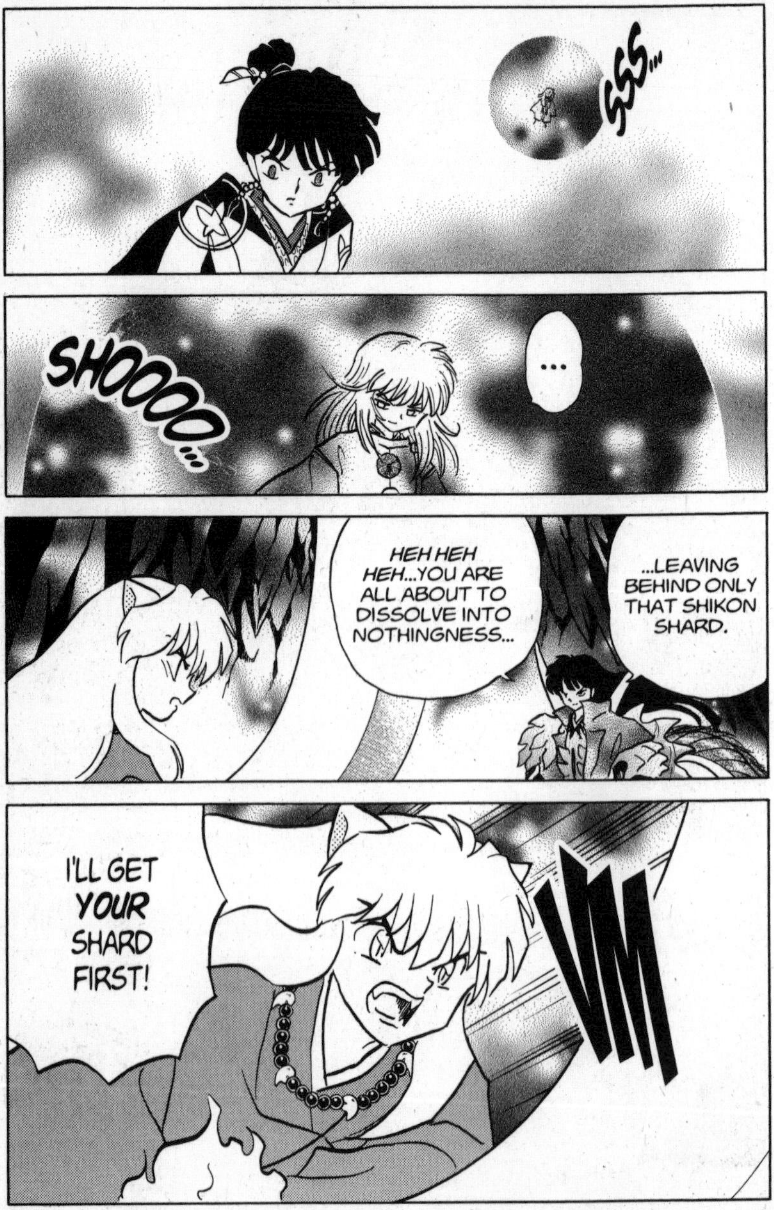
SSS...
SHOOOO...
...
HEH HEH HEH...YOU ARE ALL ABOUT TO DISSOLVE INTO NOTHINGNESS...
...LEAVING BEHIND ONLY THAT SHIKON SHARD.
I'LL GET **YOUR** SHARD FIRST!
VM

SCROLL 6

THE INDESTRUCTIBLE WALL

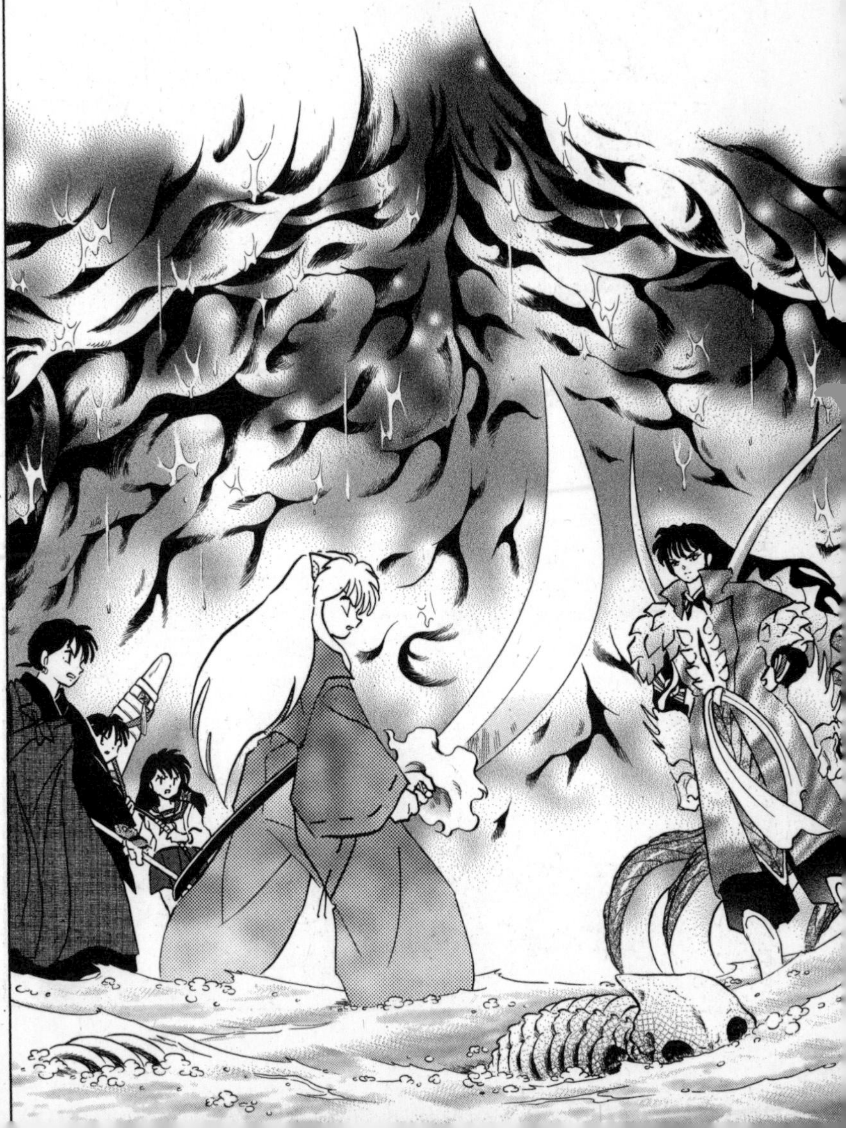

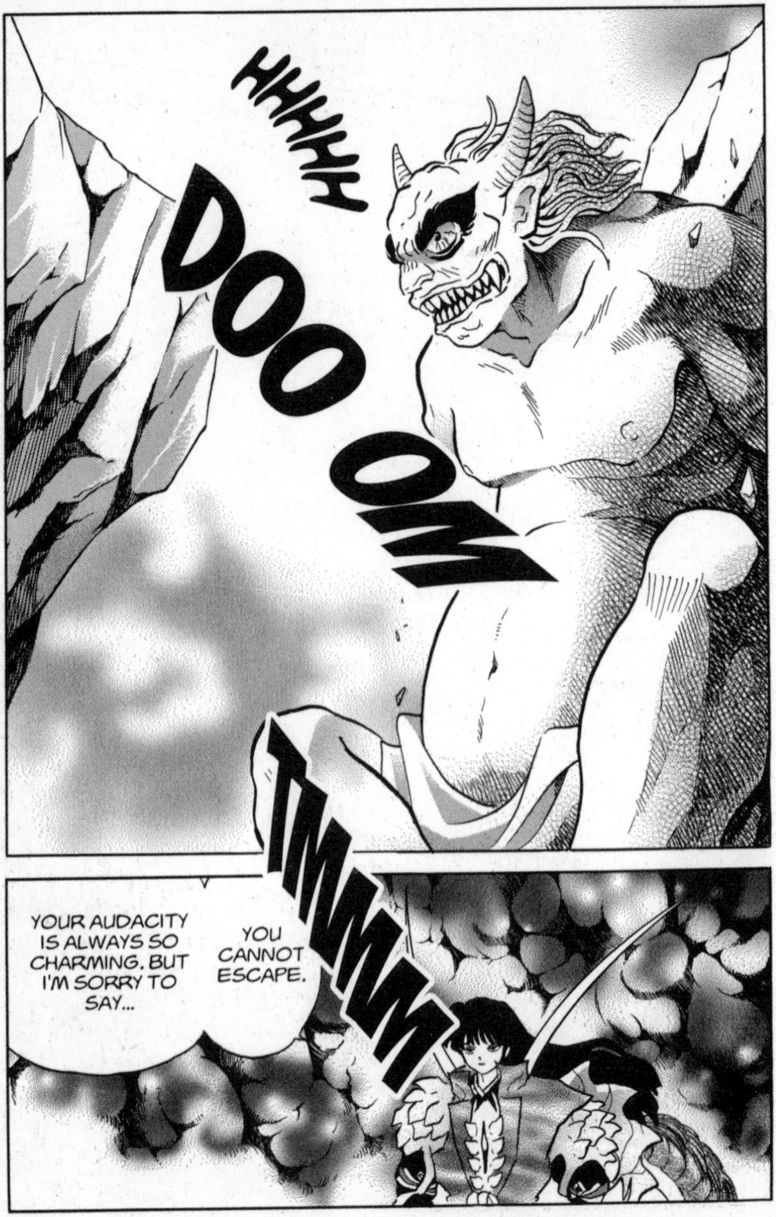
HHHHHH
DOO OM
YOUR AUDACITY IS ALWAYS SO CHARMING. BUT I'M SORRY TO SAY...
YOU CANNOT ESCAPE.
MMMMM

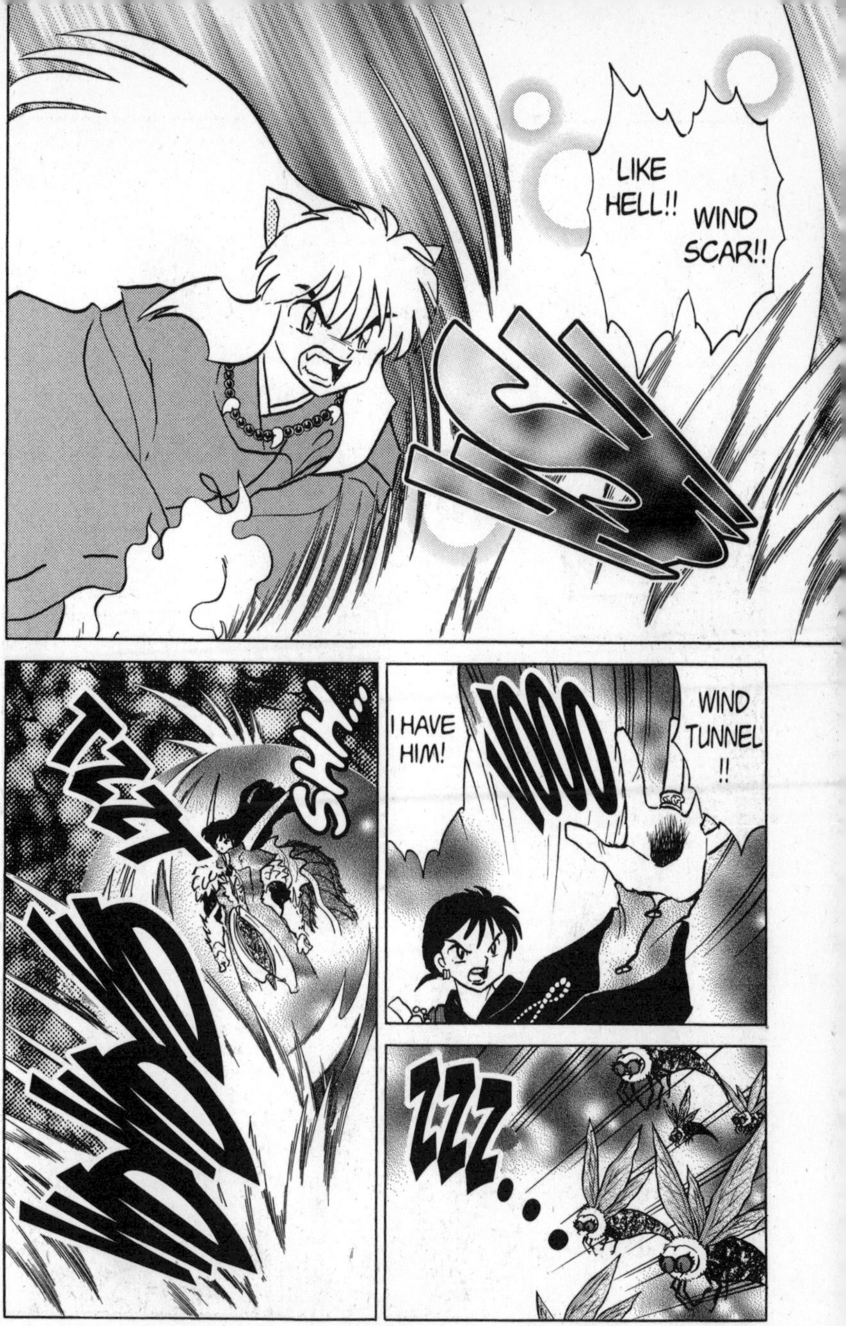
LIKE HELL!!
WIND SCAR!!
SHH...
I HAVE HIM!
WIND TUNNEL!!
ZZZ...

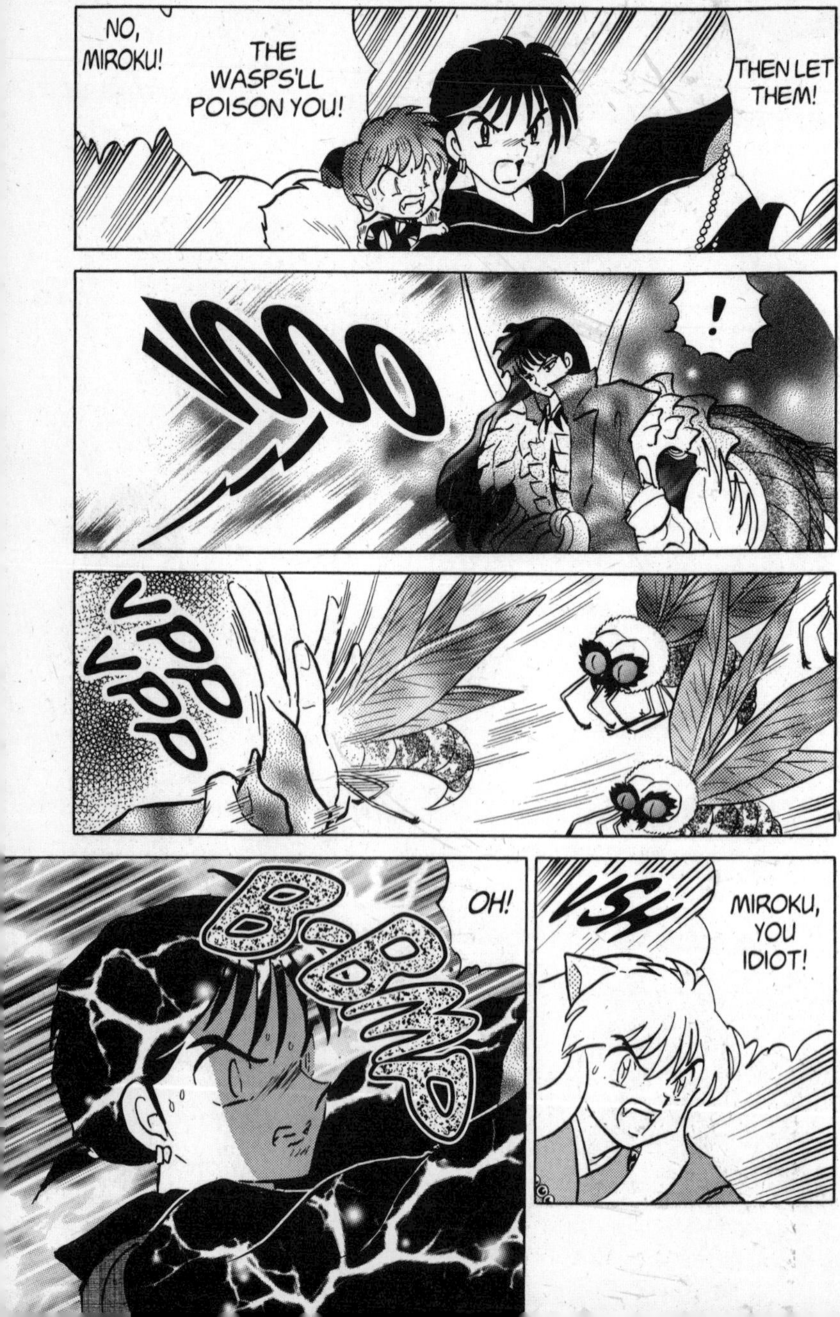
NO, MIROKU!
THE WASPS'LL POISON YOU!
THEN LET THEM!
VOOOO
!
VPP VPP
BOMP
OH!
VSH
MIROKU, YOU IDIOT!

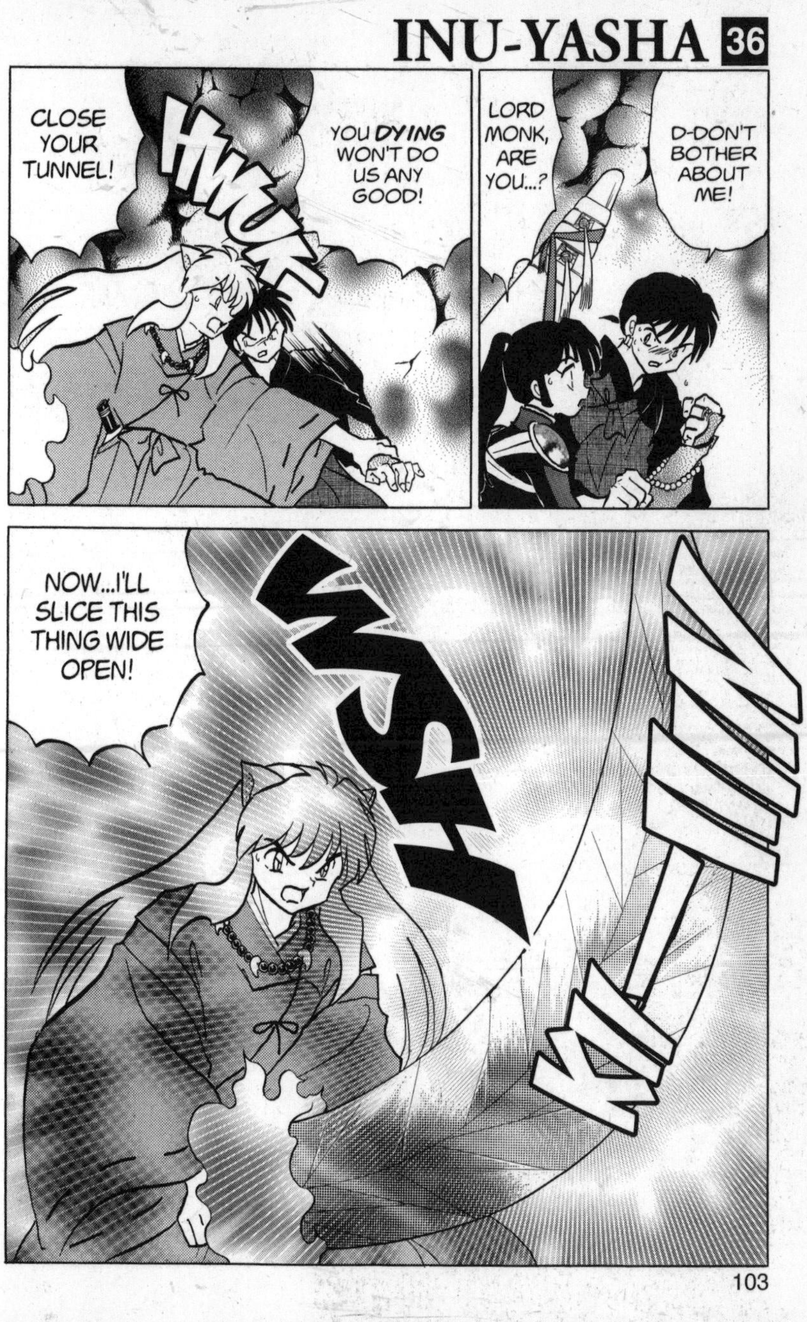
CLOSE YOUR TUNNEL!
HWUK
YOU **DYING** WON'T DO US ANY GOOD!
LORD MONK, ARE YOU...?
D-DON'T BOTHER ABOUT ME!
NOW...I'LL SLICE THIS THING WIDE OPEN!
WSH
KIIIIIIIN

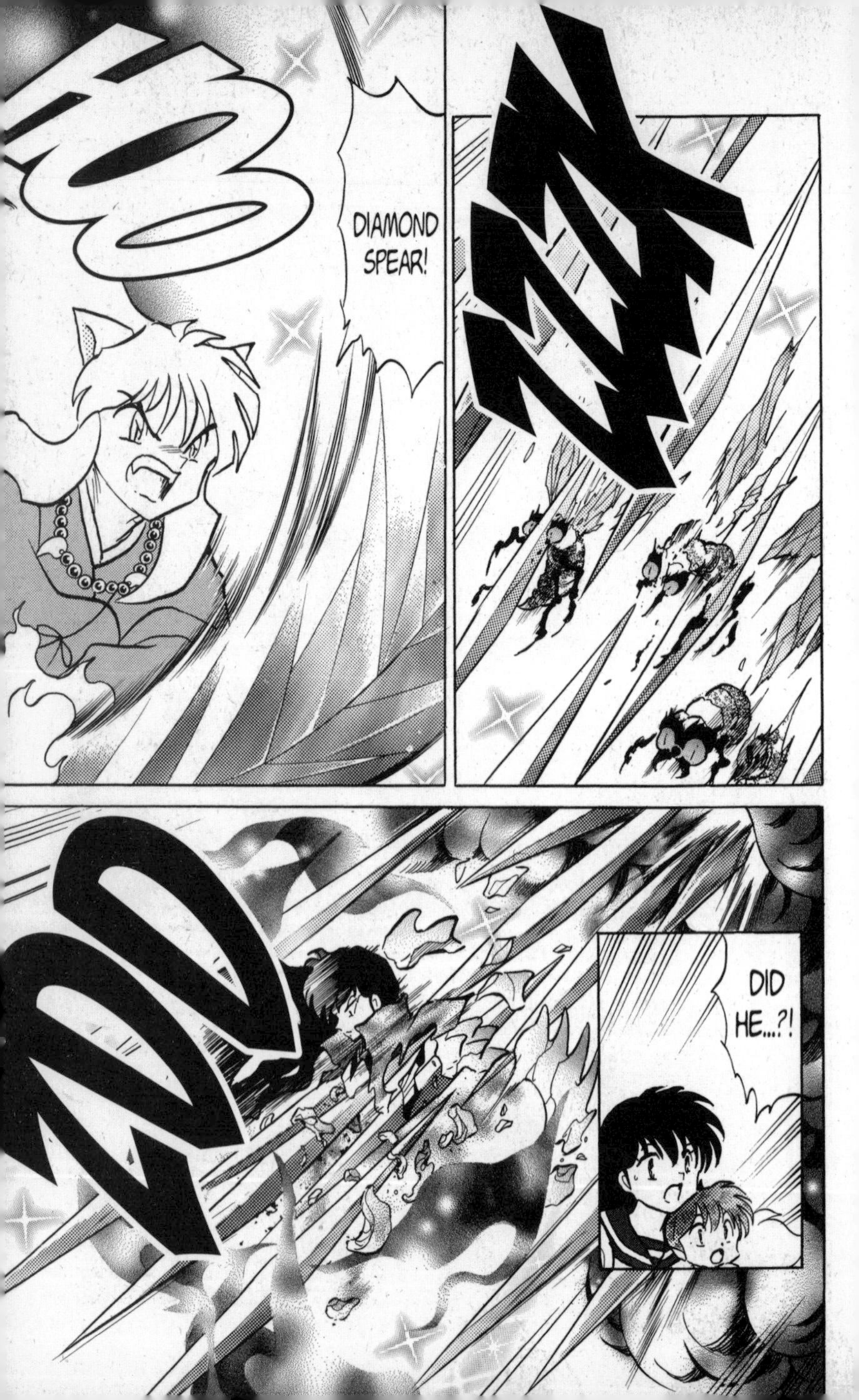
DIAMOND SPEAR!
DID HE...?!

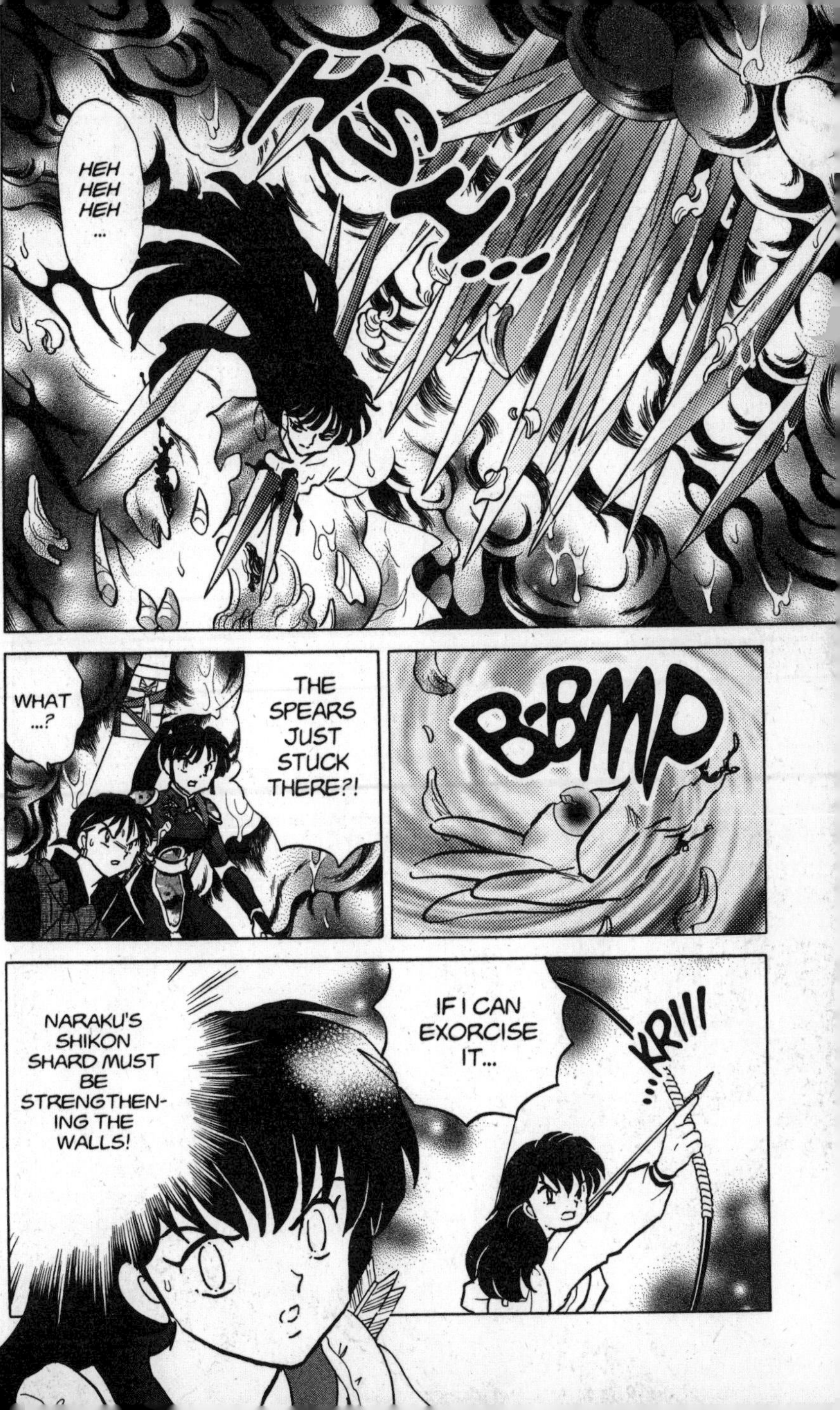
HEH HEH HEH ...
HSS...
WHAT ...?
THE SPEARS JUST STUCK THERE?!
B-BMP
NARAKU'S SHIKON SHARD MUST BE STRENGTHEN-ING THE WALLS!
IF I CAN EXORCISE IT...
KRIII...

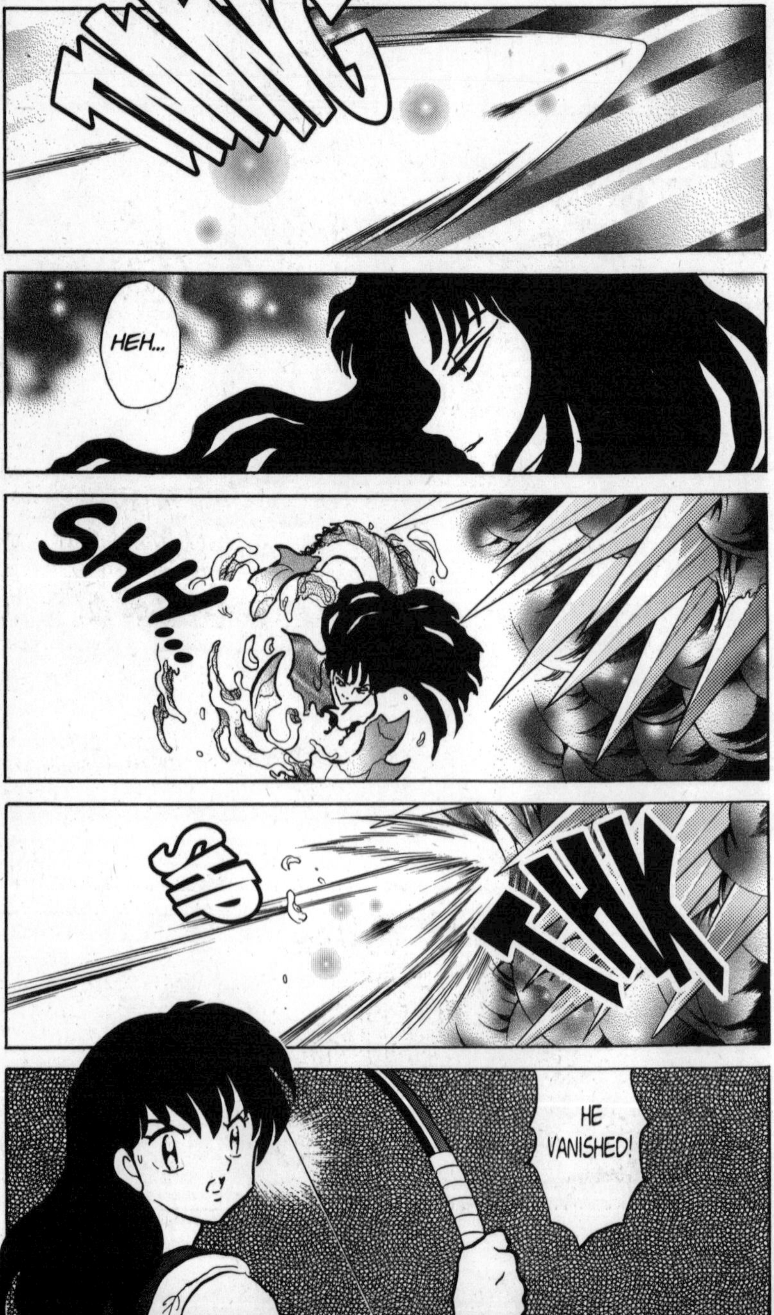
TWANG
HEH...
SHH...
SHP
THK
HE VANISHED!

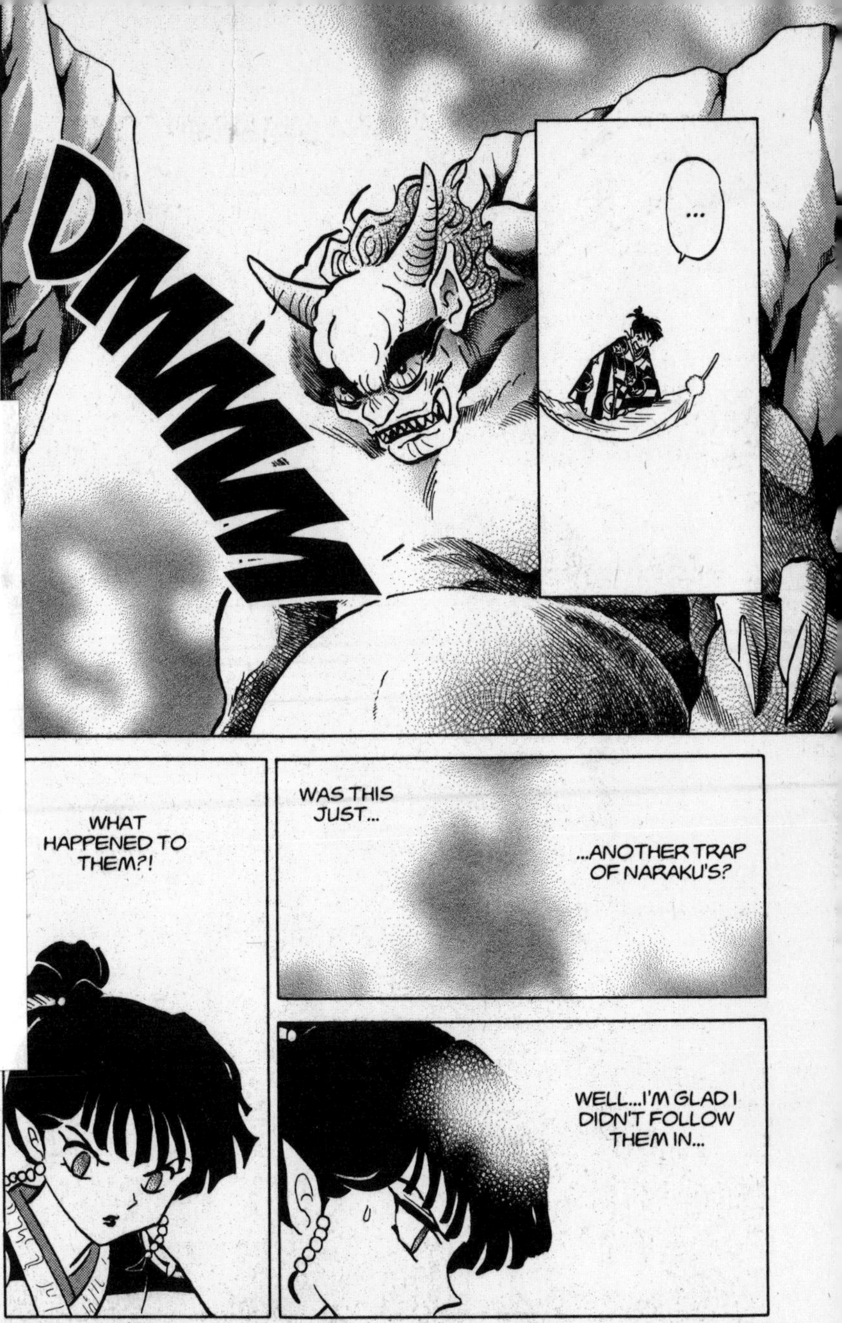
DMMMM
...
WHAT HAPPENED TO THEM?!
WAS THIS JUST...
...ANOTHER TRAP OF NARAKU'S?
WELL...I'M GLAD I DIDN'T FOLLOW THEM IN...

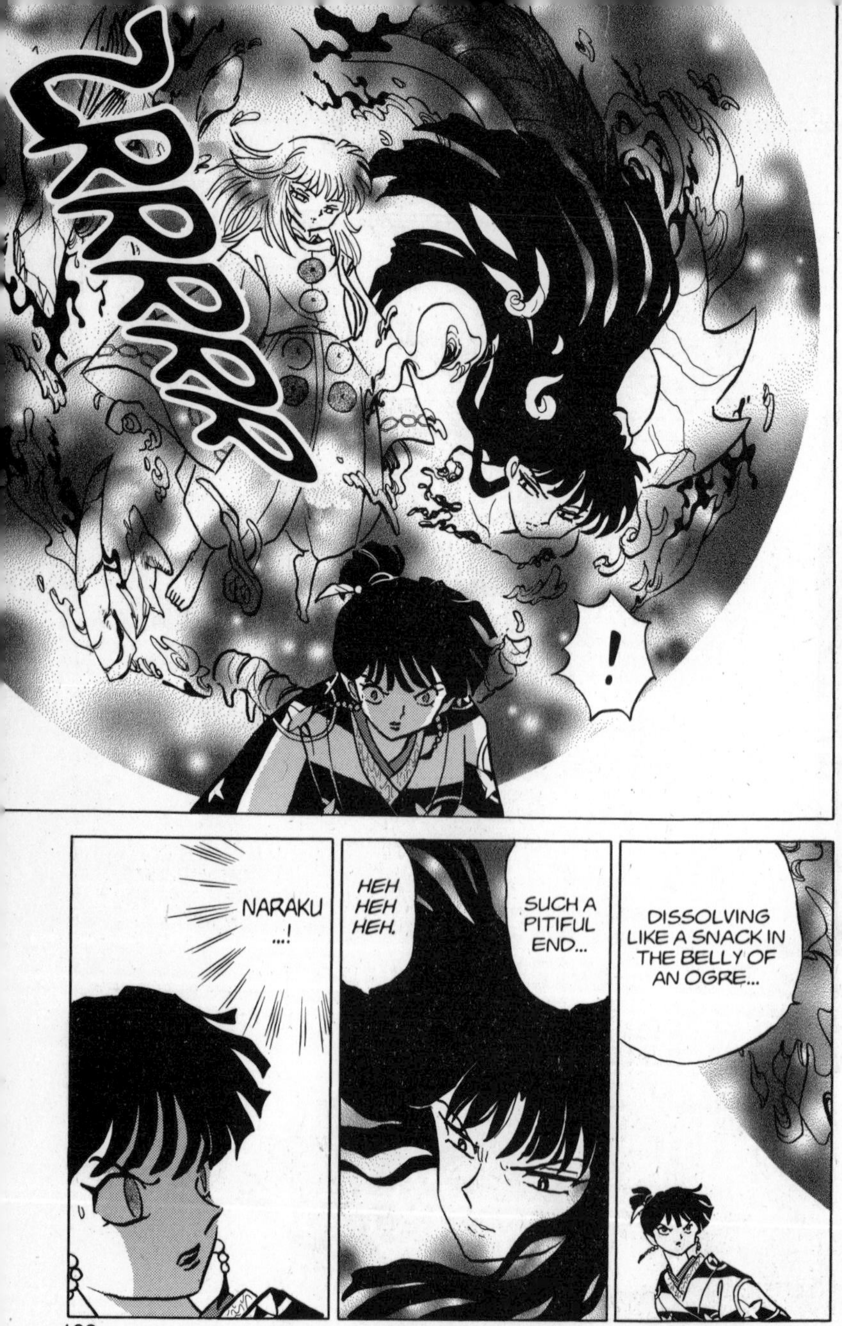
ZRRRRR
!
NARAKU ...!
HEH HEH HEH.
SUCH A PITIFUL END...
DISSOLVING LIKE A SNACK IN THE BELLY OF AN OGRE...

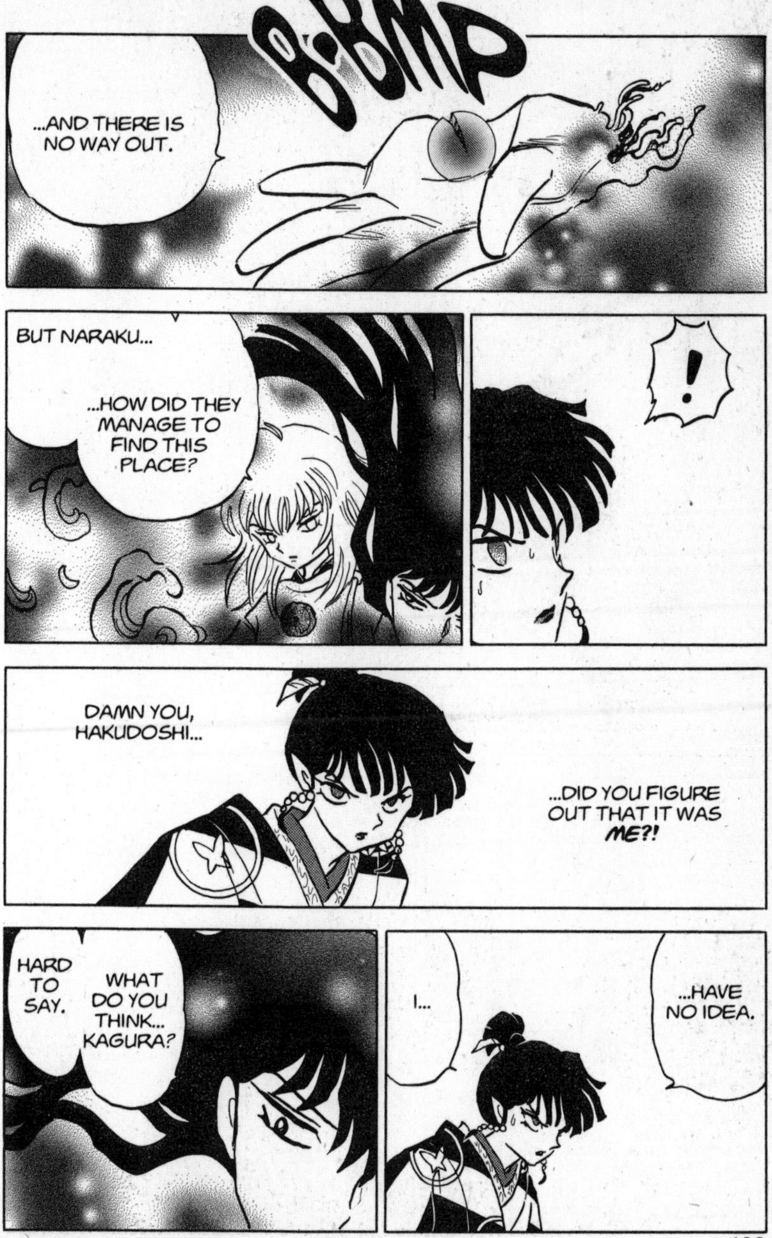
...AND THERE IS NO WAY OUT.
B-BMP
BUT NARAKU...
...HOW DID THEY MANAGE TO FIND THIS PLACE?
!
DAMN YOU, HAKUDOSHI...
...DID YOU FIGURE OUT THAT IT WAS *ME*?!
HARD TO SAY.
WHAT DO YOU THINK... KAGURA?
I...
...HAVE NO IDEA.

SSSSS...

PLIP

SSSSSS

AGHH!

PLIP PLIP

SSSSS

BLUP BLUP BLUP

THE ACID'S GETTING STRONGER!

CH-CHOKING...

KOF

SSSSS

BLP BLP BLP

IT'S SEEPING OUT OF THE WALLS!

AT THIS RATE...

BLUP

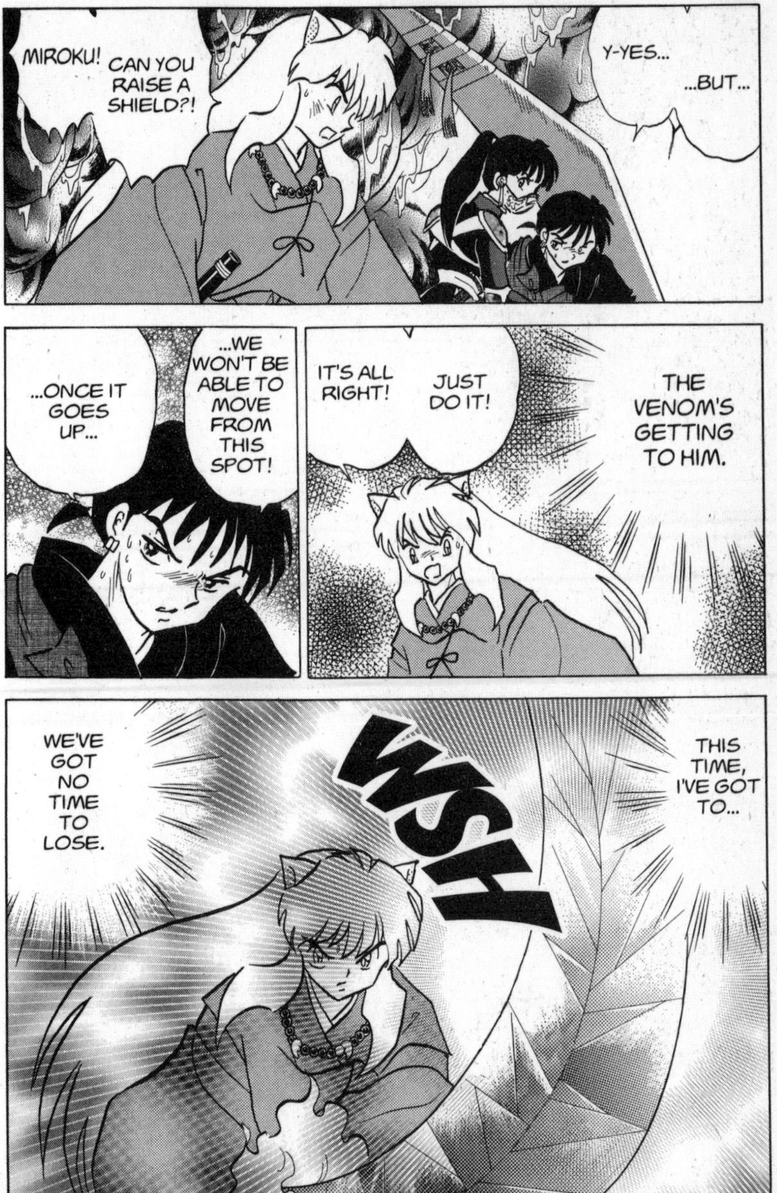
MIROKU!
CAN YOU RAISE A SHIELD?!
Y-YES...
...BUT...
...ONCE IT GOES UP...
...WE WON'T BE ABLE TO MOVE FROM THIS SPOT!
IT'S ALL RIGHT!
JUST DO IT!
THE VENOM'S GETTING TO HIM.
WE'VE GOT NO TIME TO LOSE.
WSH
THIS TIME, I'VE GOT TO...

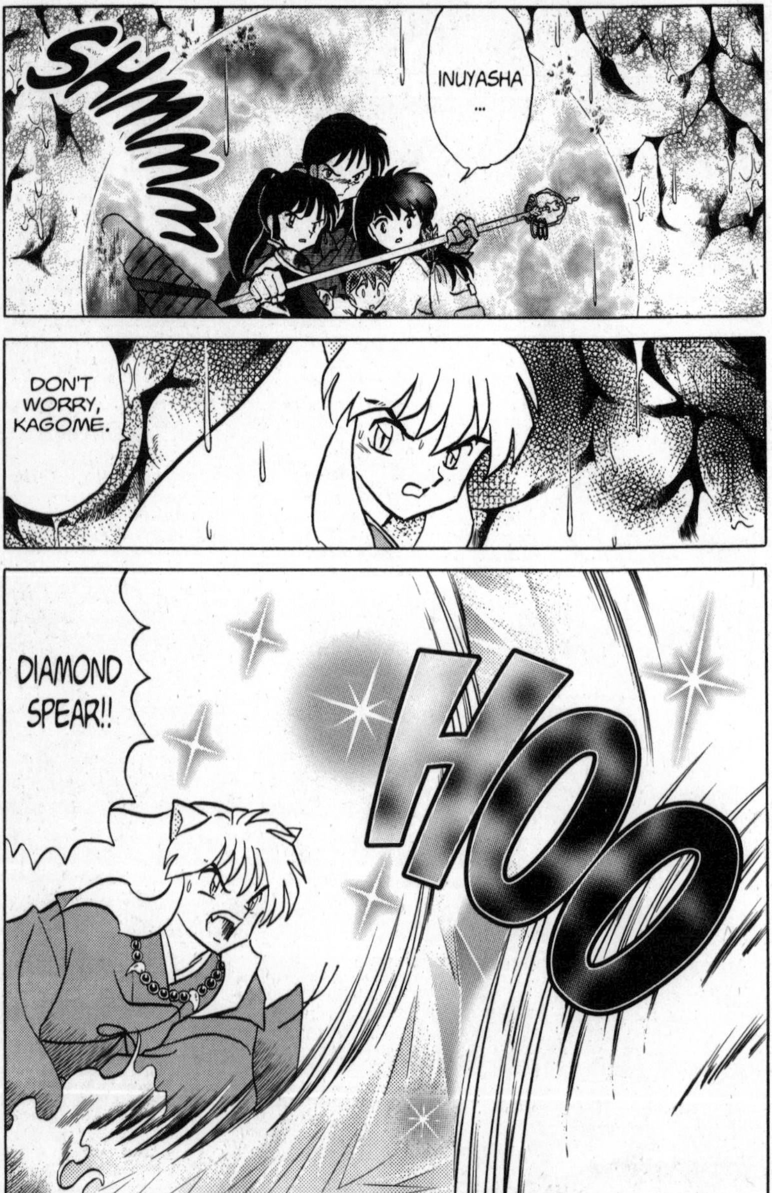
SHMMM
INUYASHA ...
DON'T WORRY, KAGOME.
DIAMOND SPEAR!!
HOO

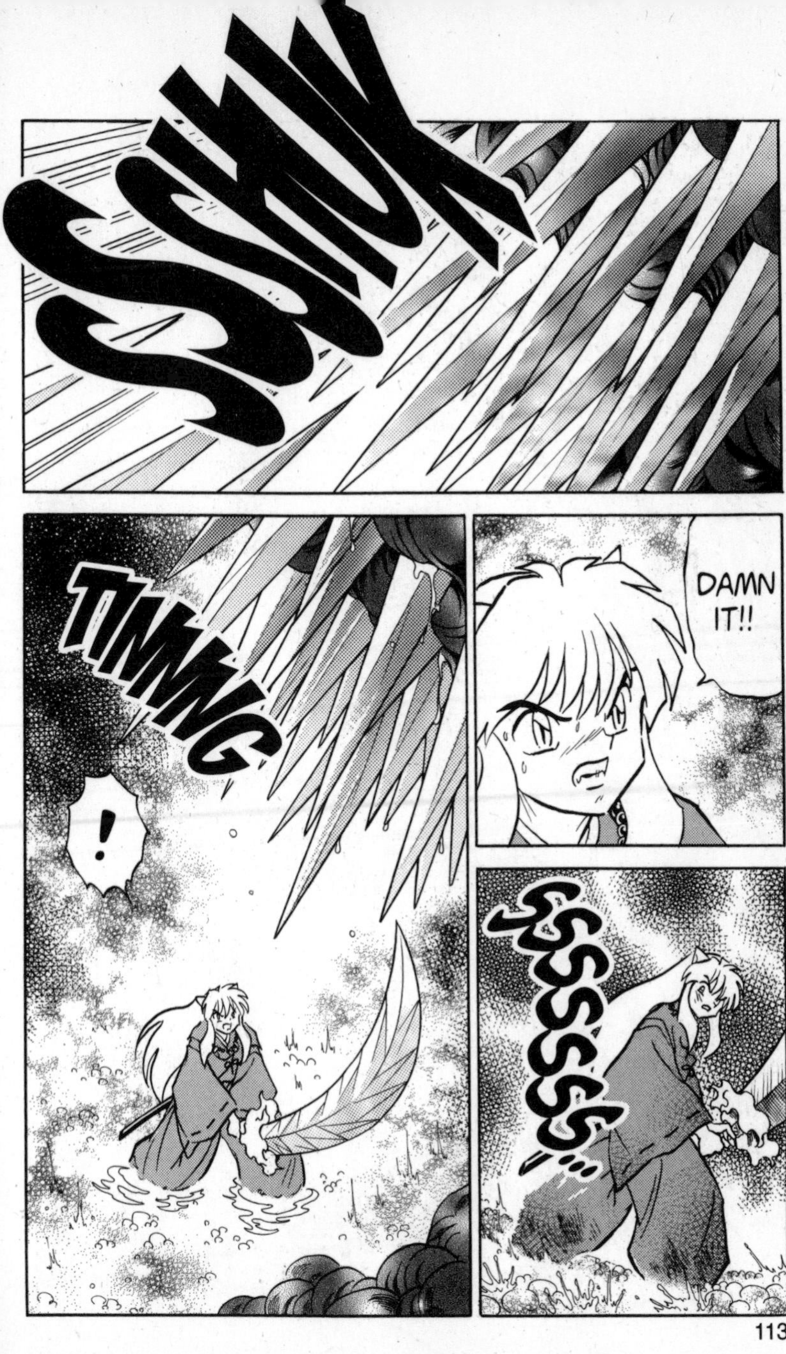
SSHIK
DAMN IT!!
SSSSSS...
TINNG
!

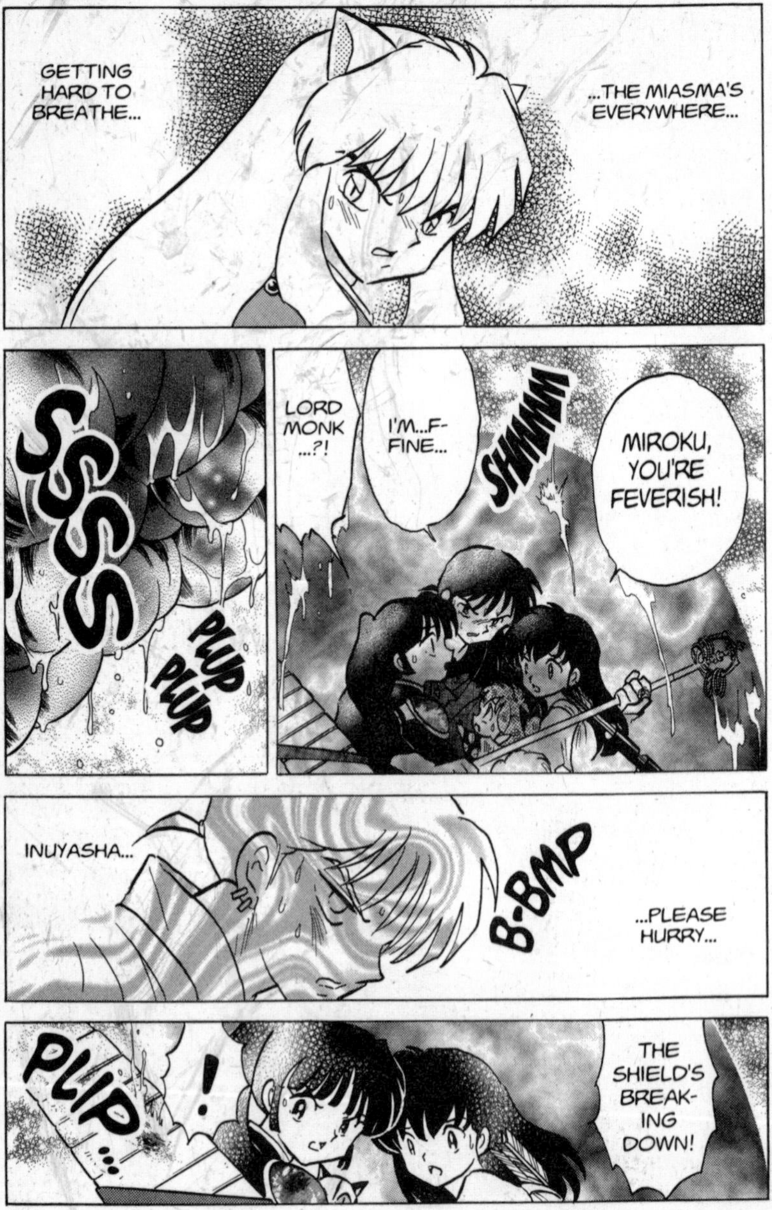
GETTING HARD TO BREATHE...
...THE MIASMA'S EVERYWHERE...
SSSS
PLUP PLUP
LORD MONK ...?!
I'M...F-FINE...
SHMMM
MIROKU, YOU'RE FEVERISH!
INUYASHA...
B-BMP
...PLEASE HURRY...
PLIP...
!
THE SHIELD'S BREAK-ING DOWN!

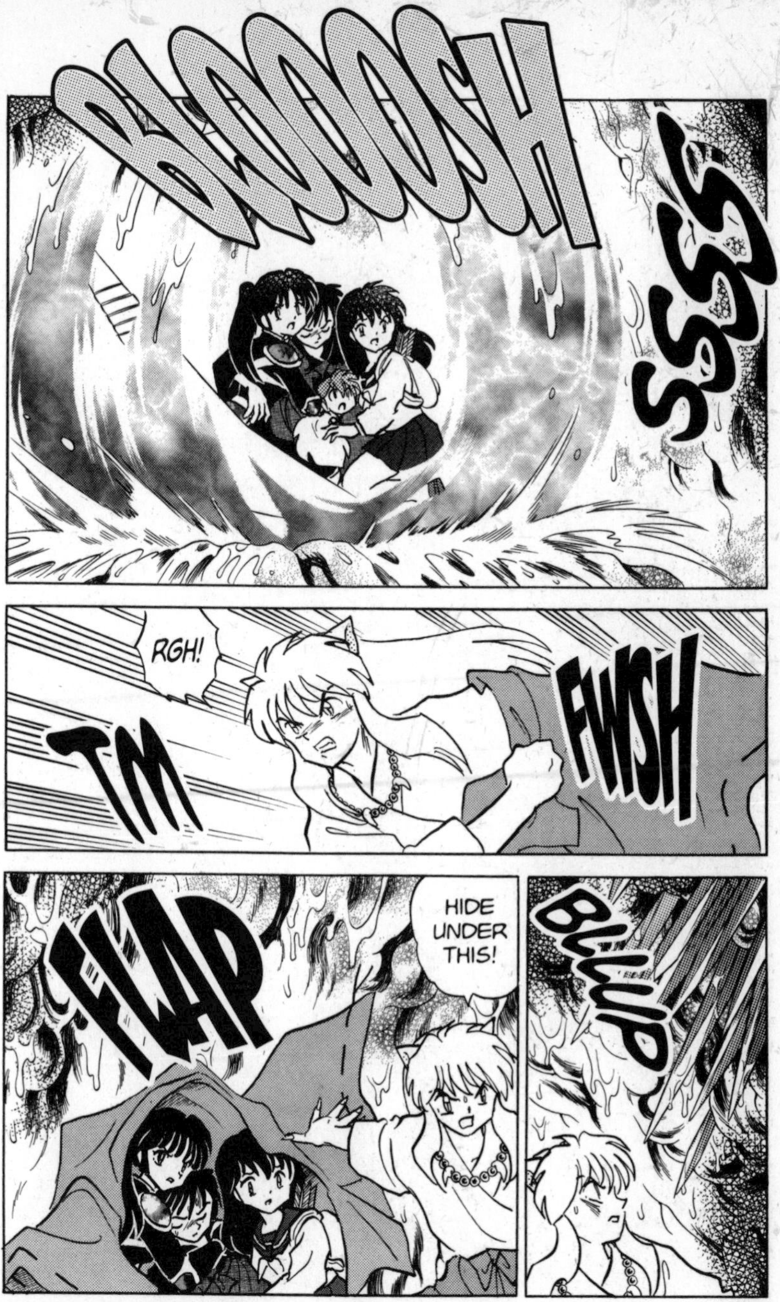
BLOOOSH
SSSSS
RGH!
TM
FWSH
FLAP
HIDE UNDER THIS!
BLUUP

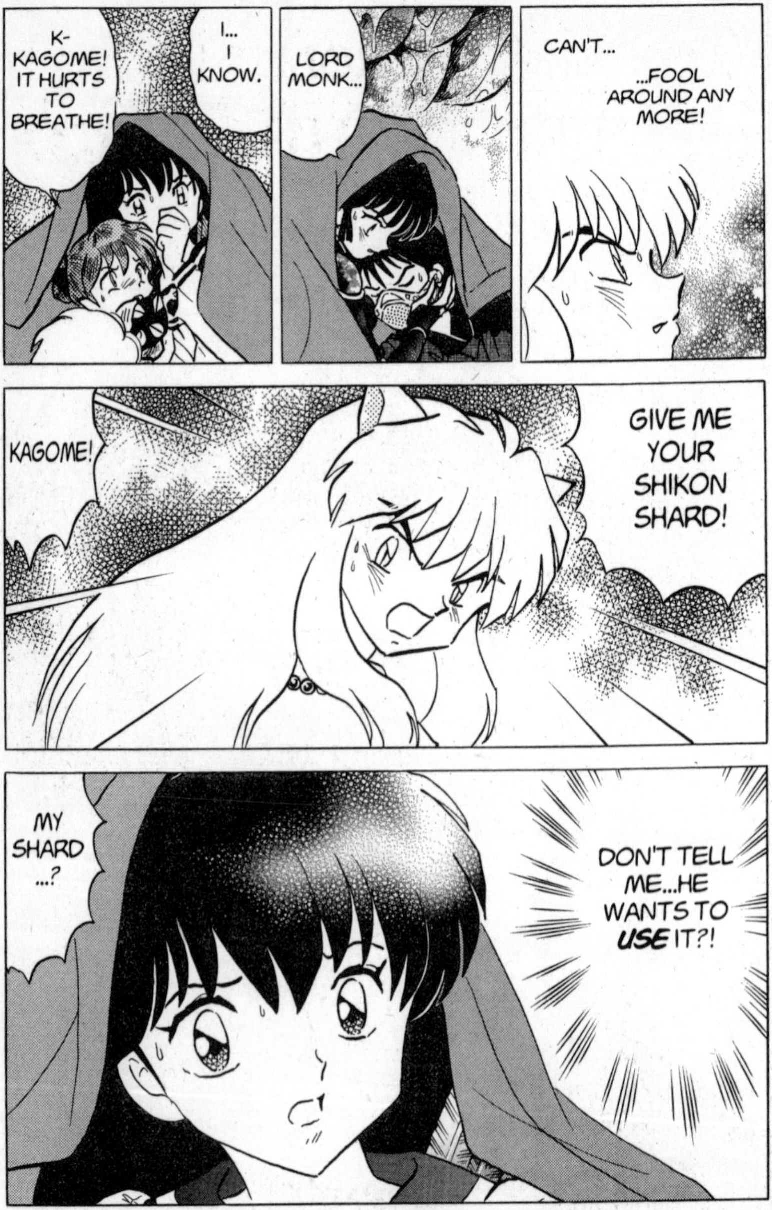
K-KAGOME! IT HURTS TO BREATHE!
I... I KNOW.
LORD MONK...
CAN'T...
...FOOL AROUND ANY MORE!
KAGOME!
GIVE ME YOUR SHIKON SHARD!
MY SHARD ...?
DON'T TELL ME...HE WANTS TO *USE* IT?!

SCROLL 7
USING THE SHARD

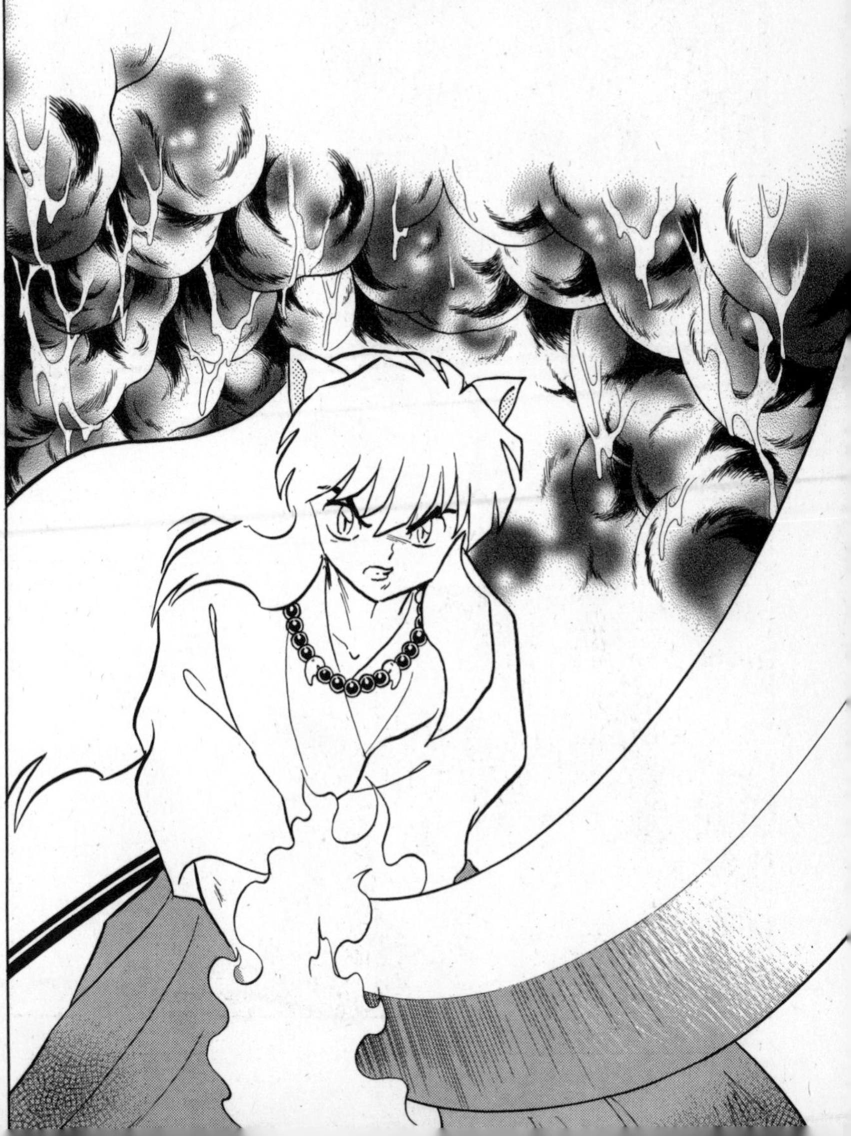

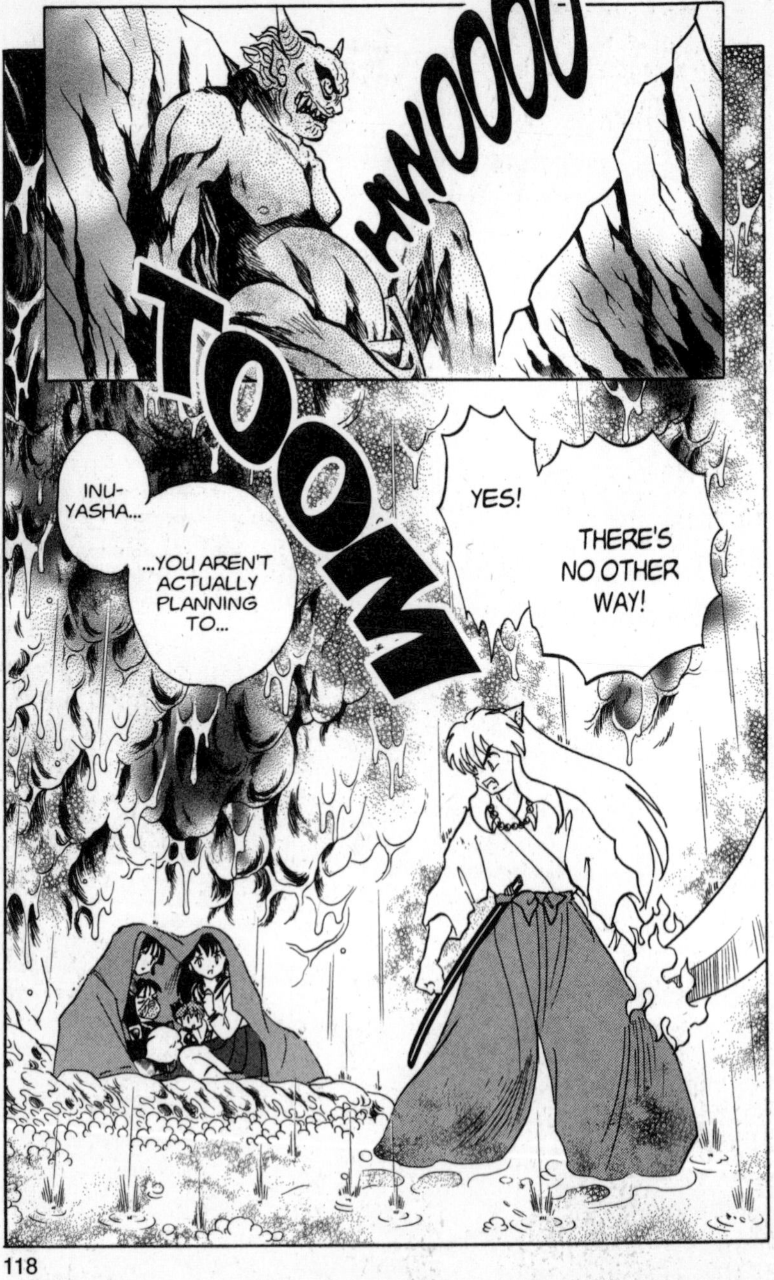
HWOOOO
TOOOM
INU-YASHA...
...YOU AREN'T ACTUALLY PLANNING TO...
YES!
THERE'S NO OTHER WAY!

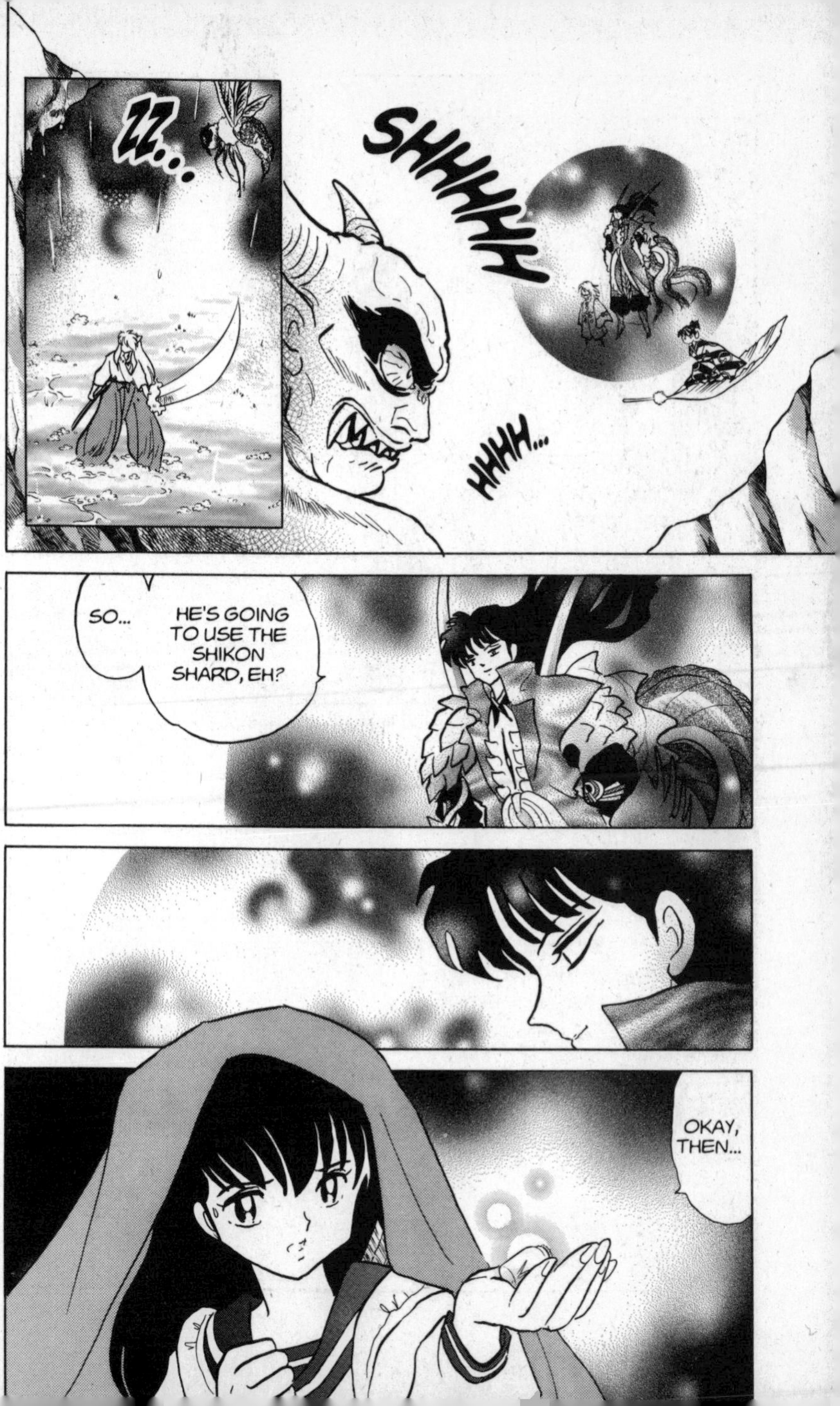
ZZ...
SHHHHHHHHHHH...
SO... HE'S GOING TO USE THE SHIKON SHARD, EH?
OKAY, THEN...

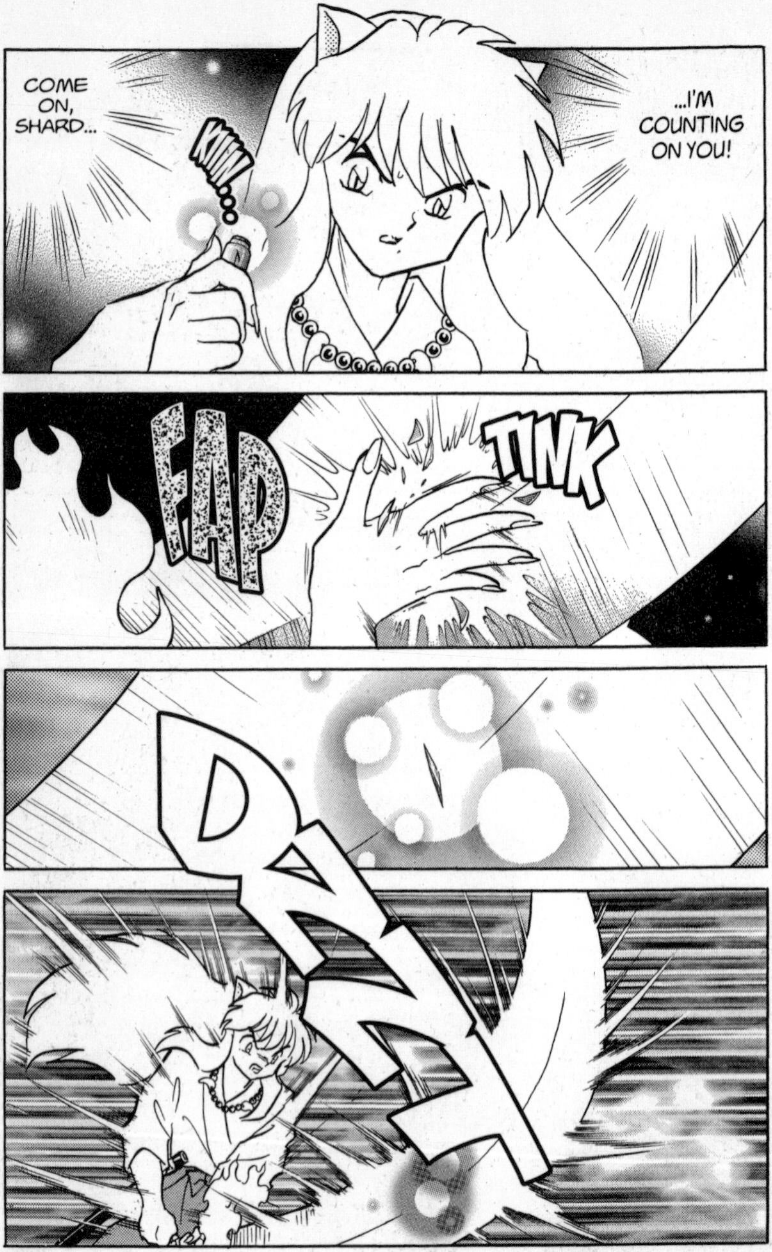
COME ON, SHARD...
KIIN
...I'M COUNTING ON YOU!
FAP
TINK

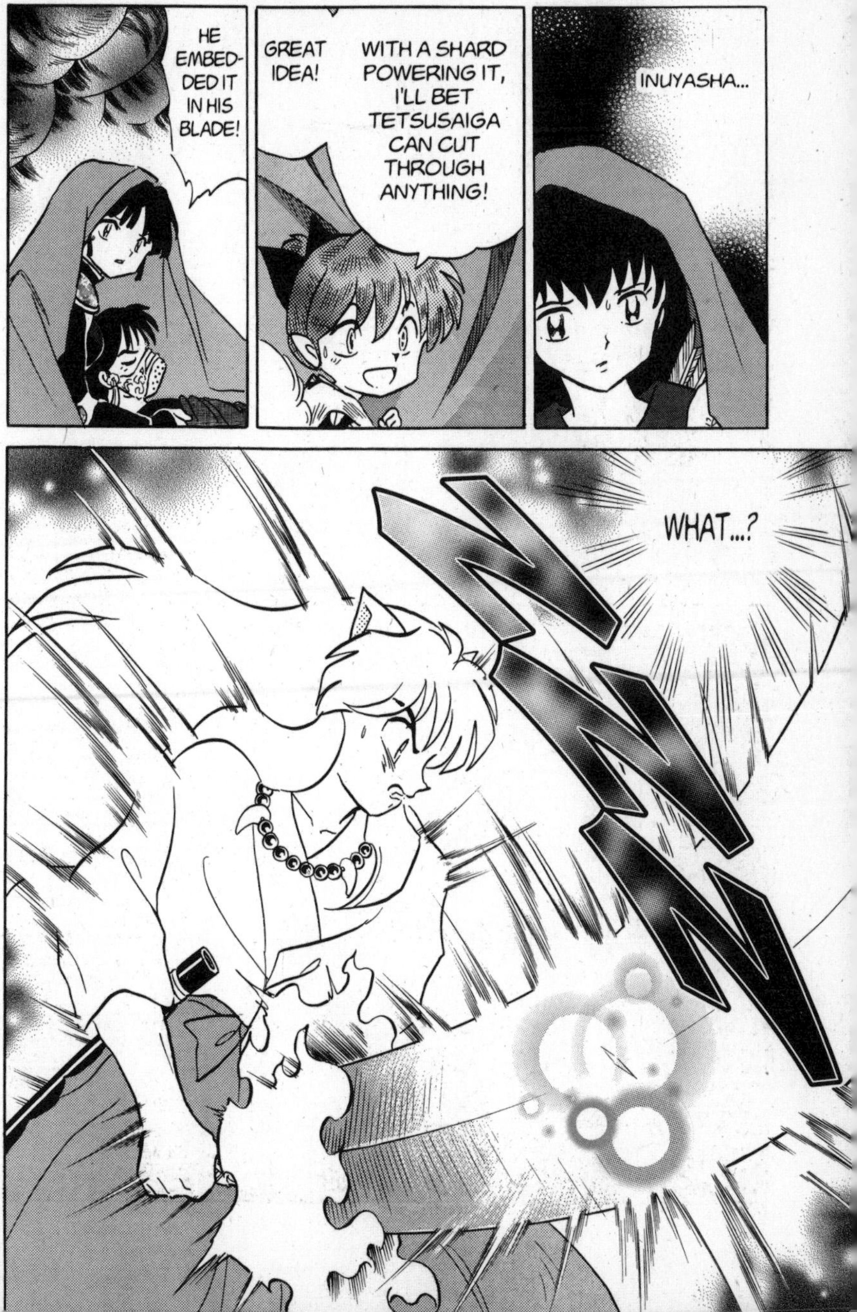
HE EMBEDDED IT IN HIS BLADE!
GREAT IDEA!
WITH A SHARD POWERING IT, I'LL BET TETSUSAIGA CAN CUT THROUGH ANYTHING!
INUYASHA...
WHAT...?

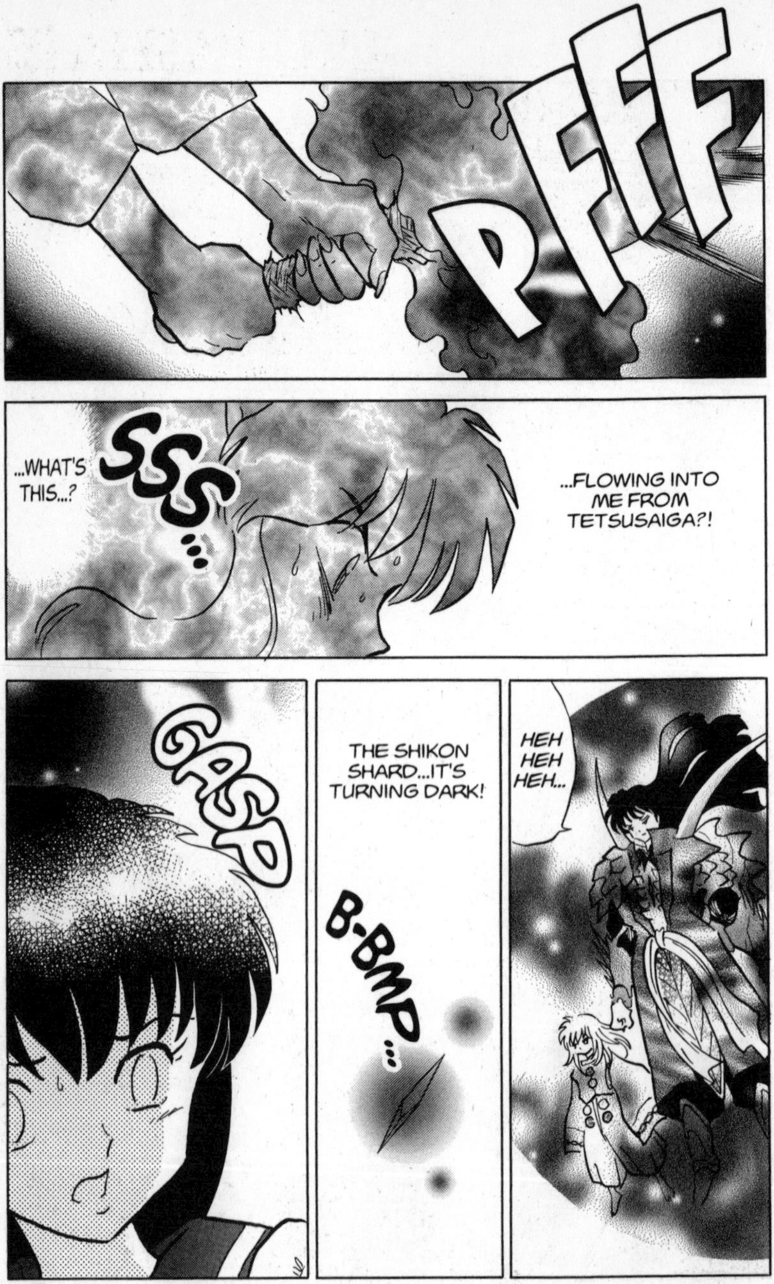
PFFF
...WHAT'S THIS...?
SSS...
...FLOWING INTO ME FROM TETSUSAIGA?!
GASP
THE SHIKON SHARD...IT'S TURNING DARK!
B-BMP...
HEH HEH HEH...

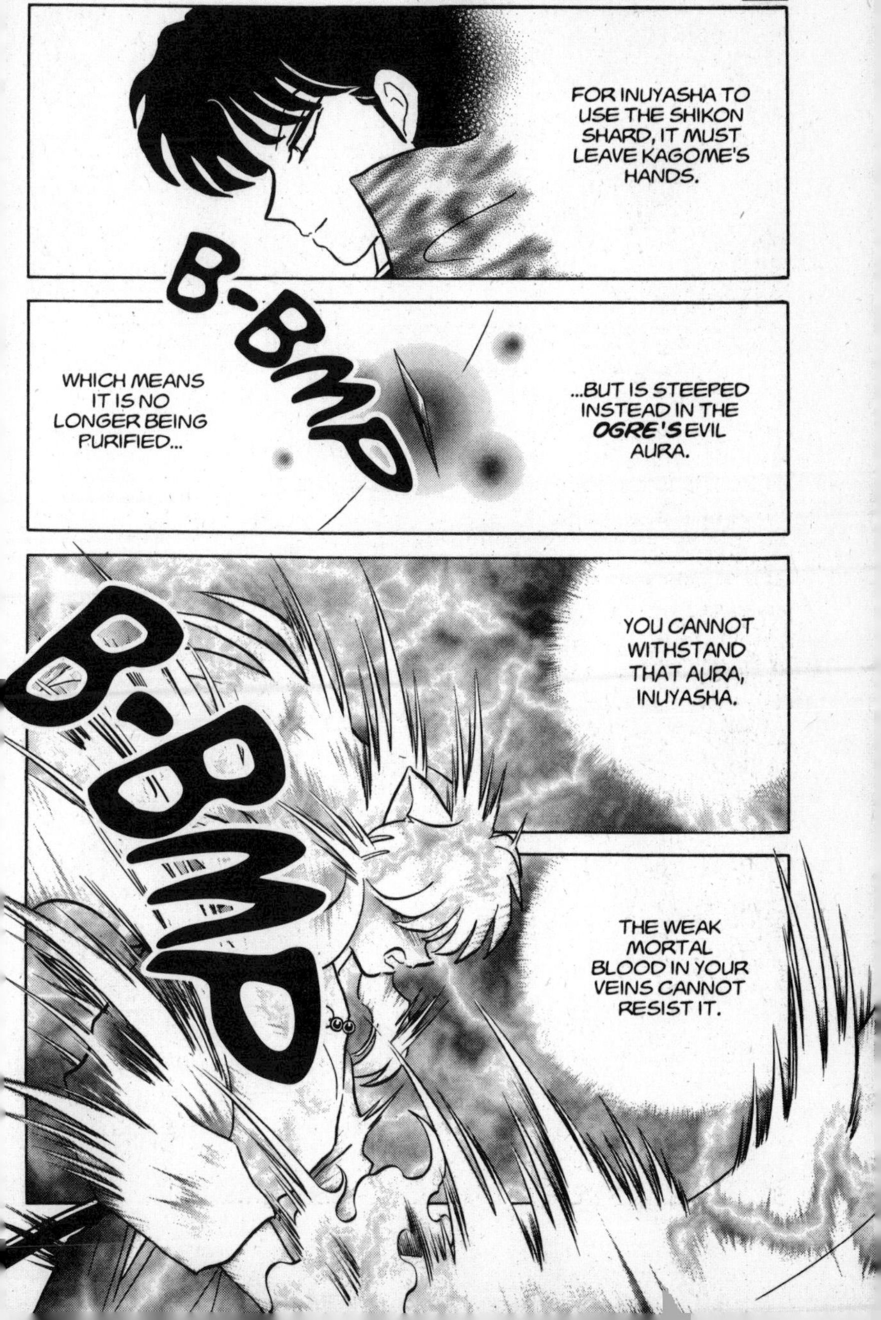
FOR INUYASHA TO USE THE SHIKON SHARD, IT MUST LEAVE KAGOME'S HANDS.
B-BMP
WHICH MEANS IT IS NO LONGER BEING PURIFIED...
...BUT IS STEEPED INSTEAD IN THE ***OGRE'S*** EVIL AURA.
B-BMP
YOU CANNOT WITHSTAND THAT AURA, INUYASHA.
THE WEAK MORTAL BLOOD IN YOUR VEINS CANNOT RESIST IT.

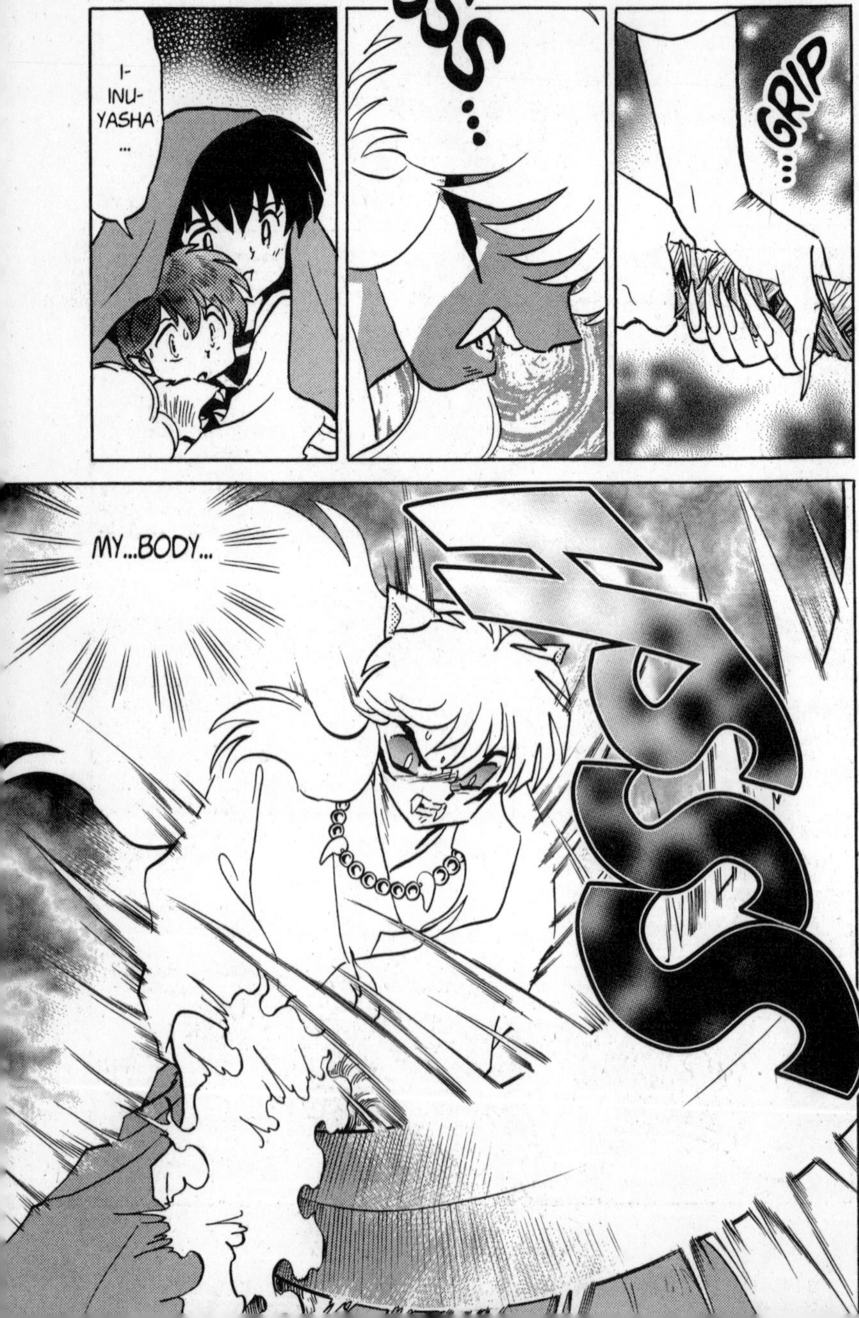
I-
INU-
YASHA
...
SSS...
...GRIP
MY...BODY...

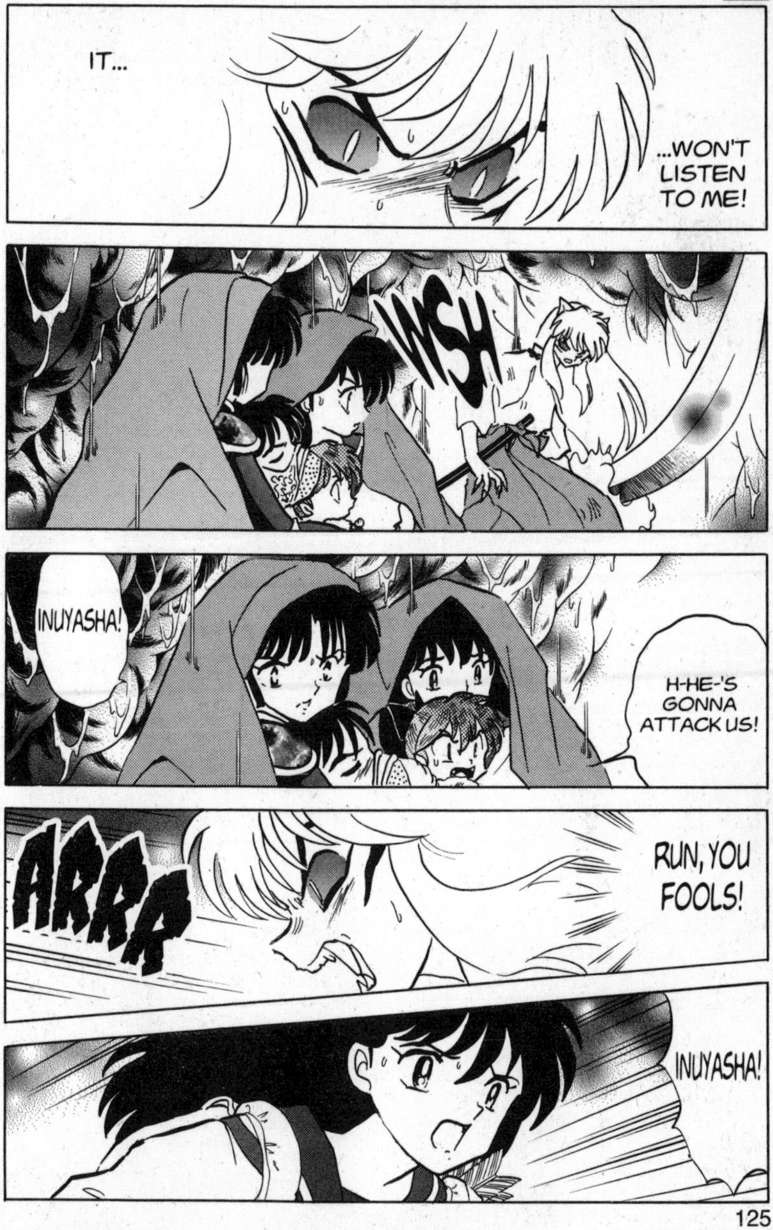
IT...
...WON'T LISTEN TO ME!
WSH
INUYASHA!
H-HE-'S GONNA ATTACK US!
ARRR
RUN, YOU FOOLS!
INUYASHA!

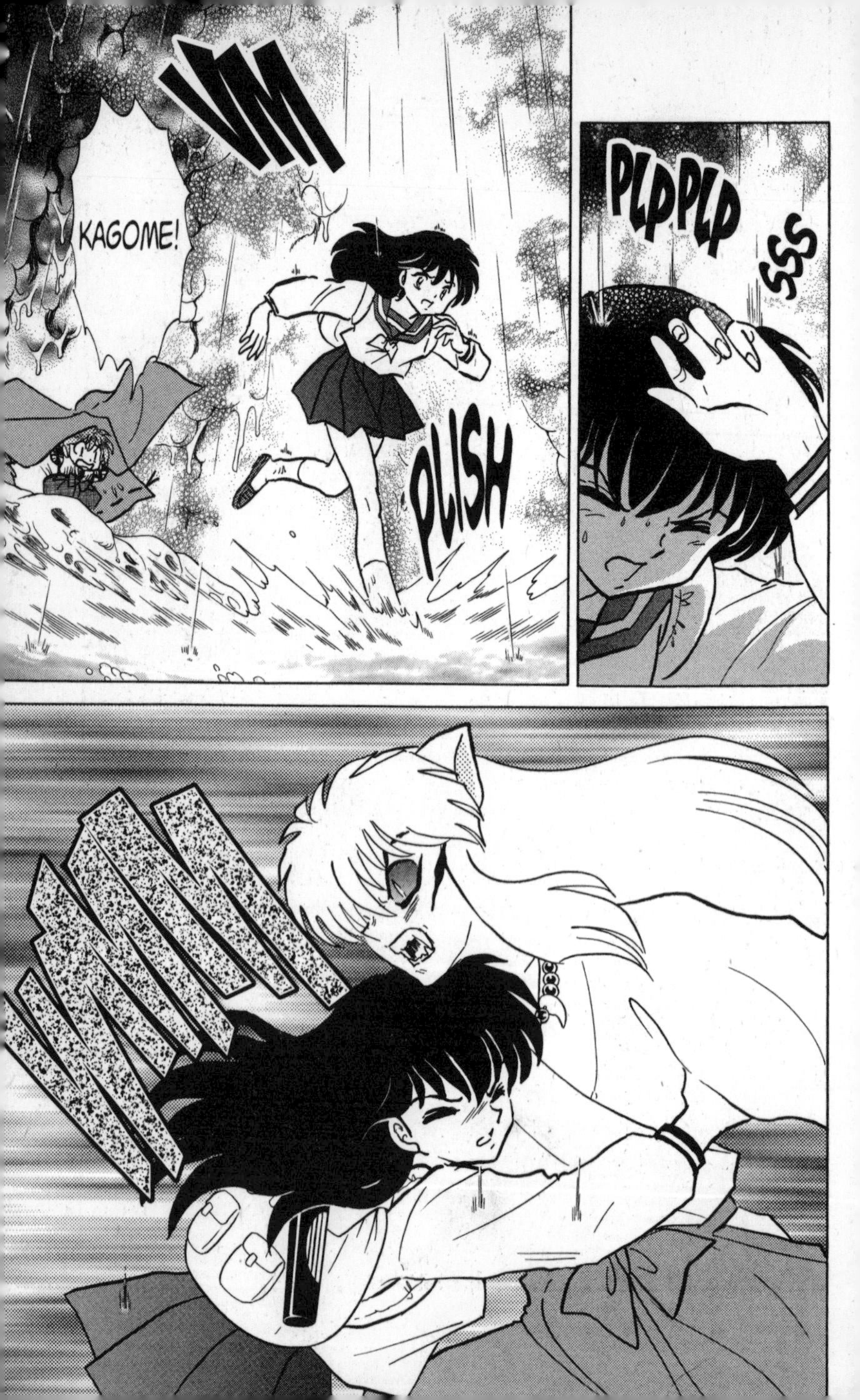
VM
KAGOME!
PLISH
PLP PLP
SSS

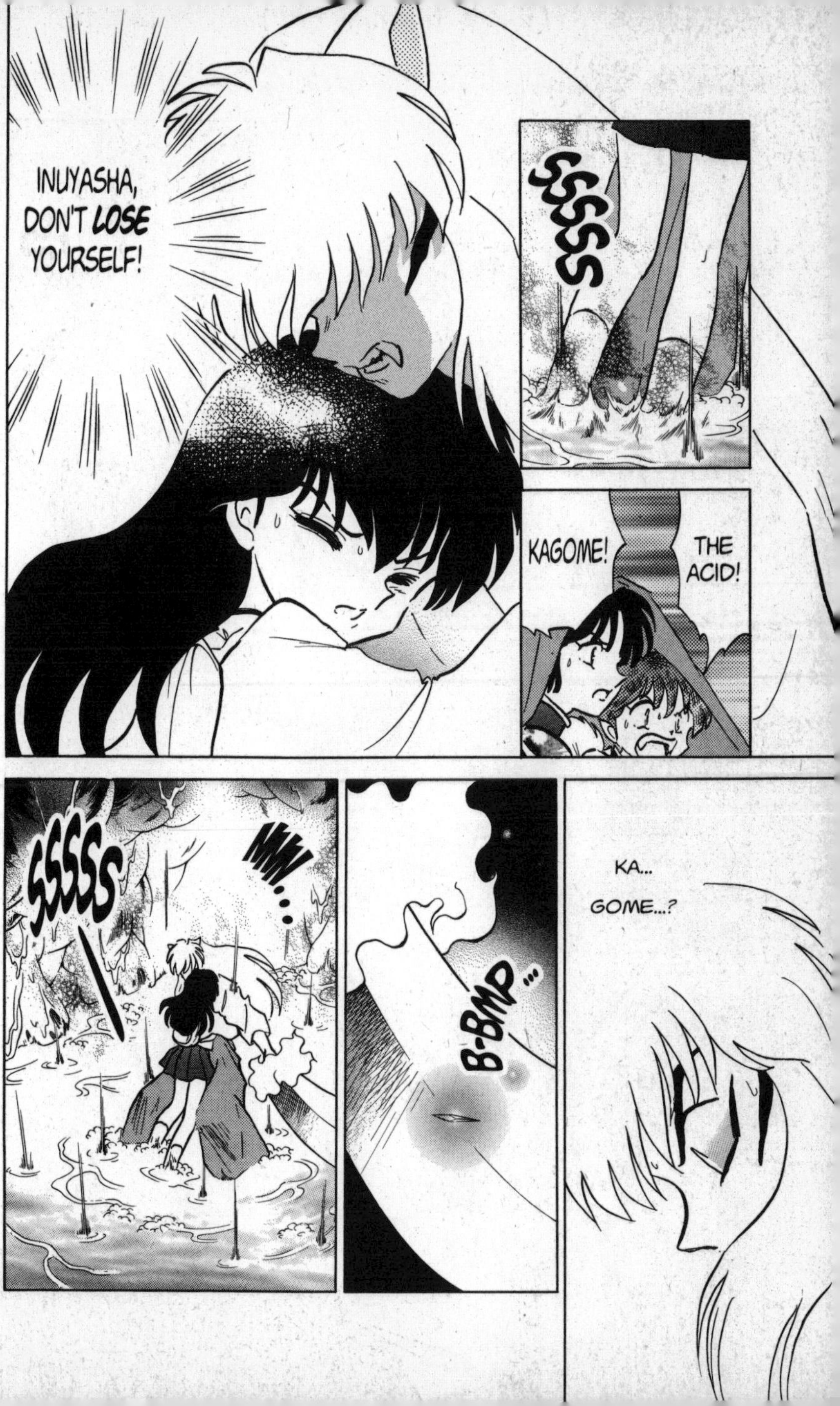
INUYASHA, DON'T LOSE YOURSELF!
SSSSS
KAGOME!
THE ACID!
SSSSS
MM...
B-BMP...
KA...
GOME...?

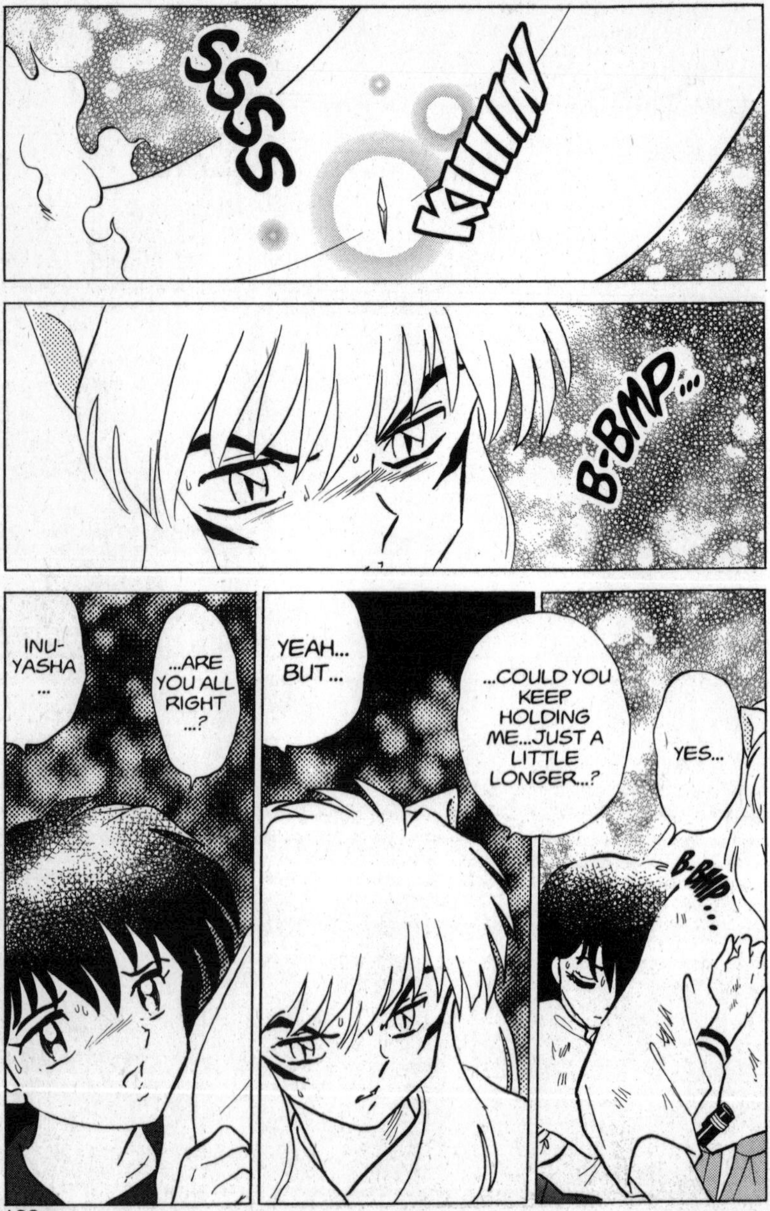

SSSS
KIIIIN
B-BMP...
INU-YASHA...
...ARE YOU ALL RIGHT...?
YEAH... BUT...
...COULD YOU KEEP HOLDING ME...JUST A LITTLE LONGER...?
YES...
B-BMP...

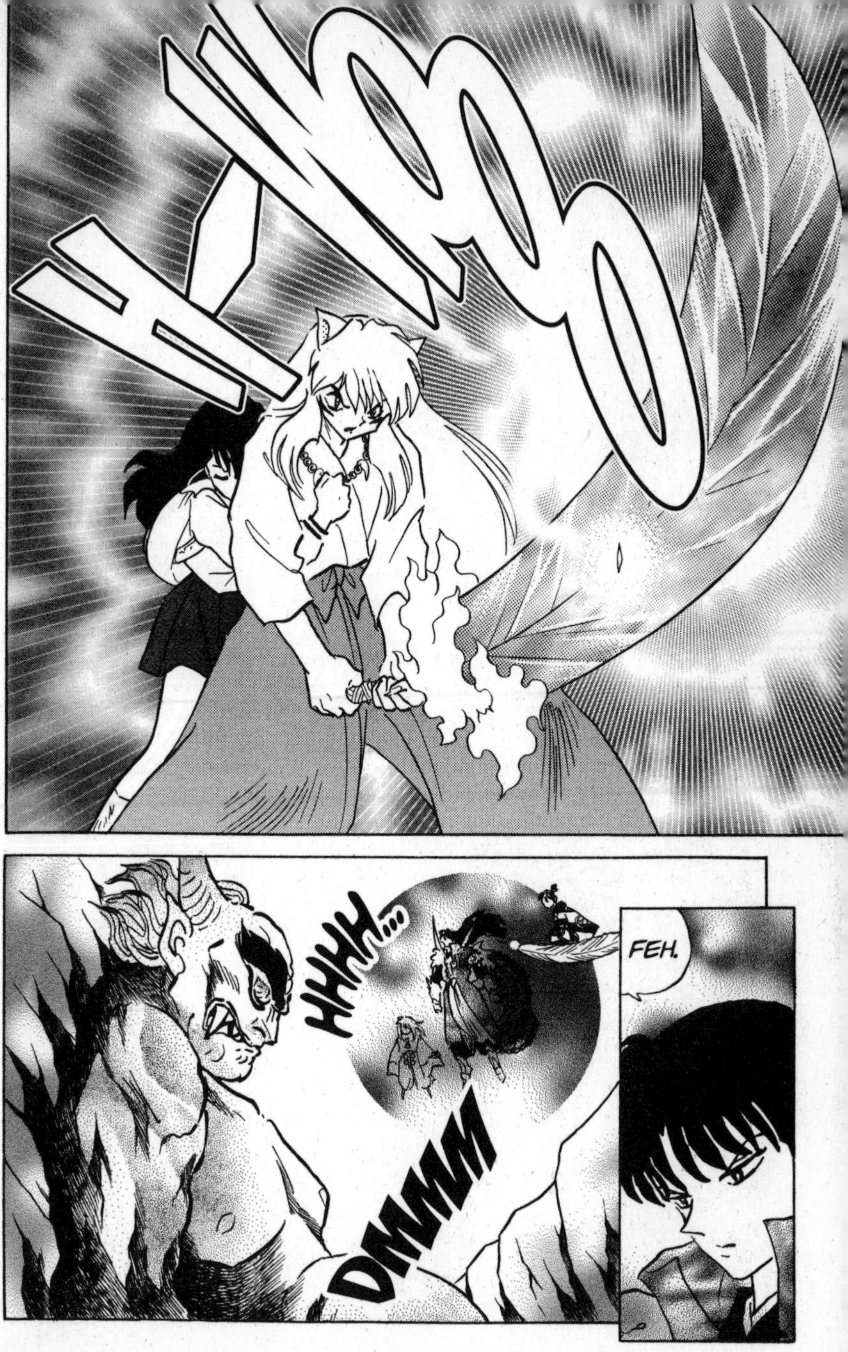
HYOOO
FEH.
HHHH...
DMMMM

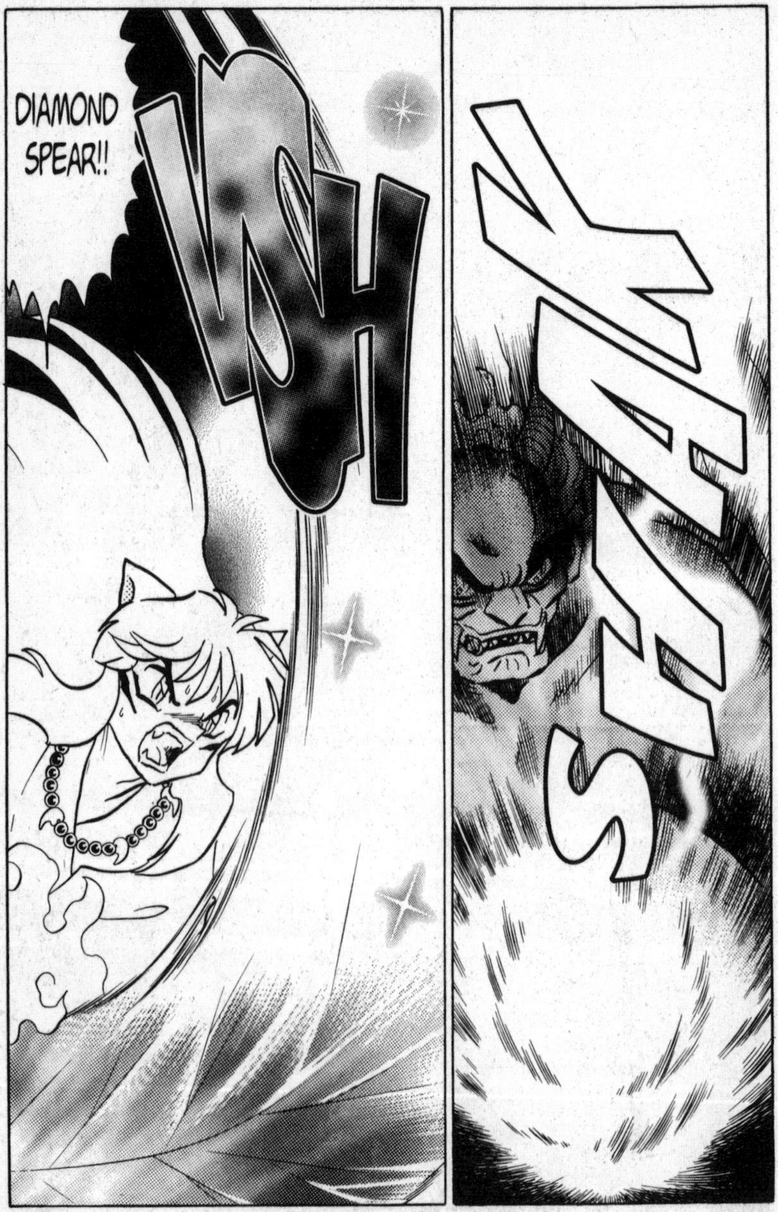
DIAMOND SPEAR!!

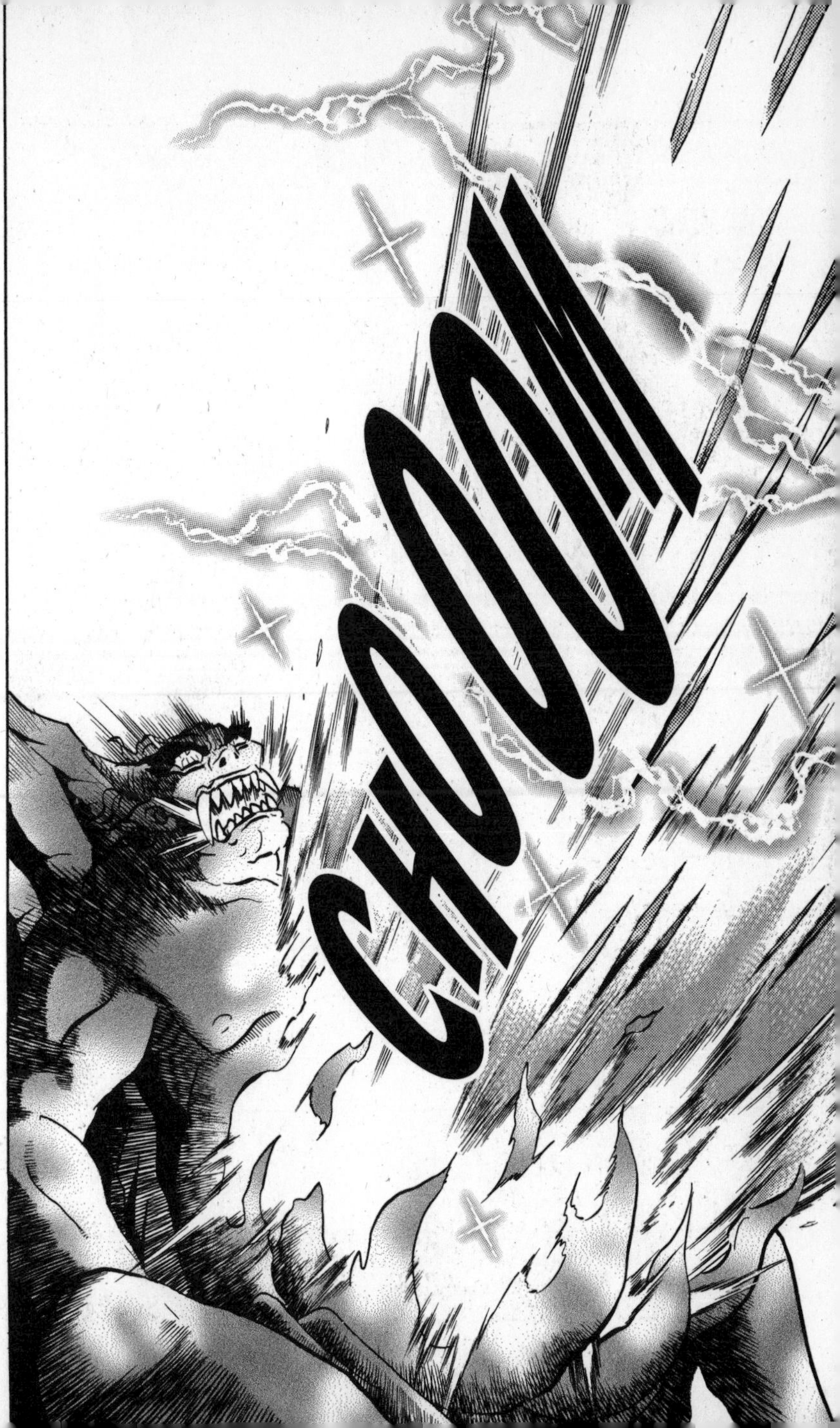
CHOOM

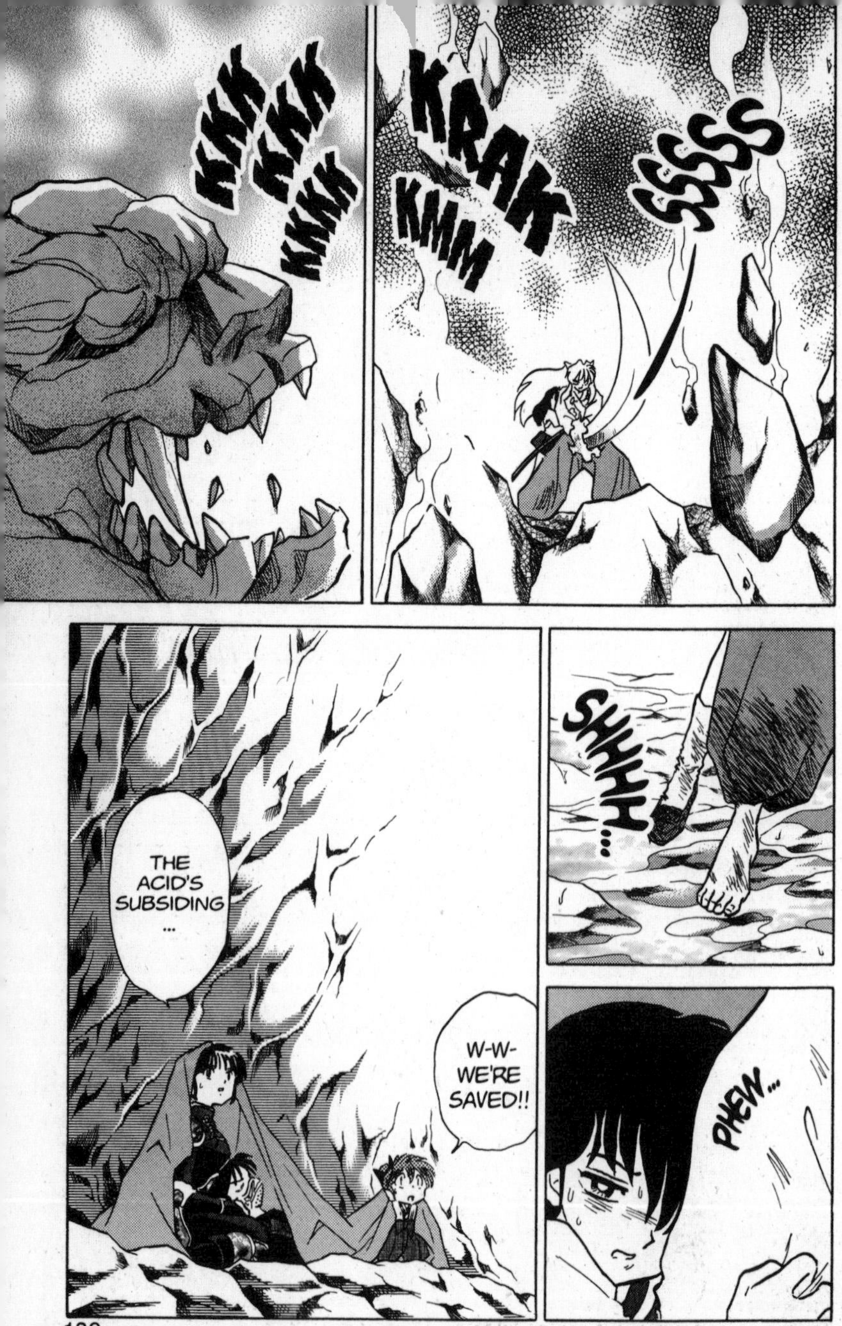
KRAK
KMM
SSSSS
THE ACID'S SUBSIDING ...
W-W-WE'RE SAVED!!
SHHHH...
PHEW...

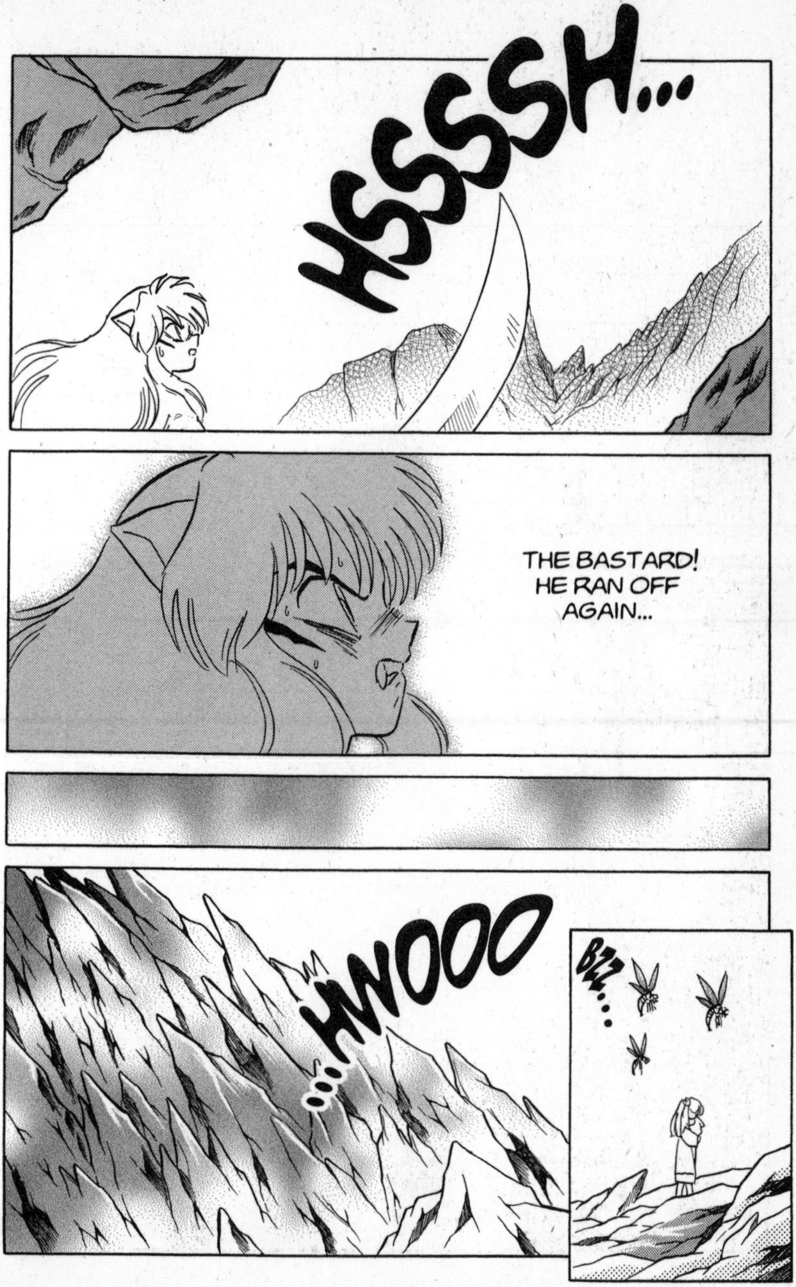
HSSSSH...
THE BASTARD! HE RAN OFF AGAIN...
...HWOOO
BZZ...

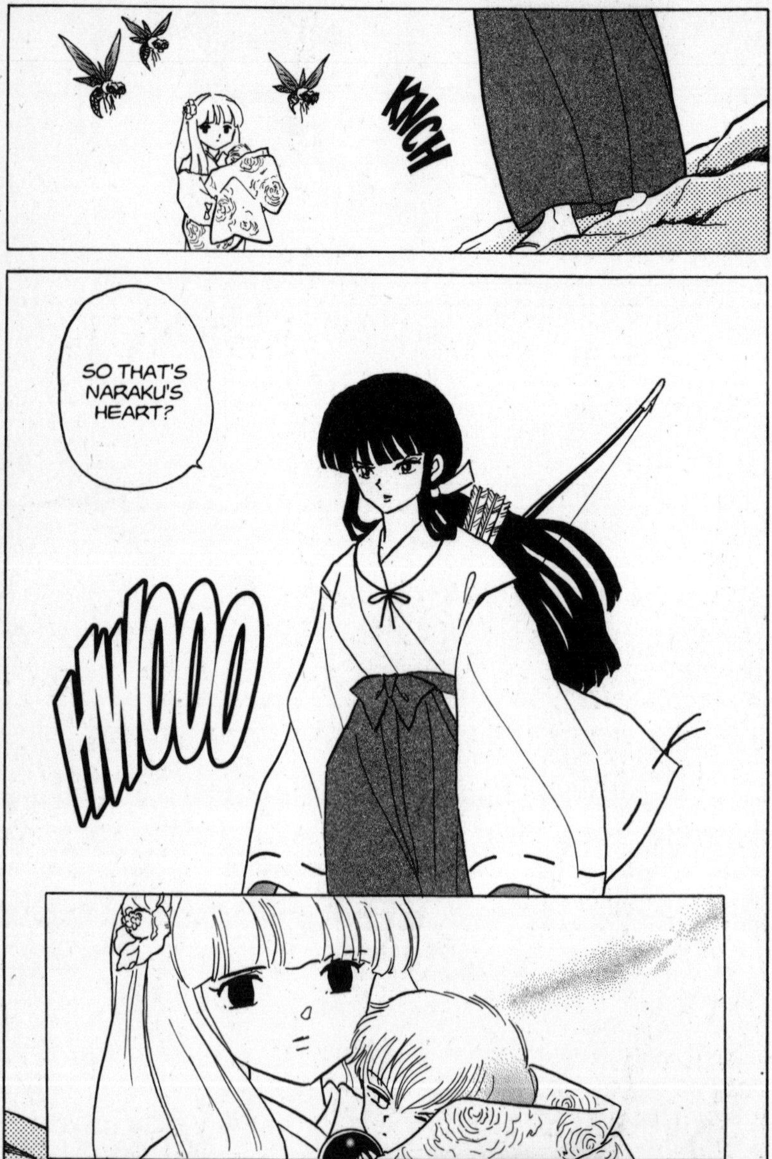
KNICH
SO THAT'S NARAKU'S HEART?
HWOOO

SCROLL 8

THE EVIL PRESENCE

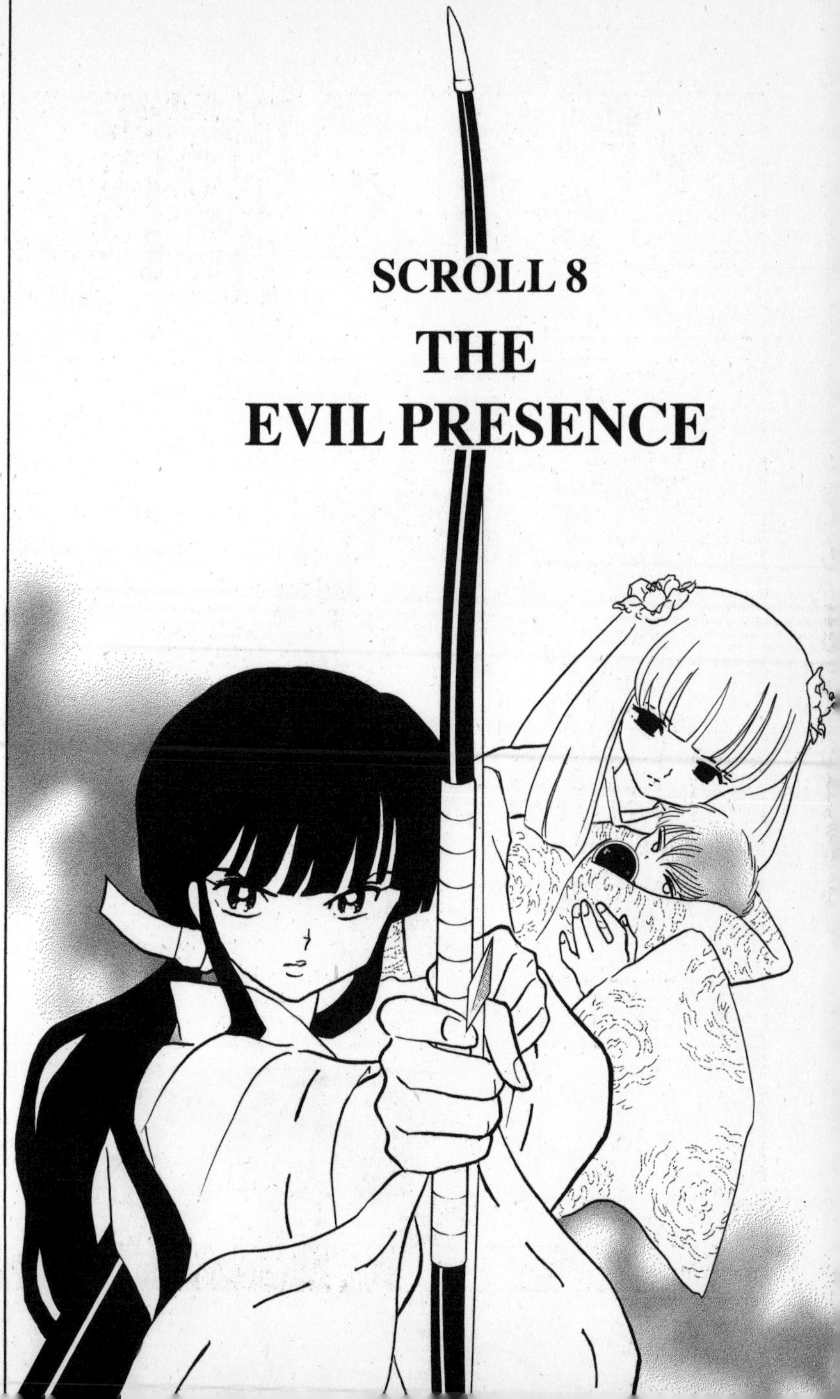

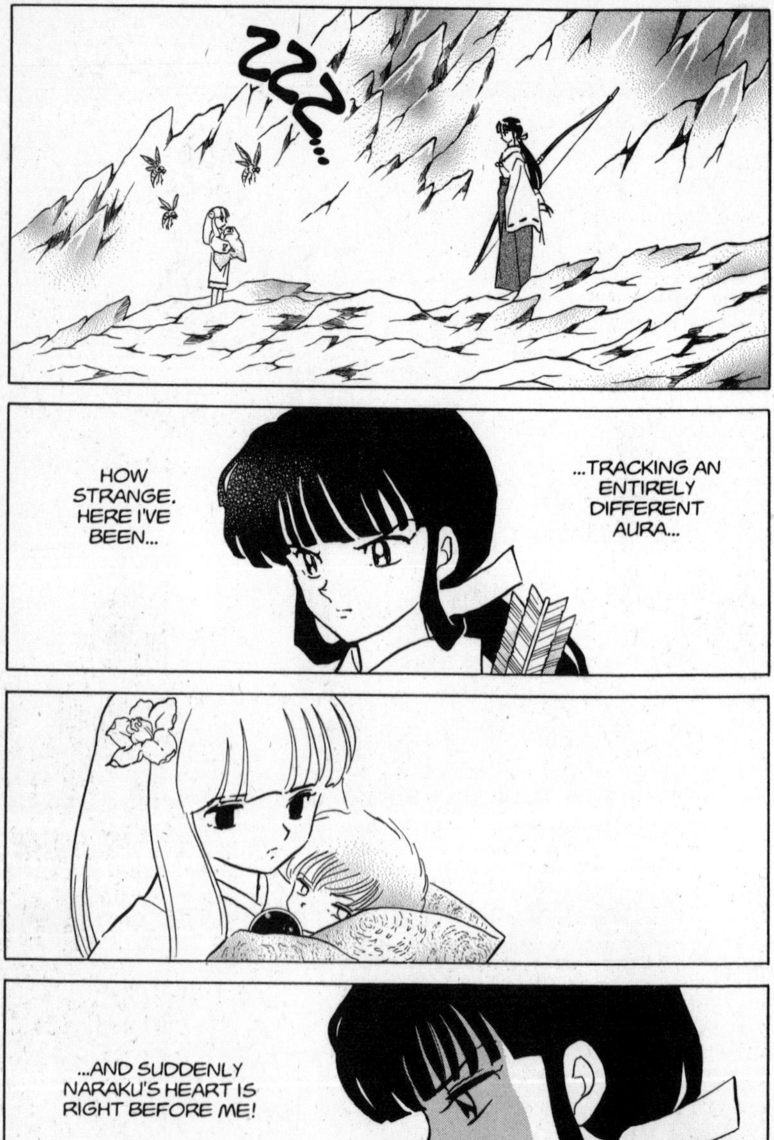
ZZZ...
HOW STRANGE. HERE I'VE BEEN...
...TRACKING AN ENTIRELY DIFFERENT AURA...
...AND SUDDENLY NARAKU'S HEART IS RIGHT BEFORE ME!

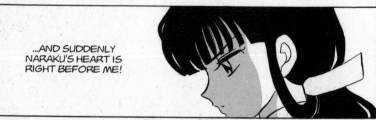

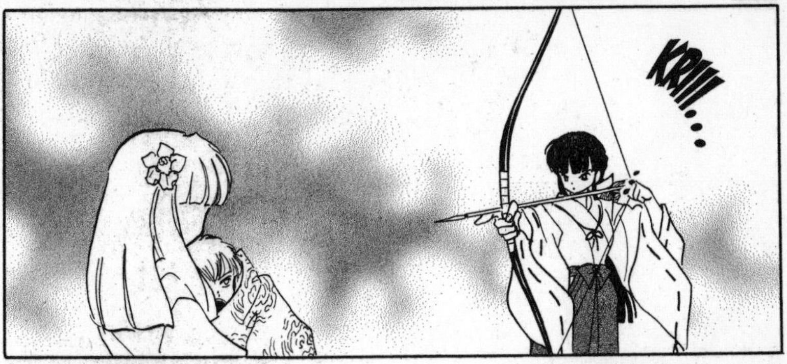
KRIII...

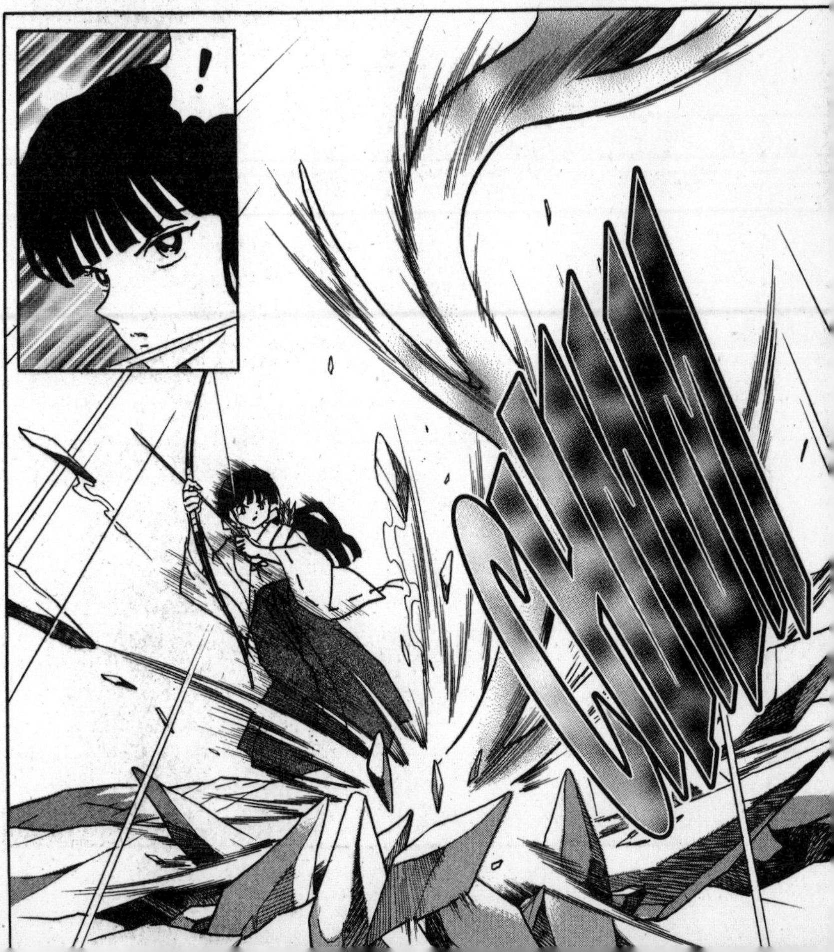
!

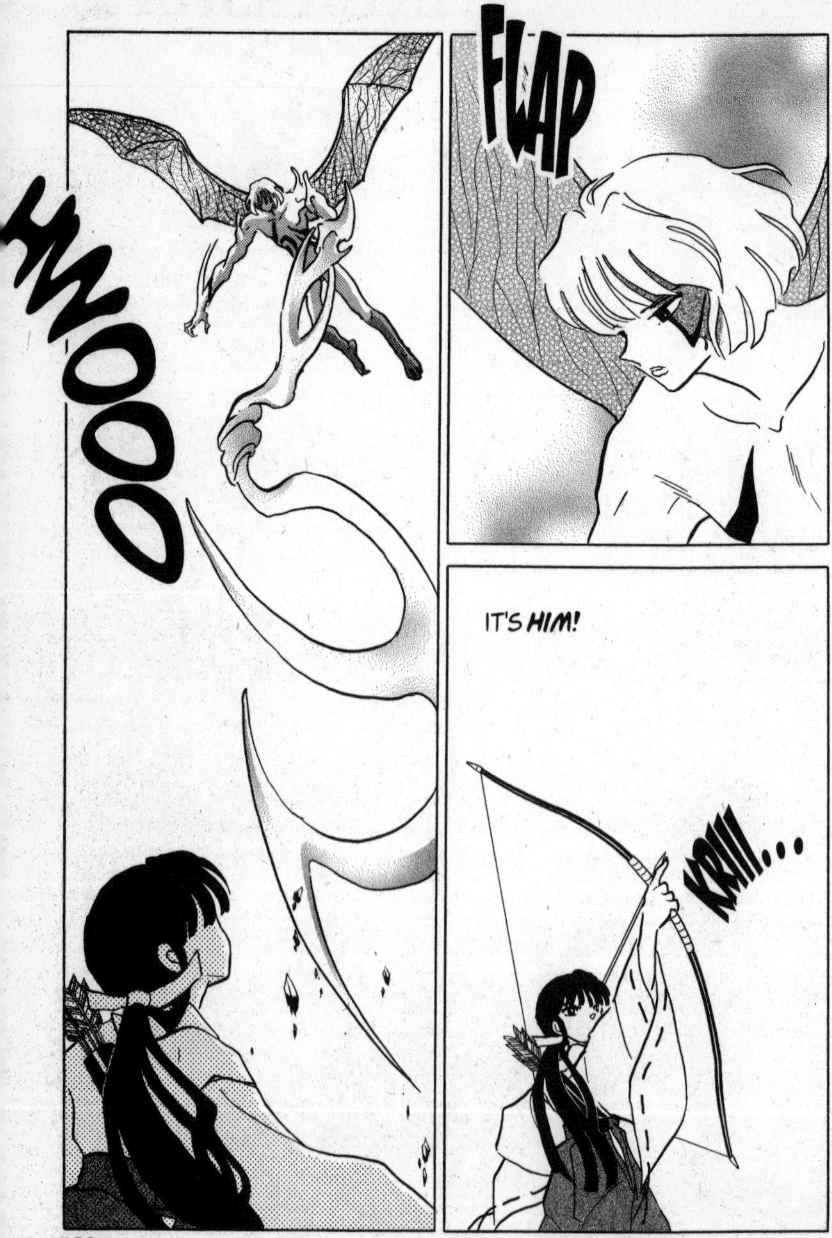
WHOOOO
FLAP
IT'S *HIM!*
KRIII...

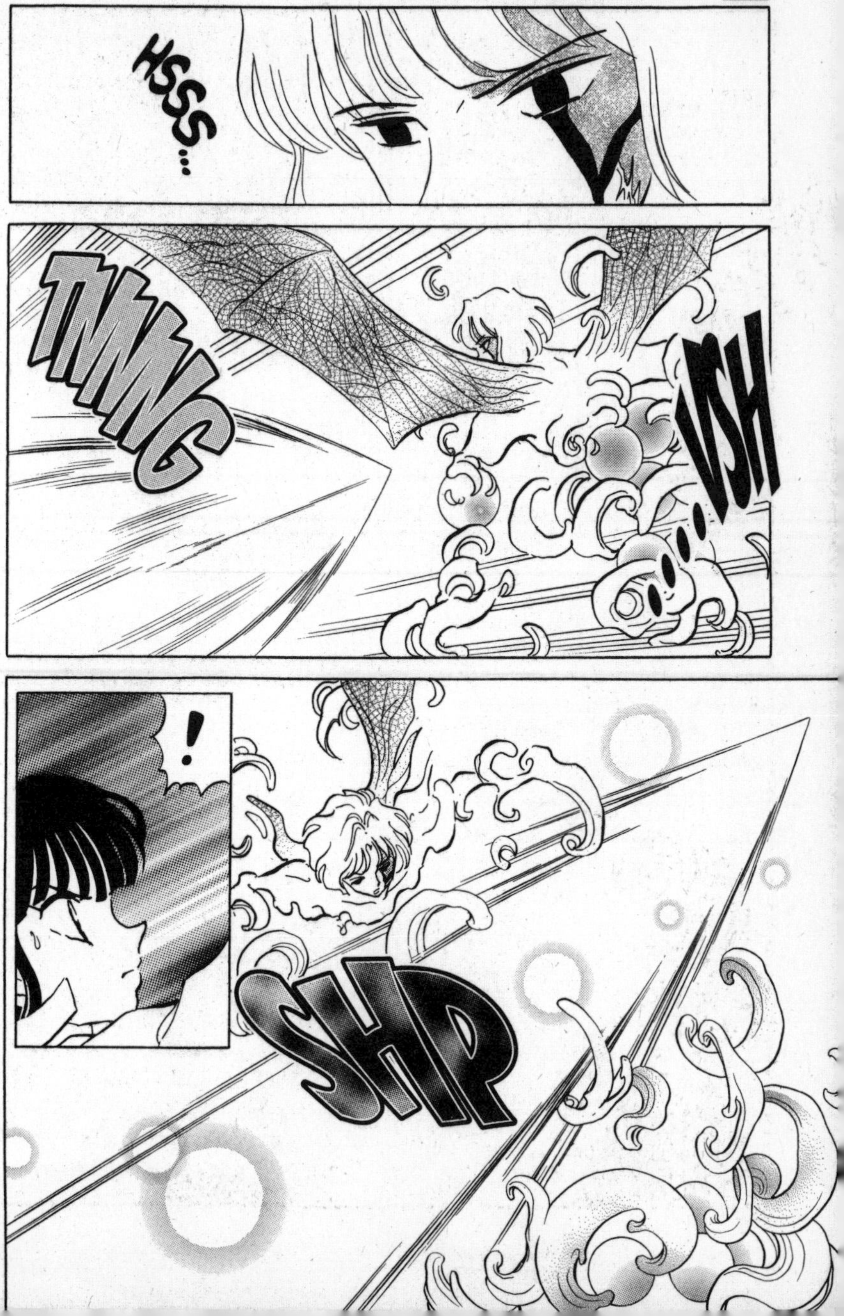
HSSS...
TWNG
...VSH
!
SHP

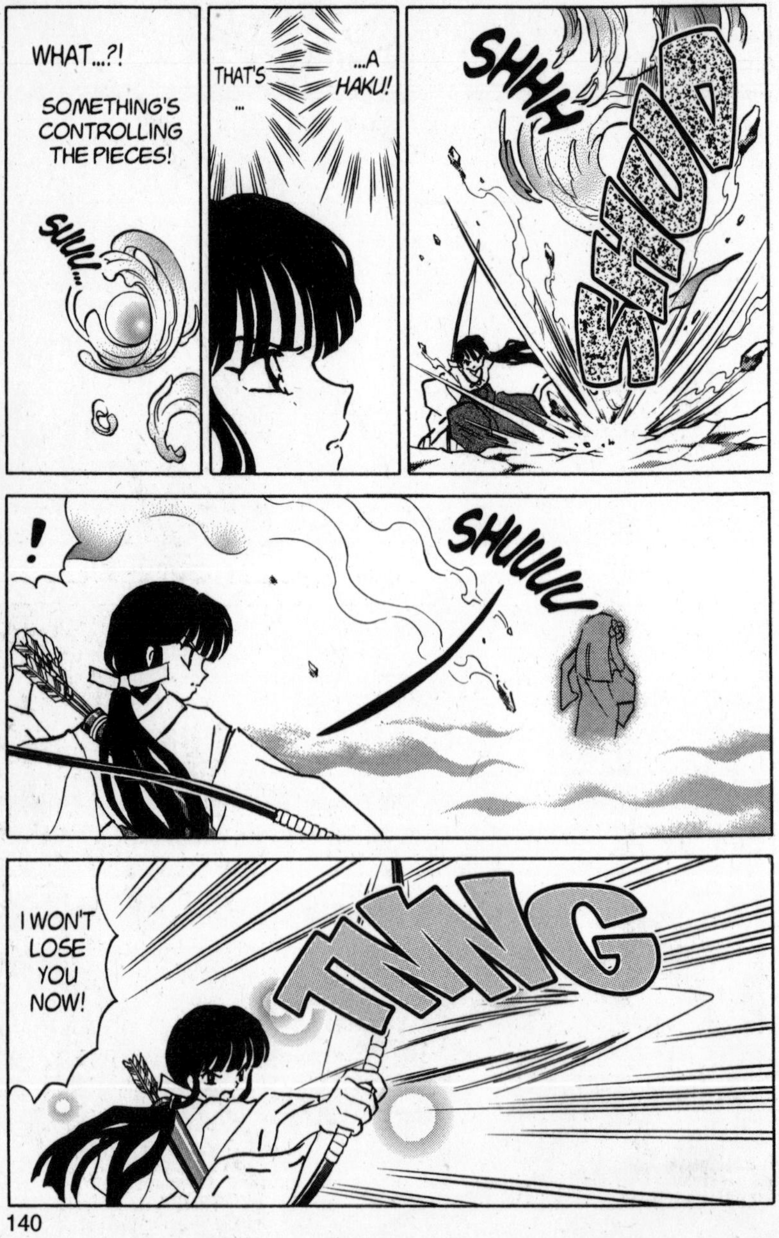
WHAT...?!
SOMETHING'S CONTROLLING THE PIECES!
SUUU...
THAT'S ...
...A HAKU!
SHHH
SHUUD
!
SHUUUU
I WON'T LOSE YOU NOW!
TWNG

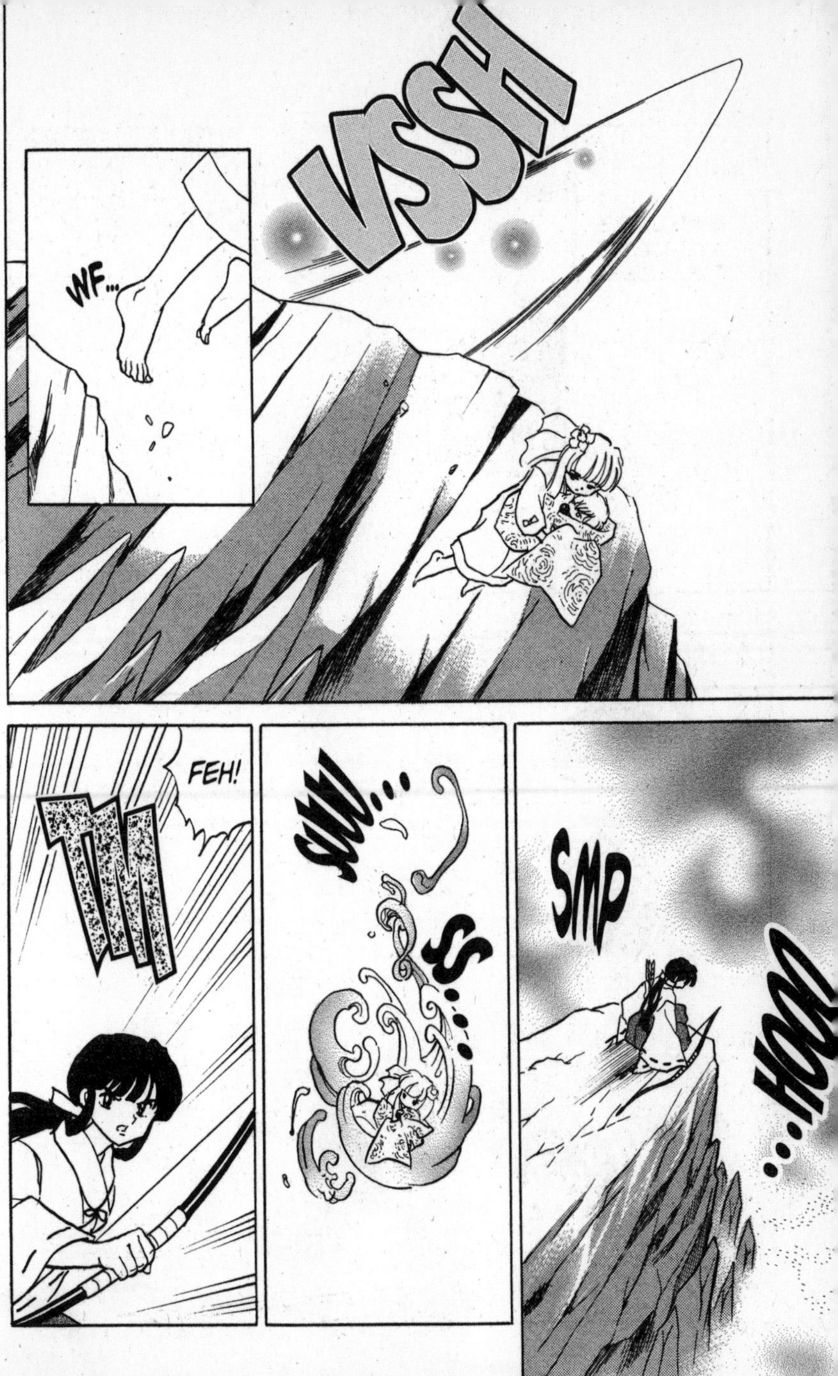

WF...
VSSH
FEH!
TM
SUUU...
SS...
SMP
...HOOO

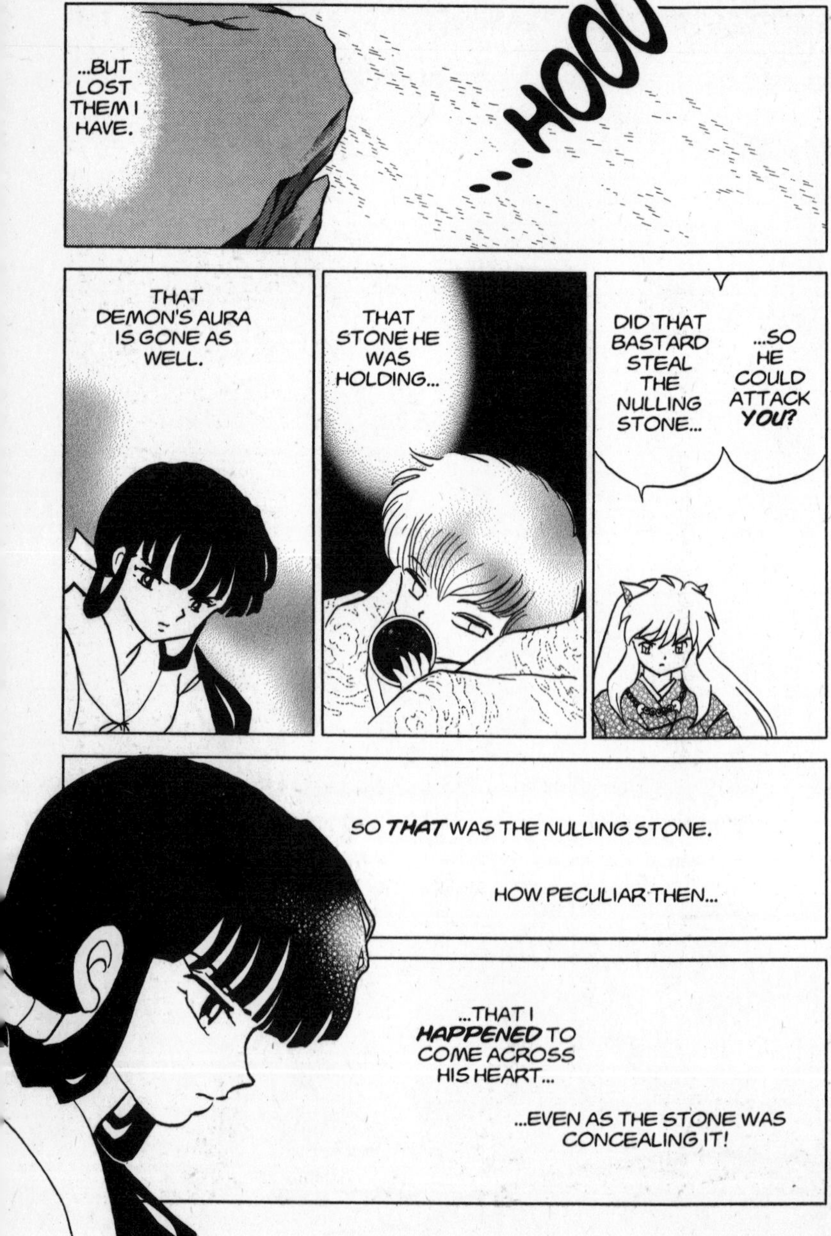

...BUT LOST THEM I HAVE.
...HOO
THAT DEMON'S AURA IS GONE AS WELL.
THAT STONE HE WAS HOLDING...
DID THAT BASTARD STEAL THE NULLING STONE...
...SO HE COULD ATTACK *YOU?*
SO *THAT* WAS THE NULLING STONE.
HOW PECULIAR THEN...
...THAT I *HAPPENED* TO COME ACROSS HIS HEART...
...EVEN AS THE STONE WAS CONCEALING IT!

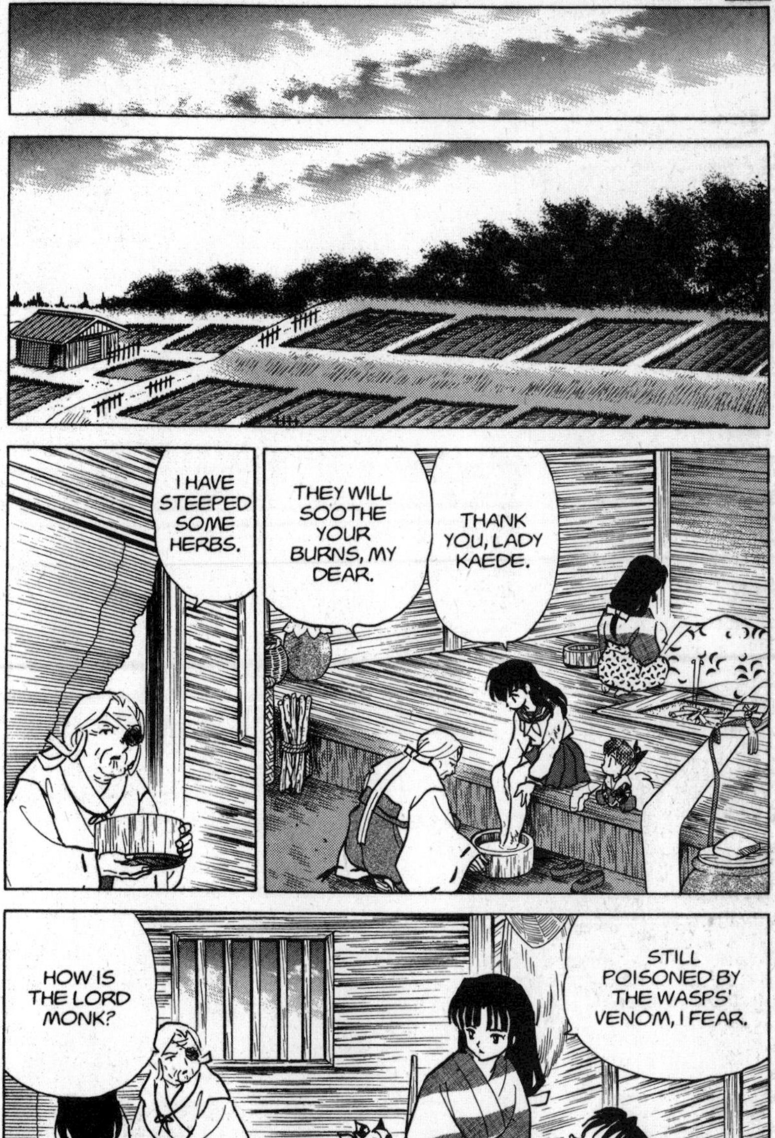
I HAVE STEEPED SOME HERBS.
THEY WILL SOOTHE YOUR BURNS, MY DEAR.
THANK YOU, LADY KAEDE.
HOW IS THE LORD MONK?
STILL POISONED BY THE WASPS' VENOM, I FEAR.

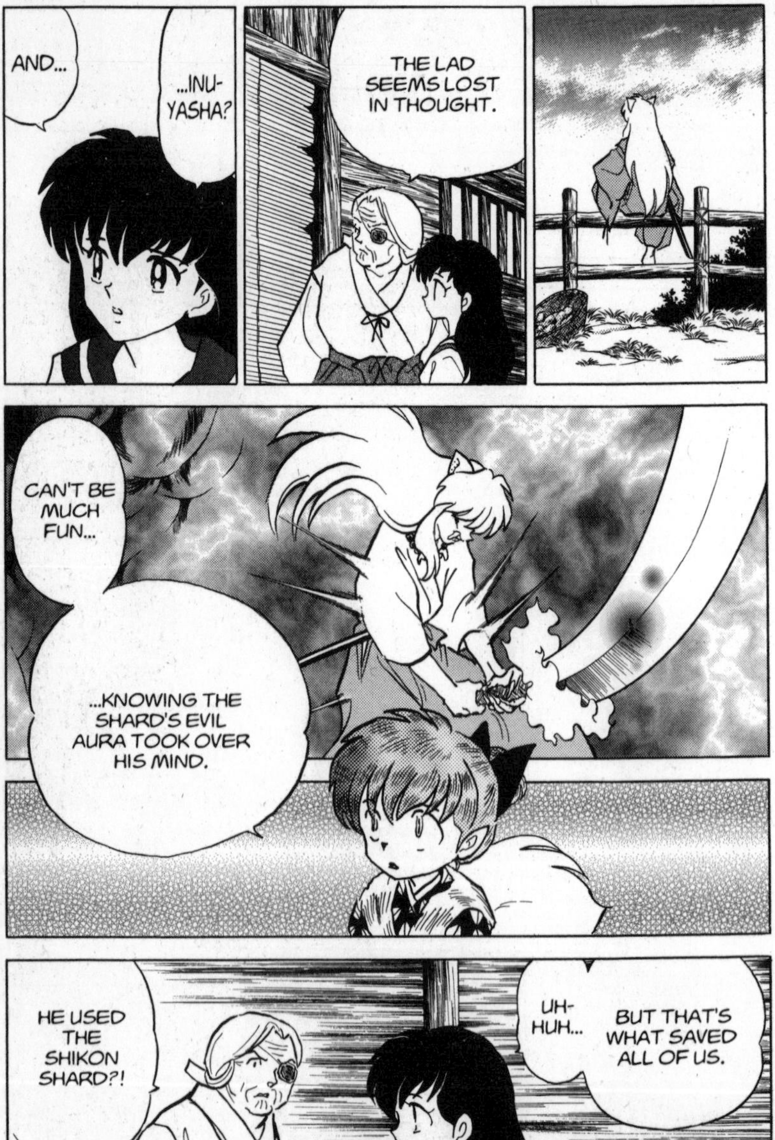
AND...
...INU-YASHA?
THE LAD SEEMS LOST IN THOUGHT.
CAN'T BE MUCH FUN...
...KNOWING THE SHARD'S EVIL AURA TOOK OVER HIS MIND.
HE USED THE SHIKON SHARD?!
UH-HUH...
BUT THAT'S WHAT SAVED ALL OF US.

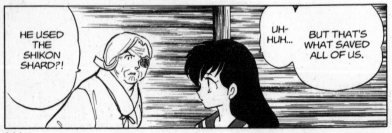

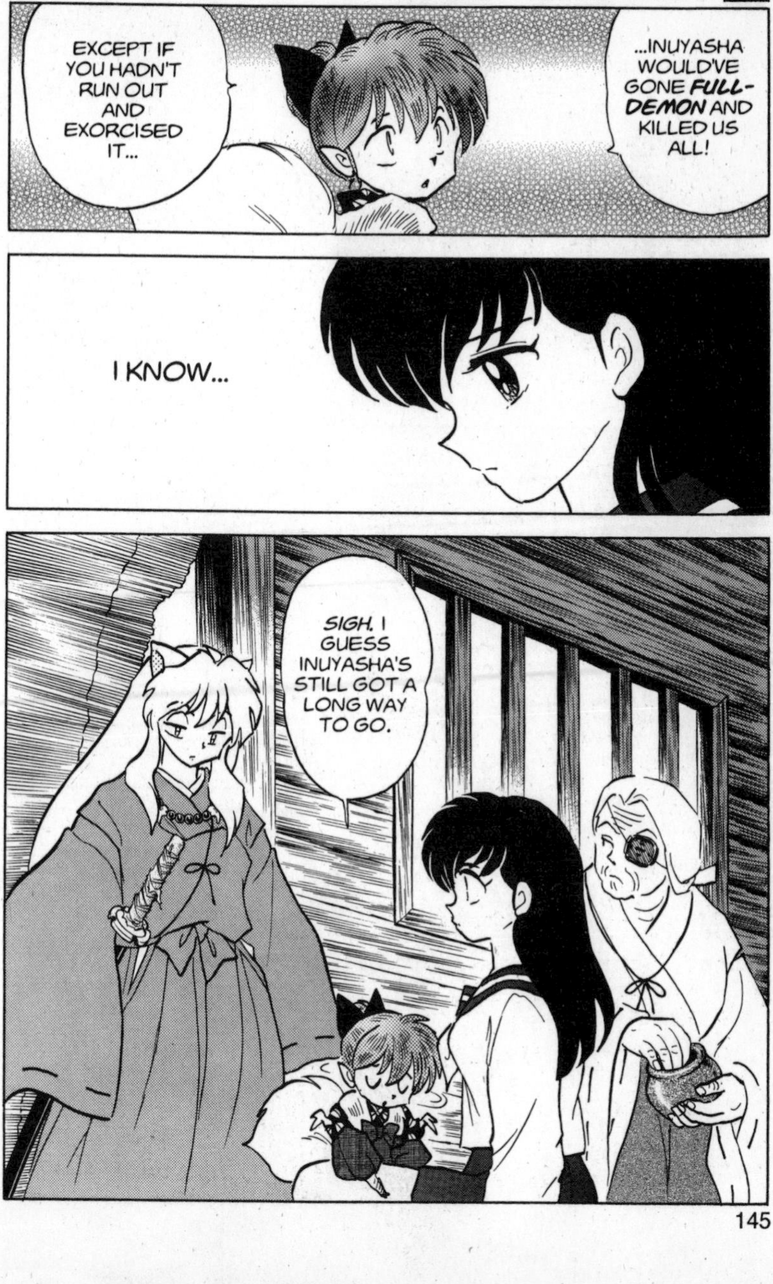
EXCEPT IF YOU HADN'T RUN OUT AND EXORCISED IT...
...INUYASHA WOULD'VE GONE FULL-DEMON AND KILLED US ALL!
I KNOW...
SIGH. I GUESS INUYASHA'S STILL GOT A LONG WAY TO GO.

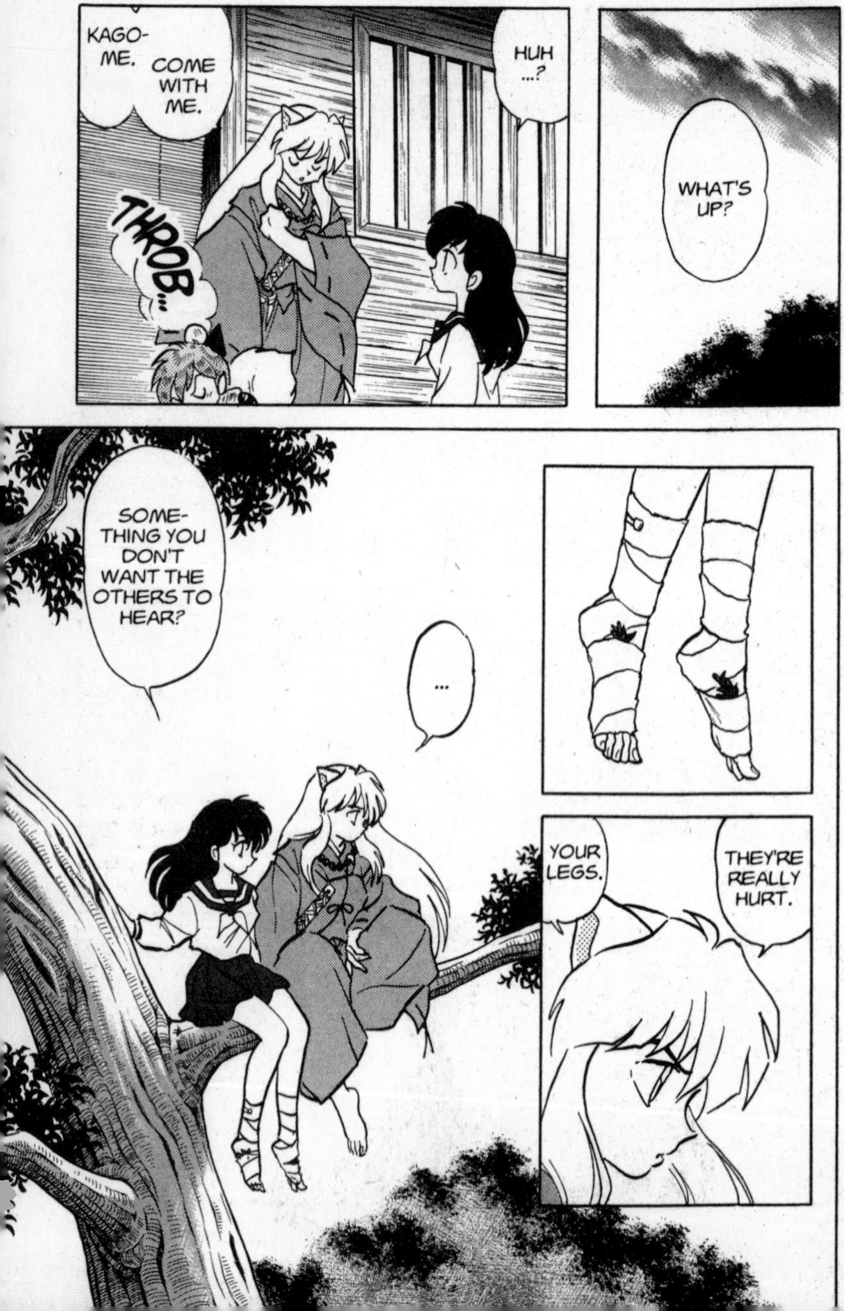
KAGO-ME.
COME WITH ME.
THROB...
HUH ...?
WHAT'S UP?
SOME-THING YOU DON'T WANT THE OTHERS TO HEAR?
...
YOUR LEGS.
THEY'RE REALLY HURT.

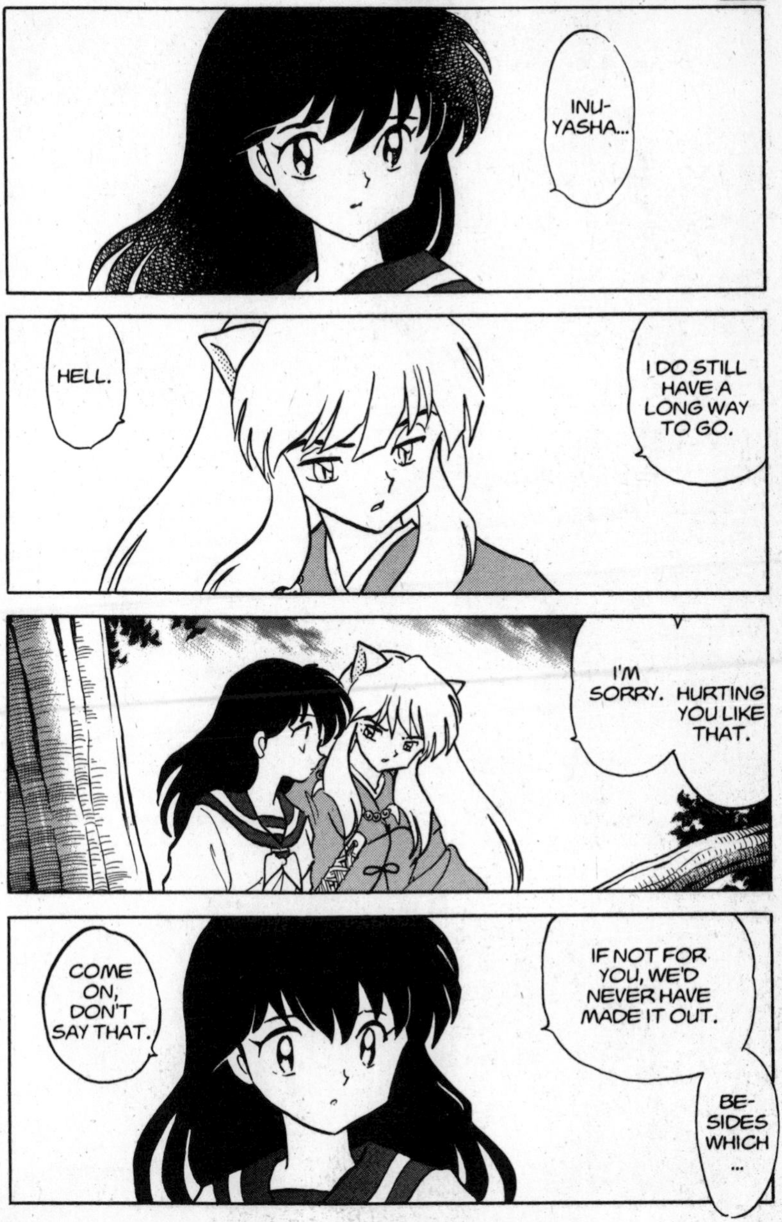
INU-
YASHA...
HELL.
I DO STILL
HAVE A
LONG WAY
TO GO.
I'M
SORRY.
HURTING
YOU LIKE
THAT.
COME
ON,
DON'T
SAY THAT.
IF NOT FOR
YOU, WE'D
NEVER HAVE
MADE IT OUT.
BE-
SIDES
WHICH
...

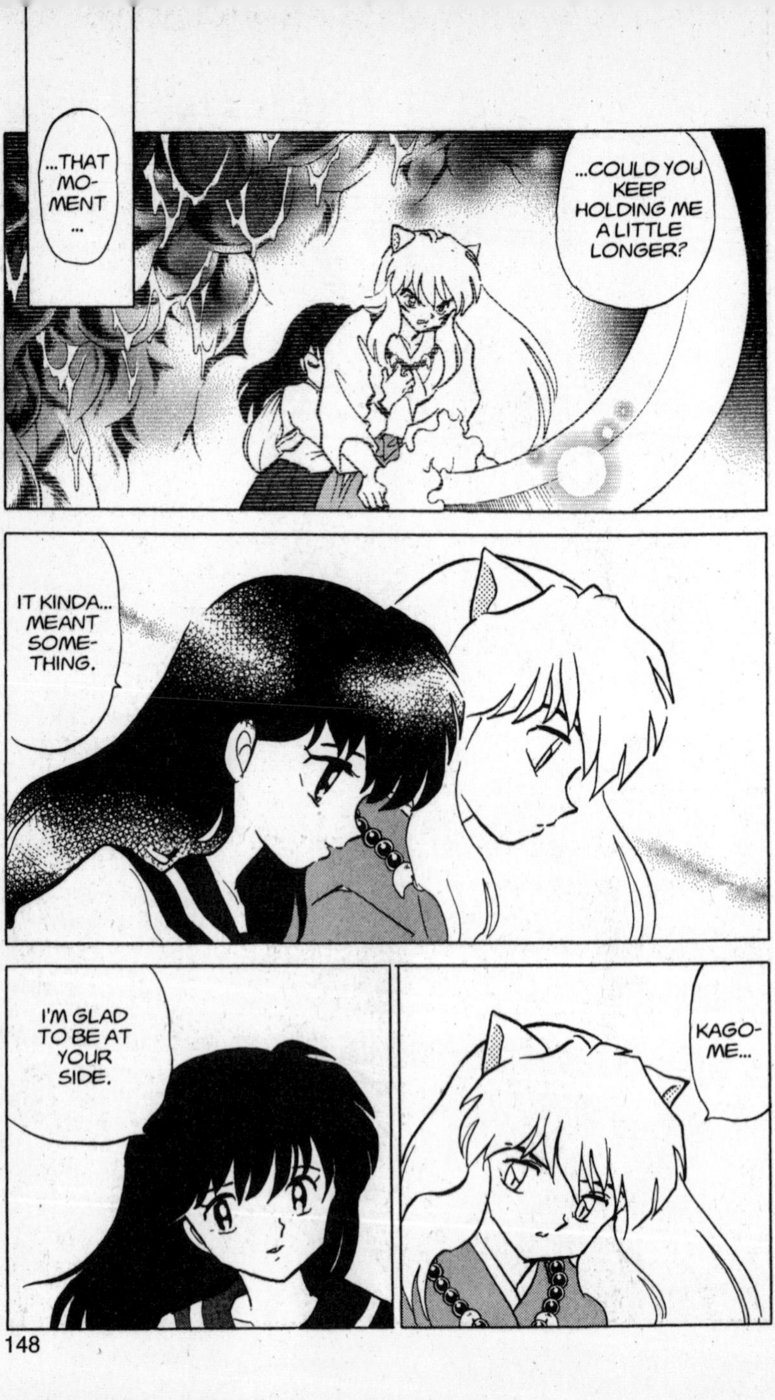
...THAT MOMENT ...
...COULD YOU KEEP HOLDING ME A LITTLE LONGER?
IT KINDA... MEANT SOMETHING.
I'M GLAD TO BE AT YOUR SIDE.
KAGOME...

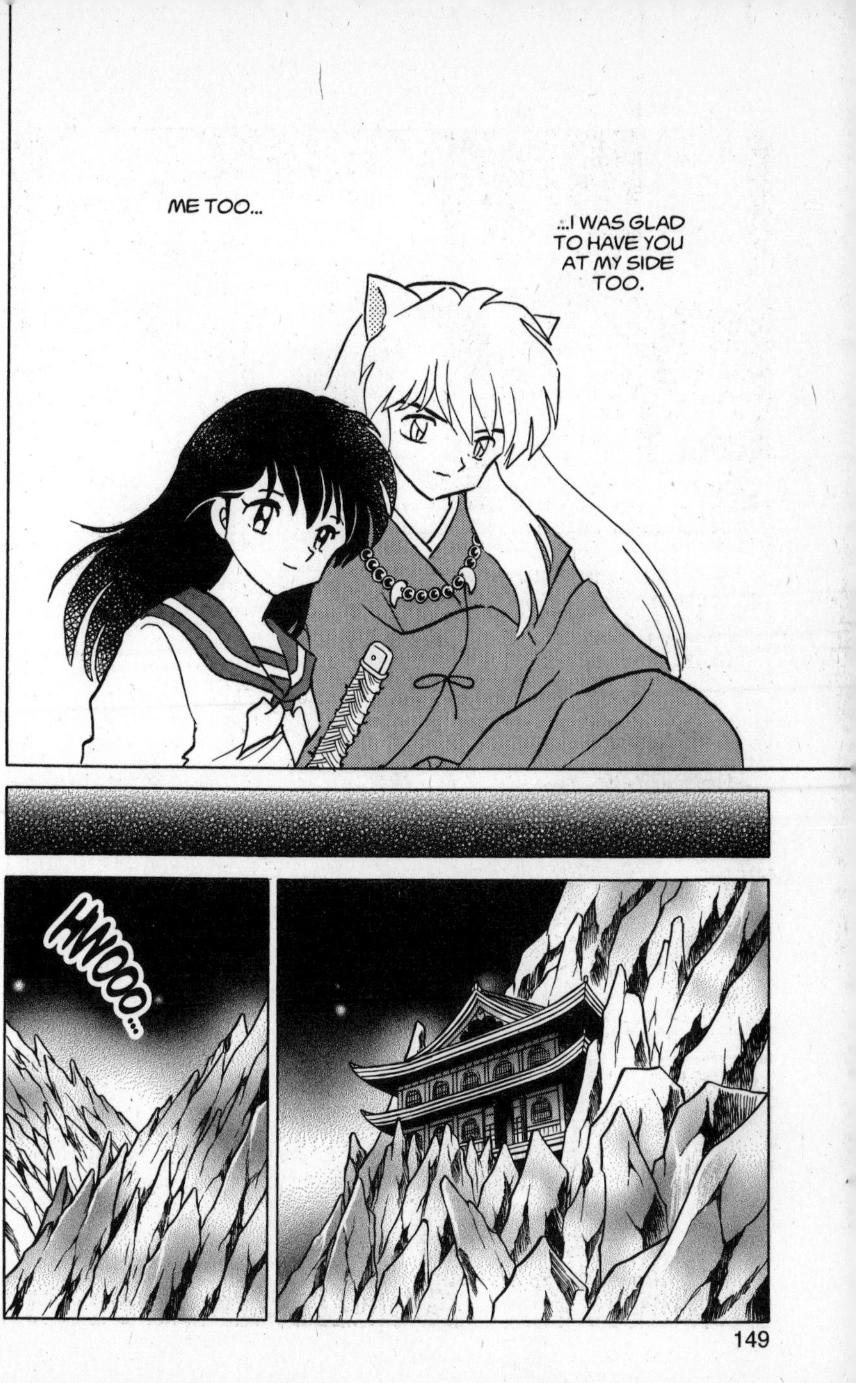
ME TOO...
...I WAS GLAD TO HAVE YOU AT MY SIDE TOO.
HWOOO...

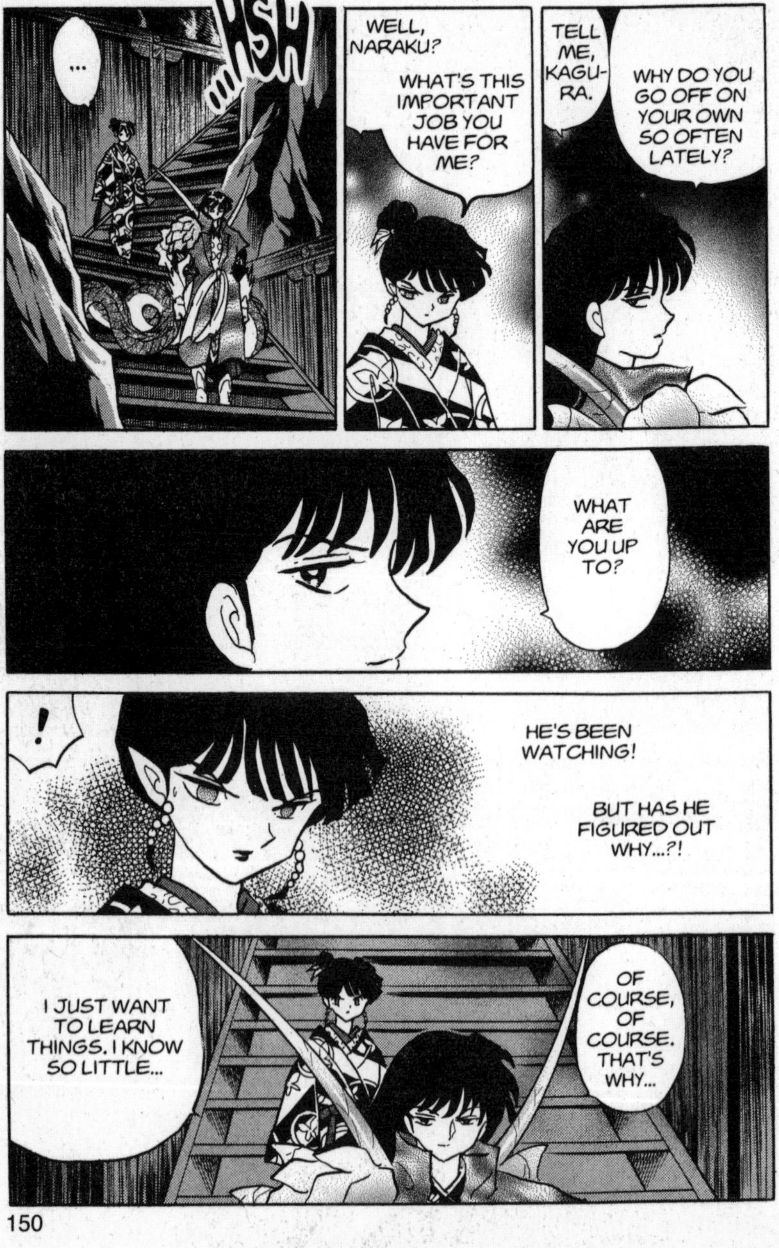
...
HSH...
WELL, NARAKU?
WHAT'S THIS IMPORTANT JOB YOU HAVE FOR ME?
TELL ME, KAGURA.
WHY DO YOU GO OFF ON YOUR OWN SO OFTEN LATELY?
WHAT ARE YOU UP TO?
!
HE'S BEEN WATCHING!
BUT HAS HE FIGURED OUT WHY...?!
I JUST WANT TO LEARN THINGS. I KNOW SO LITTLE...
OF COURSE, OF COURSE. THAT'S WHY...

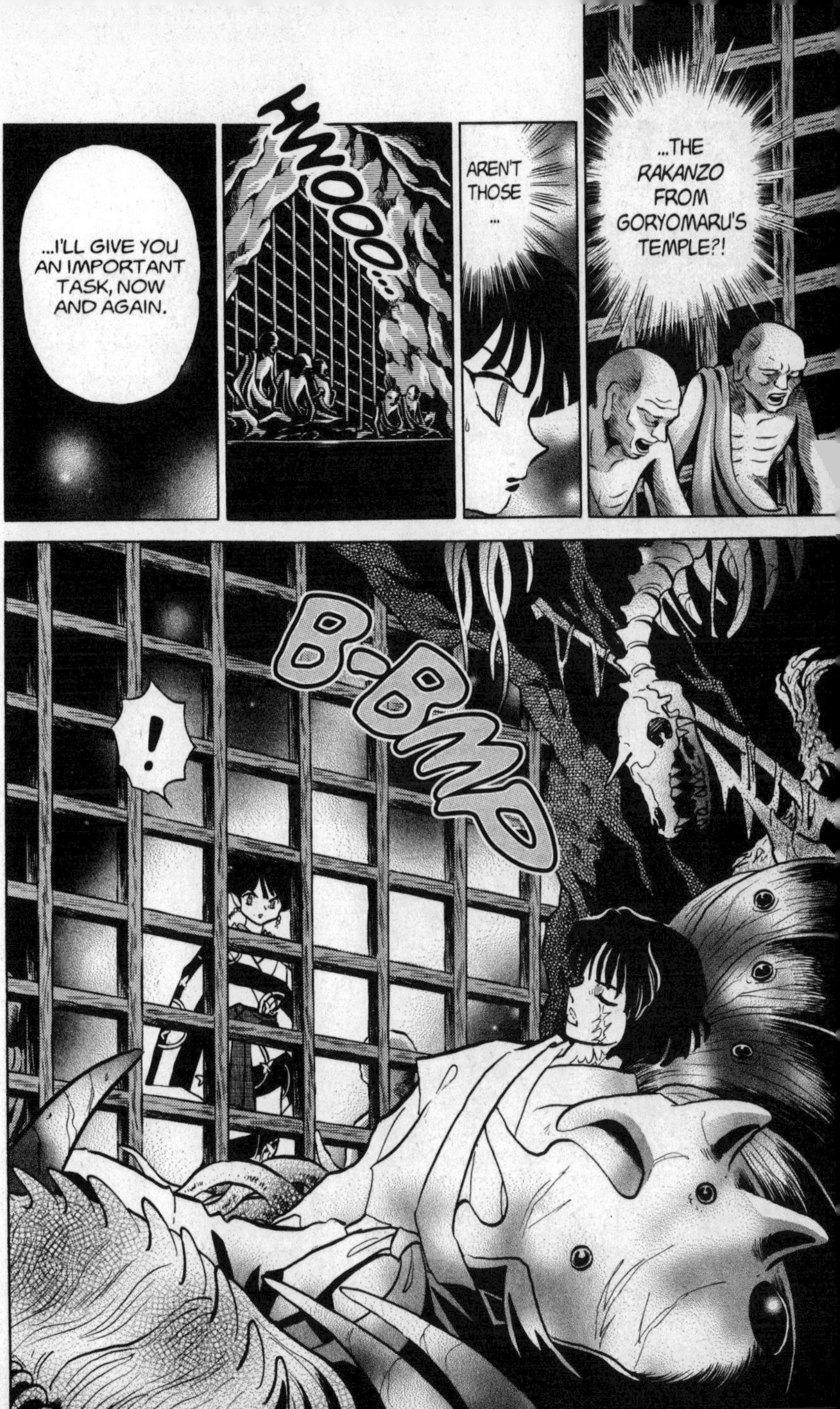

...I'LL GIVE YOU AN IMPORTANT TASK, NOW AND AGAIN.
HWOOO...
AREN'T THOSE ...
...THE RAKANZO FROM GORYOMARU'S TEMPLE?!
!
B-BMP

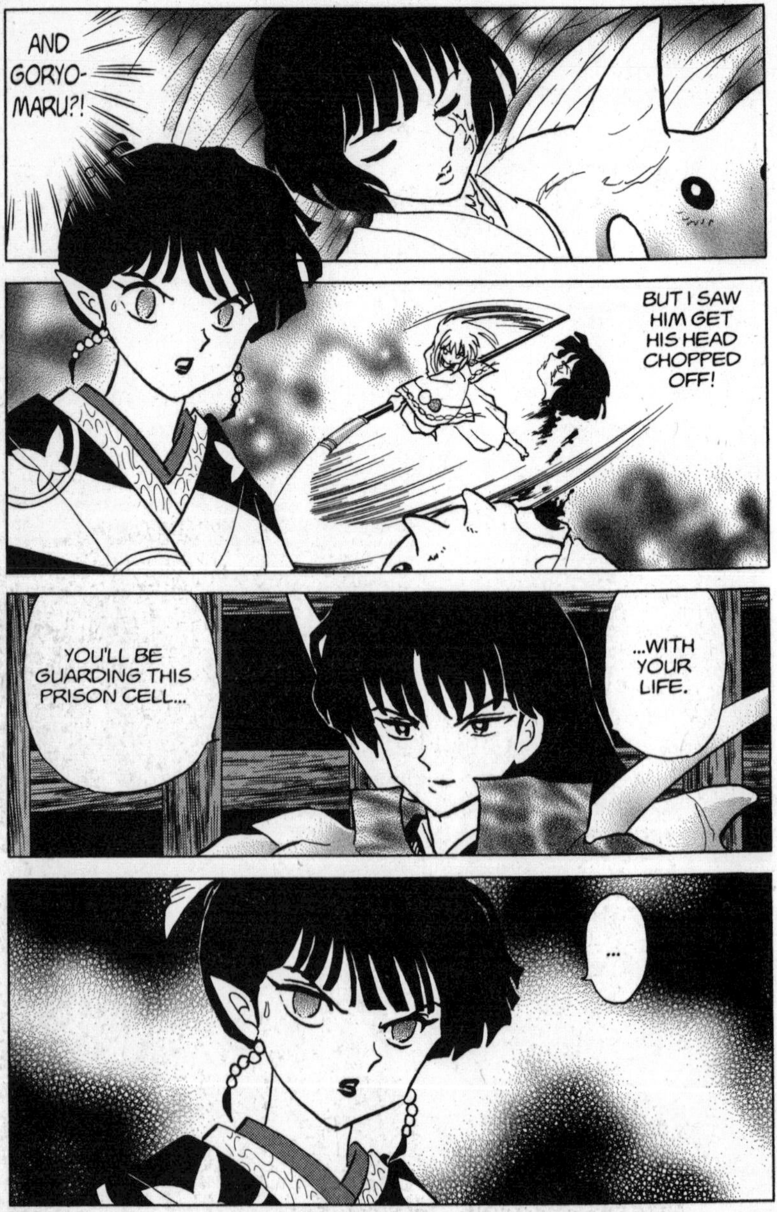
AND GORYO-MARU?!
BUT I SAW HIM GET HIS HEAD CHOPPED OFF!
YOU'LL BE GUARDING THIS PRISON CELL...
...WITH YOUR LIFE.
...

SCROLL 9
THE MEDICINE MERCHANT

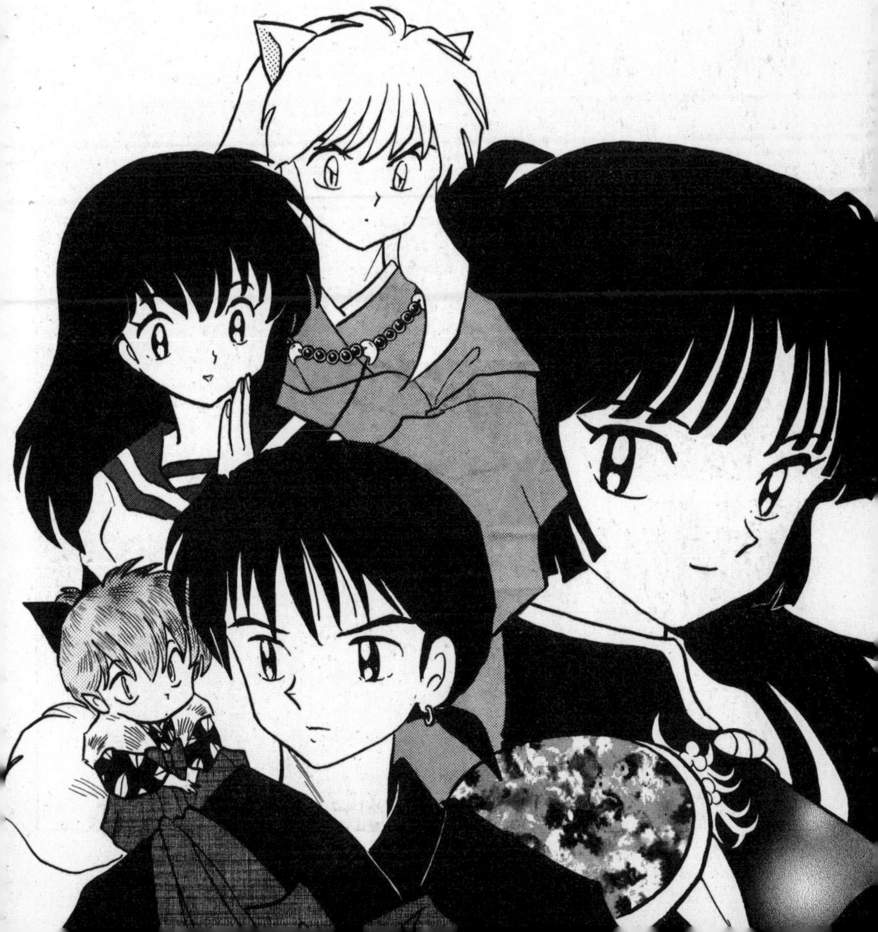

WHAT'S GOING ON, NARAKU?

THIS GORYO-MARU...

...WHAT AND WHO IS HE?!

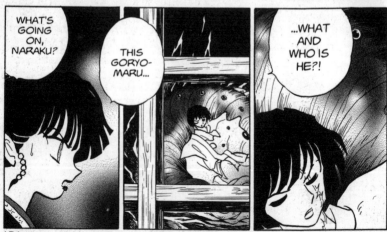

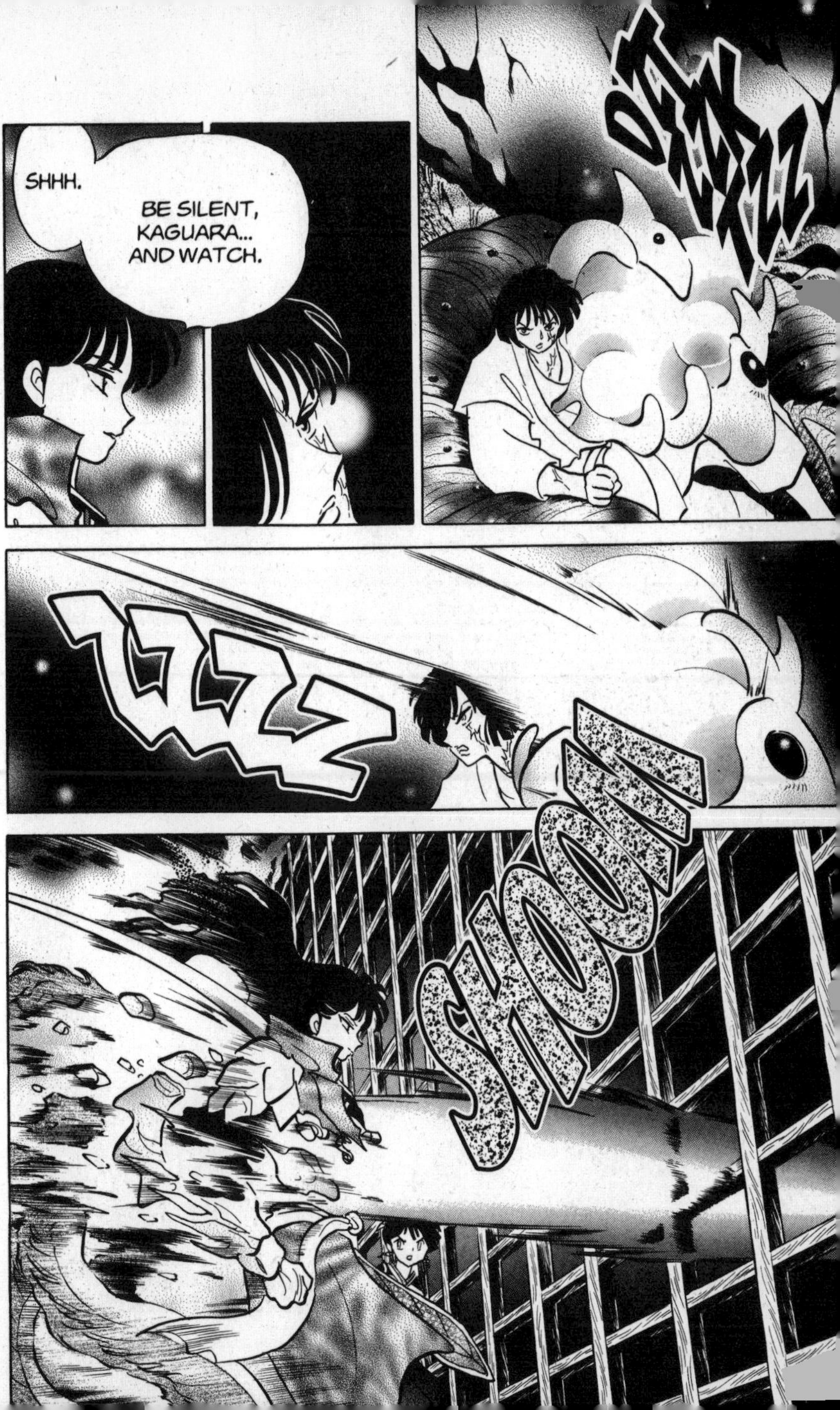
SHHH.
BE SILENT, KAGUARA... AND WATCH.
ZZZ
SHOOM

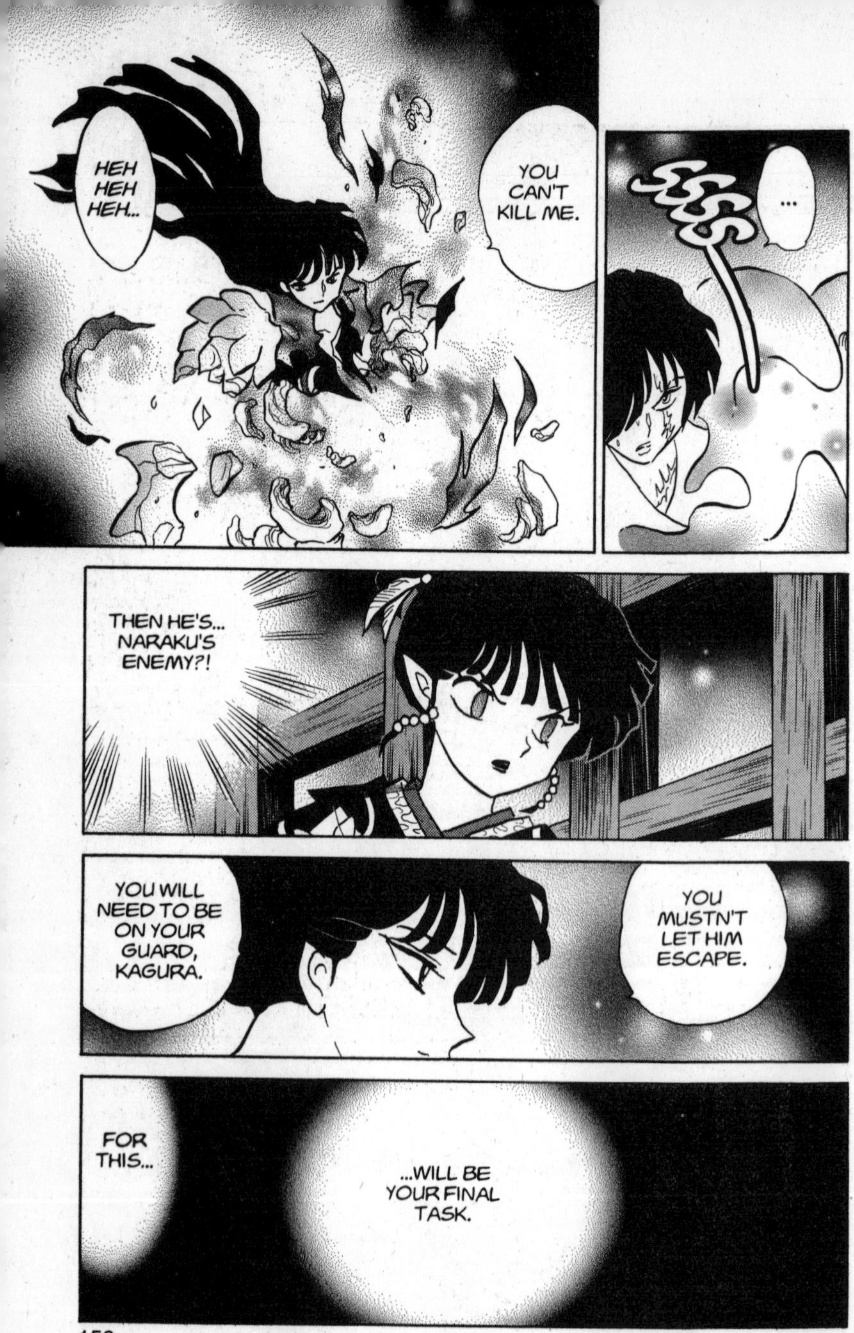
HEH HEH HEH...
YOU CAN'T KILL ME.
SSSS
...
THEN HE'S... NARAKU'S ENEMY?!
YOU WILL NEED TO BE ON YOUR GUARD, KAGURA.
YOU MUSTN'T LET HIM ESCAPE.
FOR THIS...
...WILL BE YOUR FINAL TASK.

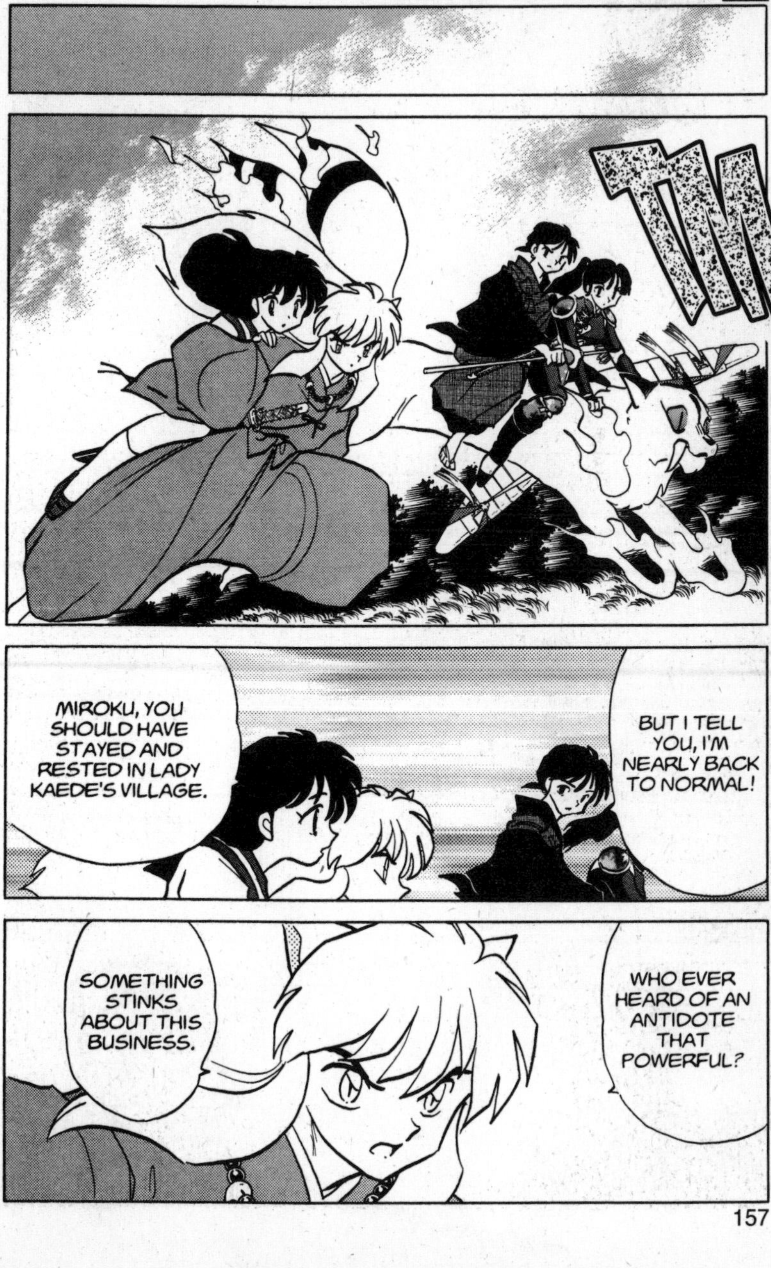
TM
MIROKU, YOU SHOULD HAVE STAYED AND RESTED IN LADY KAEDE'S VILLAGE.
BUT I TELL YOU, I'M NEARLY BACK TO NORMAL!
SOMETHING STINKS ABOUT THIS BUSINESS.
WHO EVER HEARD OF AN ANTIDOTE THAT POWERFUL?

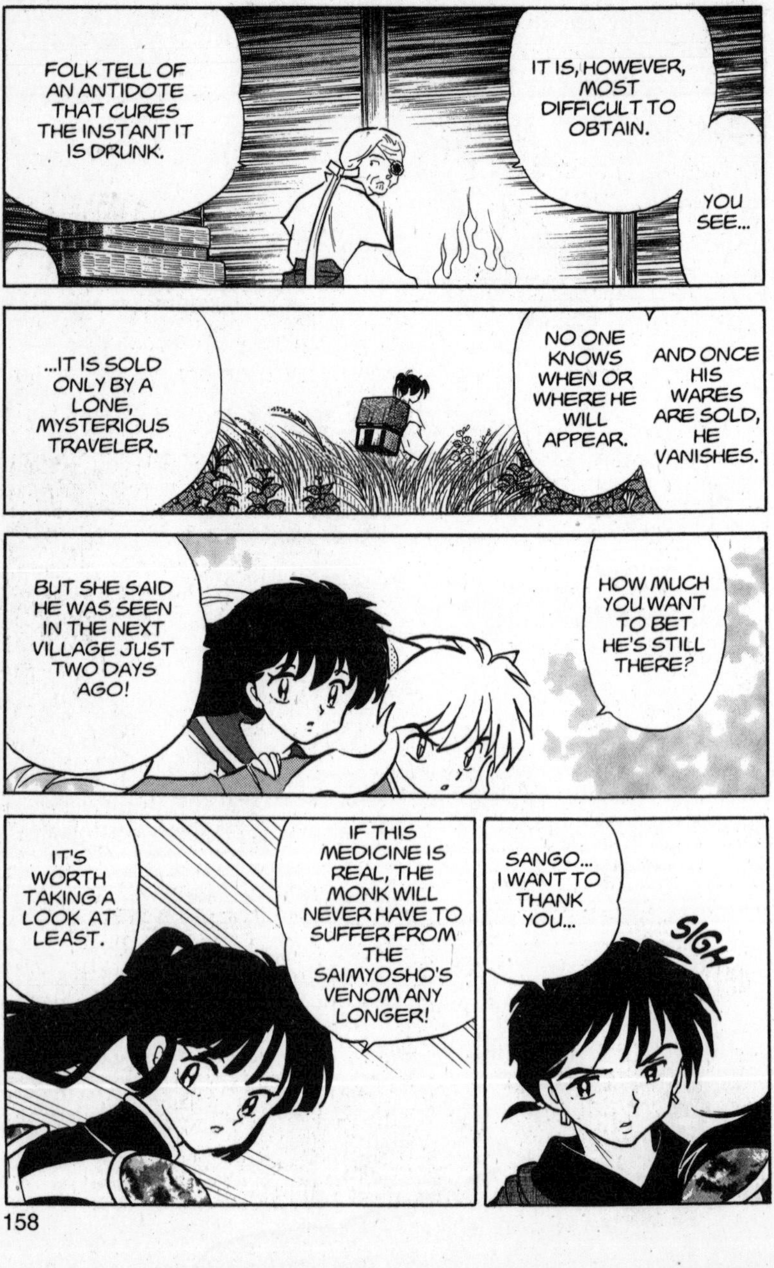
FOLK TELL OF AN ANTIDOTE THAT CURES THE INSTANT IT IS DRUNK.
IT IS, HOWEVER, MOST DIFFICULT TO OBTAIN.
YOU SEE...
...IT IS SOLD ONLY BY A LONE, MYSTERIOUS TRAVELER.
NO ONE KNOWS WHEN OR WHERE HE WILL APPEAR.
AND ONCE HIS WARES ARE SOLD, HE VANISHES.
BUT SHE SAID HE WAS SEEN IN THE NEXT VILLAGE JUST TWO DAYS AGO!
HOW MUCH YOU WANT TO BET HE'S STILL THERE?
IT'S WORTH TAKING A LOOK AT LEAST.
IF THIS MEDICINE IS REAL, THE MONK WILL NEVER HAVE TO SUFFER FROM THE SAIMYOSHO'S VENOM ANY LONGER!
SANGO... I WANT TO THANK YOU...
SIGH

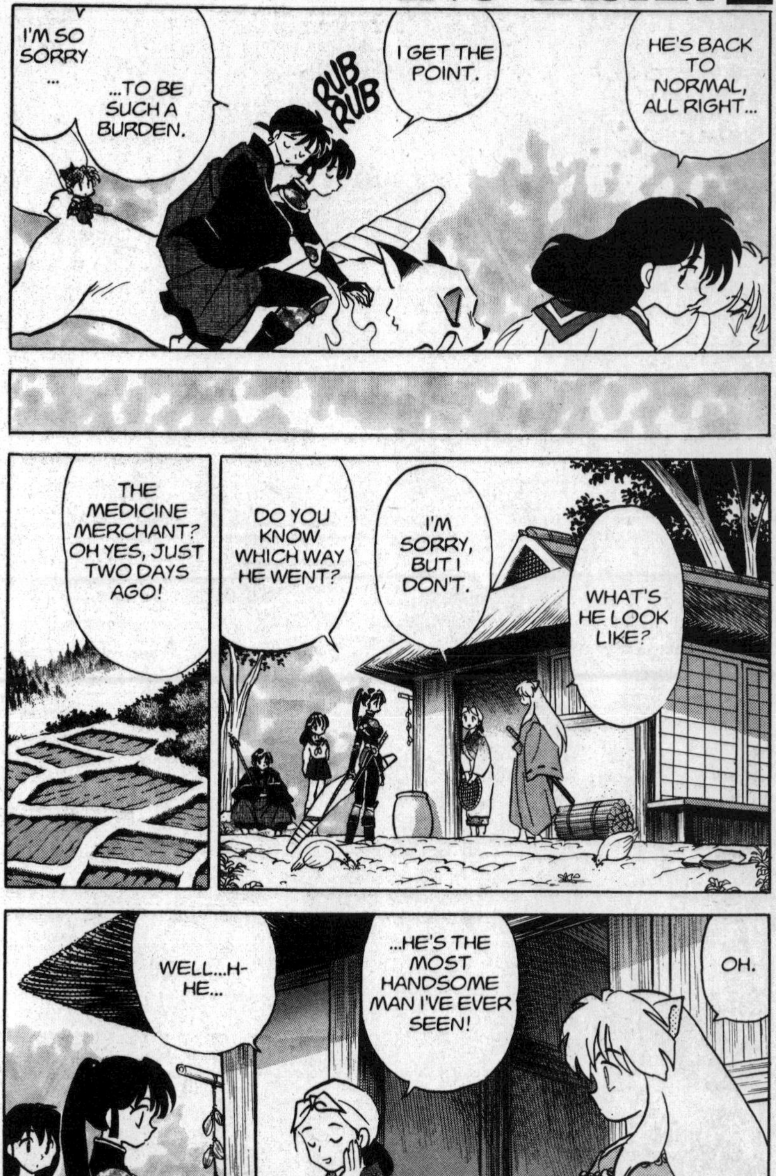
I'M SO SORRY ...
...TO BE SUCH A BURDEN.
RUB RUB
I GET THE POINT.
HE'S BACK TO NORMAL, ALL RIGHT...
THE MEDICINE MERCHANT? OH YES, JUST TWO DAYS AGO!
DO YOU KNOW WHICH WAY HE WENT?
I'M SORRY, BUT I DON'T.
WHAT'S HE LOOK LIKE?
WELL...H-HE...
...HE'S THE MOST HANDSOME MAN I'VE EVER SEEN!
OH.

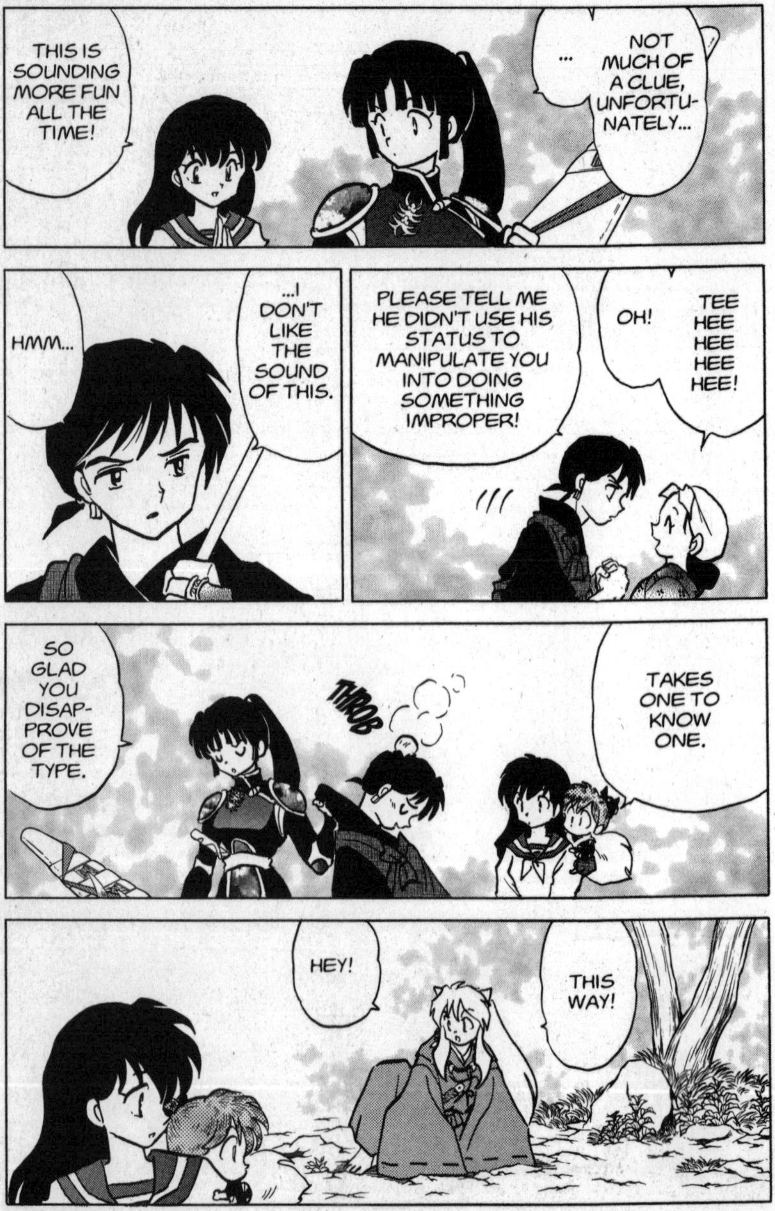
THIS IS SOUNDING MORE FUN ALL THE TIME!
...
NOT MUCH OF A CLUE, UNFORTUNATELY...
HMM...
...I DON'T LIKE THE SOUND OF THIS.
PLEASE TELL ME HE DIDN'T USE HIS STATUS TO MANIPULATE YOU INTO DOING SOMETHING IMPROPER!
OH!
TEE HEE HEE HEE HEE!
SO GLAD YOU DISAPPROVE OF THE TYPE.
THROB
TAKES ONE TO KNOW ONE.
HEY!
THIS WAY!

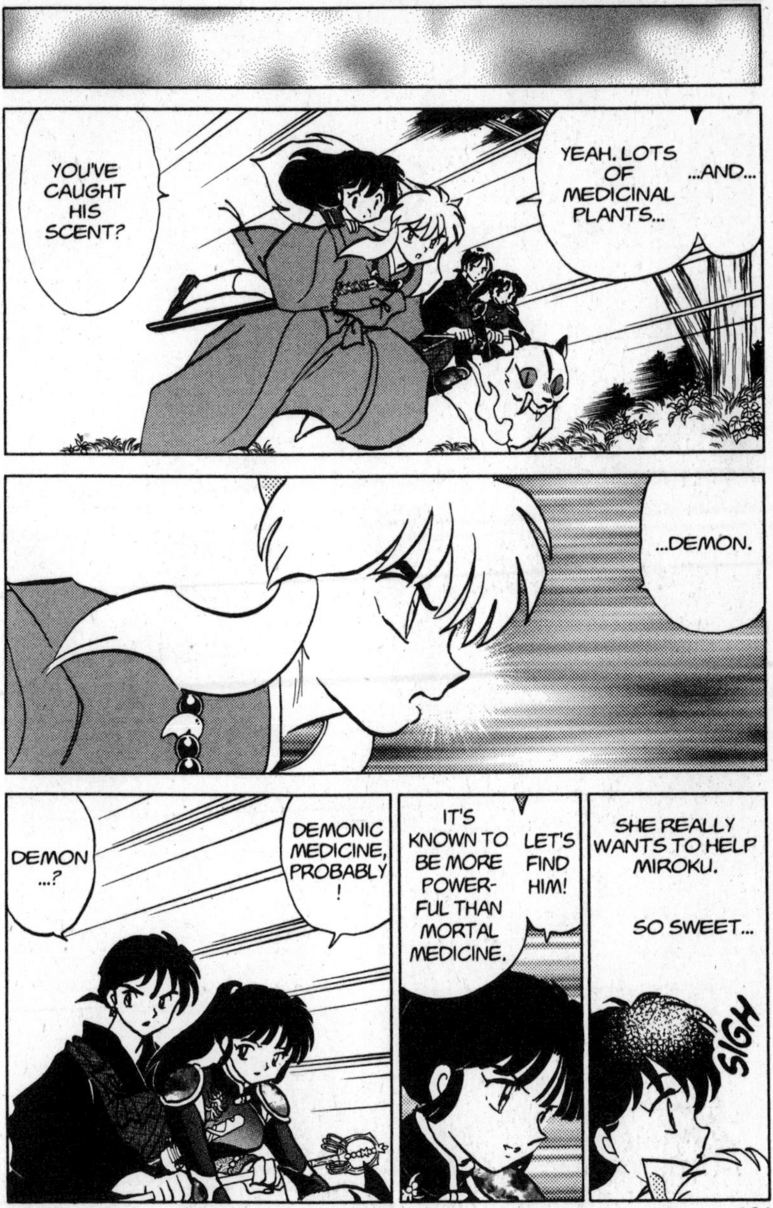
YOU'VE CAUGHT HIS SCENT?
YEAH. LOTS OF MEDICINAL PLANTS...
...AND...
...DEMON.
DEMON ...?
DEMONIC MEDICINE, PROBABLY !
IT'S KNOWN TO BE MORE POWER-FUL THAN MORTAL MEDICINE.
LET'S FIND HIM!
SHE REALLY WANTS TO HELP MIROKU.
SO SWEET...
SIGH

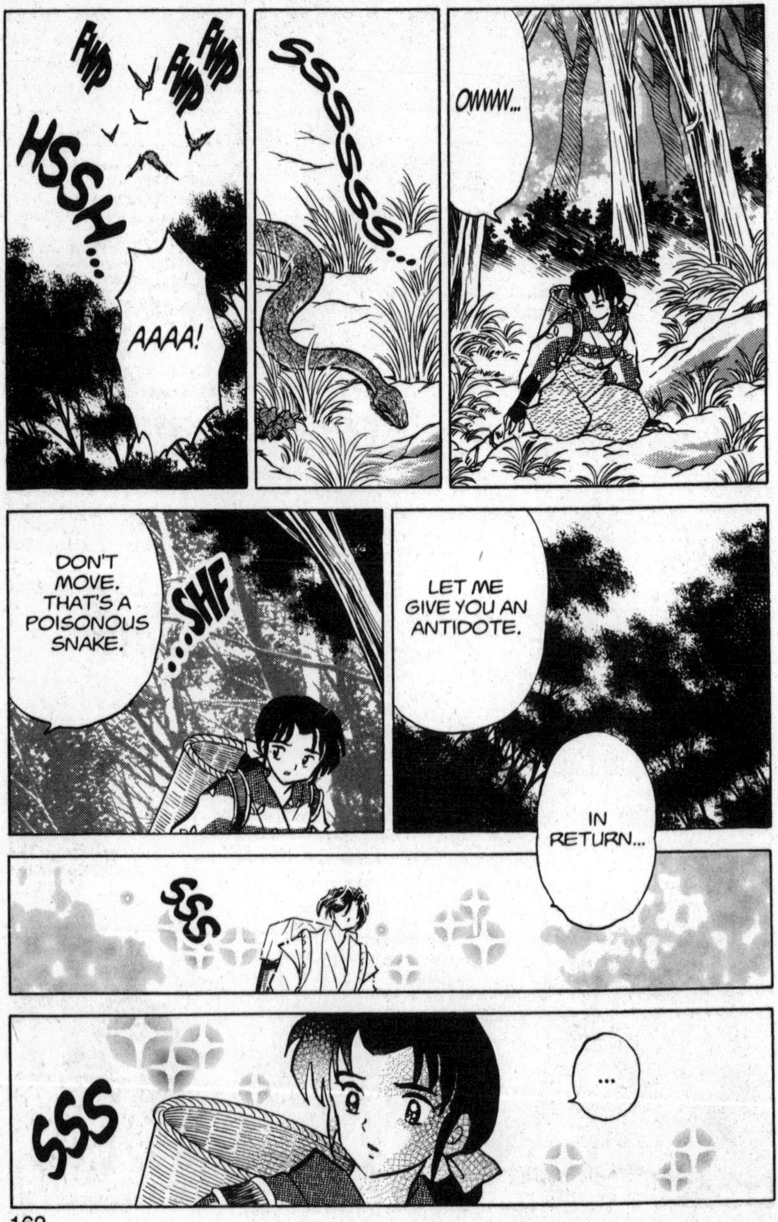
FWIP
FWIP
FWIP
HSSH...
AAAA!
SSSSSS...
OWWW...
DON'T MOVE. THAT'S A POISONOUS SNAKE.
...SHF
LET ME GIVE YOU AN ANTIDOTE.
IN RETURN...
SSS
SSS
...

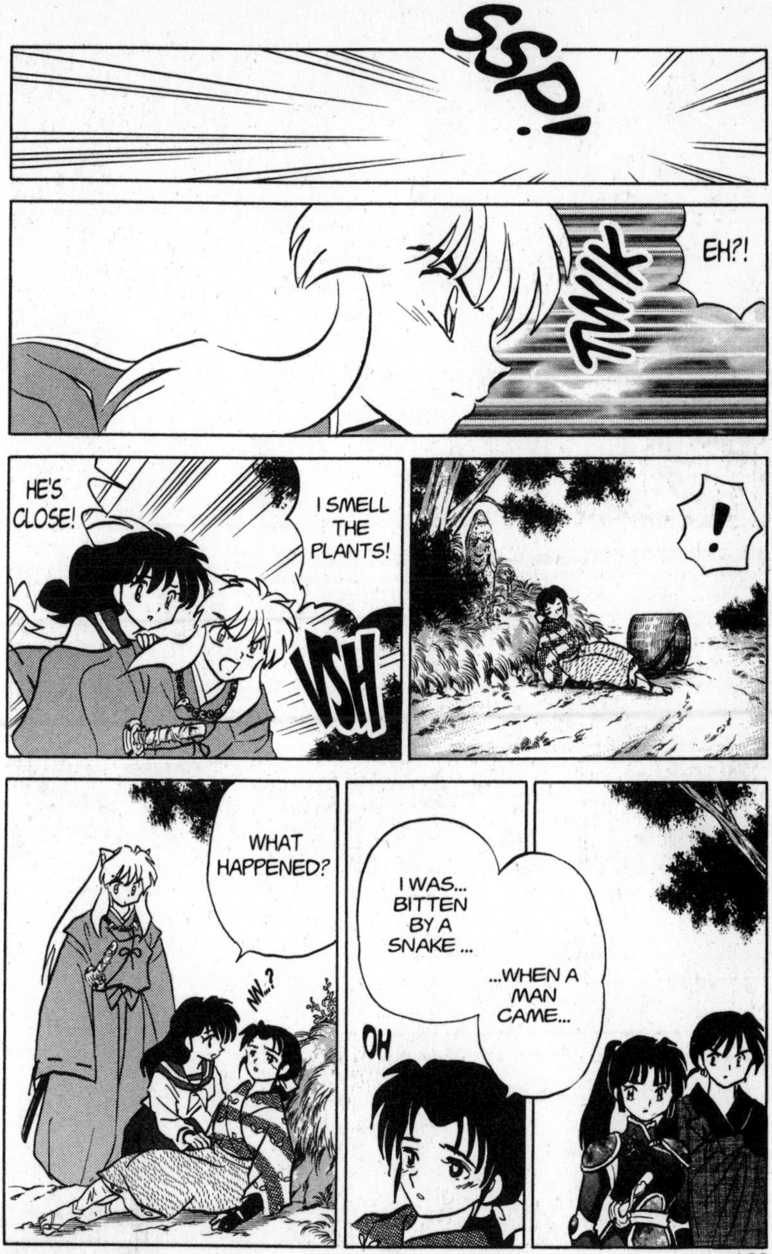
SSP!
TWIK
EH?!
HE'S CLOSE!
I SMELL THE PLANTS!
VSH
!
WHAT HAPPENED?
NN...?
I WAS... BITTEN BY A SNAKE ...
OH
...WHEN A MAN CAME...

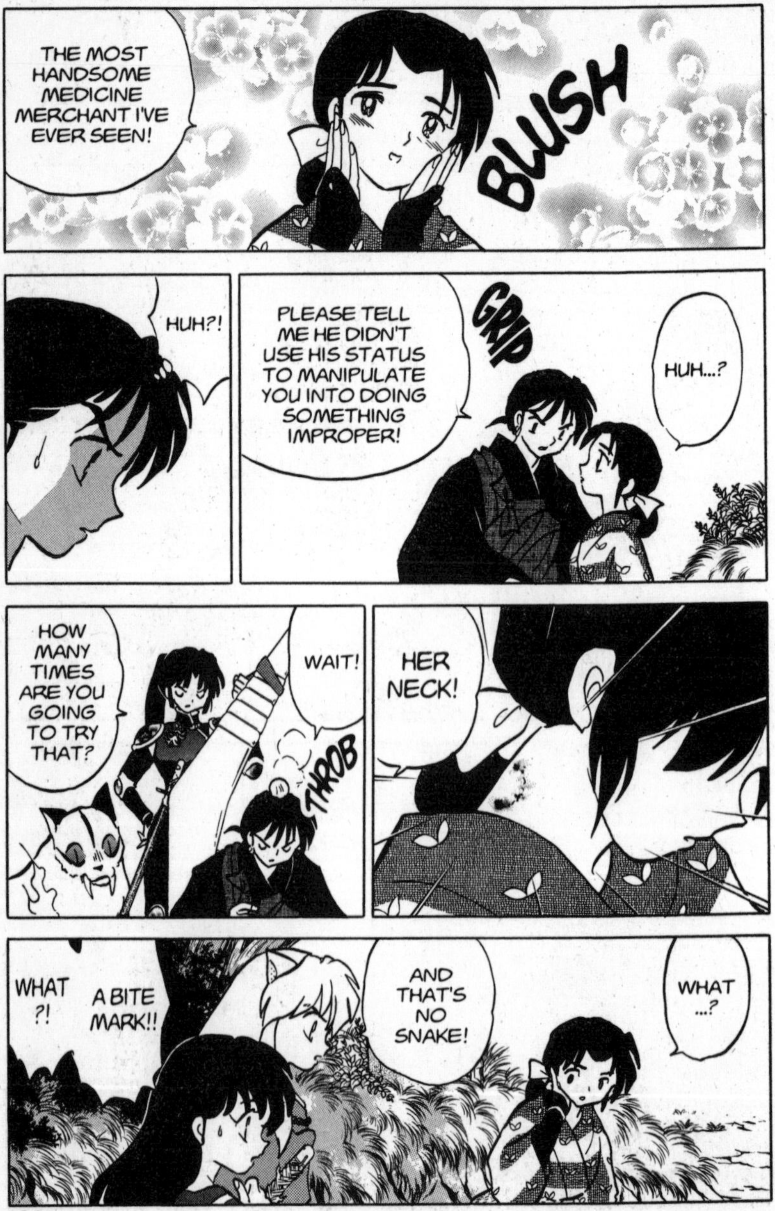
THE MOST HANDSOME MEDICINE MERCHANT I'VE EVER SEEN!
BLUSH
HUH?!
PLEASE TELL ME HE DIDN'T USE HIS STATUS TO MANIPULATE YOU INTO DOING SOMETHING IMPROPER!
GRIP
HUH...?
HOW MANY TIMES ARE YOU GOING TO TRY THAT?
WAIT!
THROB
HER NECK!
WHAT ?!
A BITE MARK!!
AND THAT'S NO SNAKE!
WHAT ...?

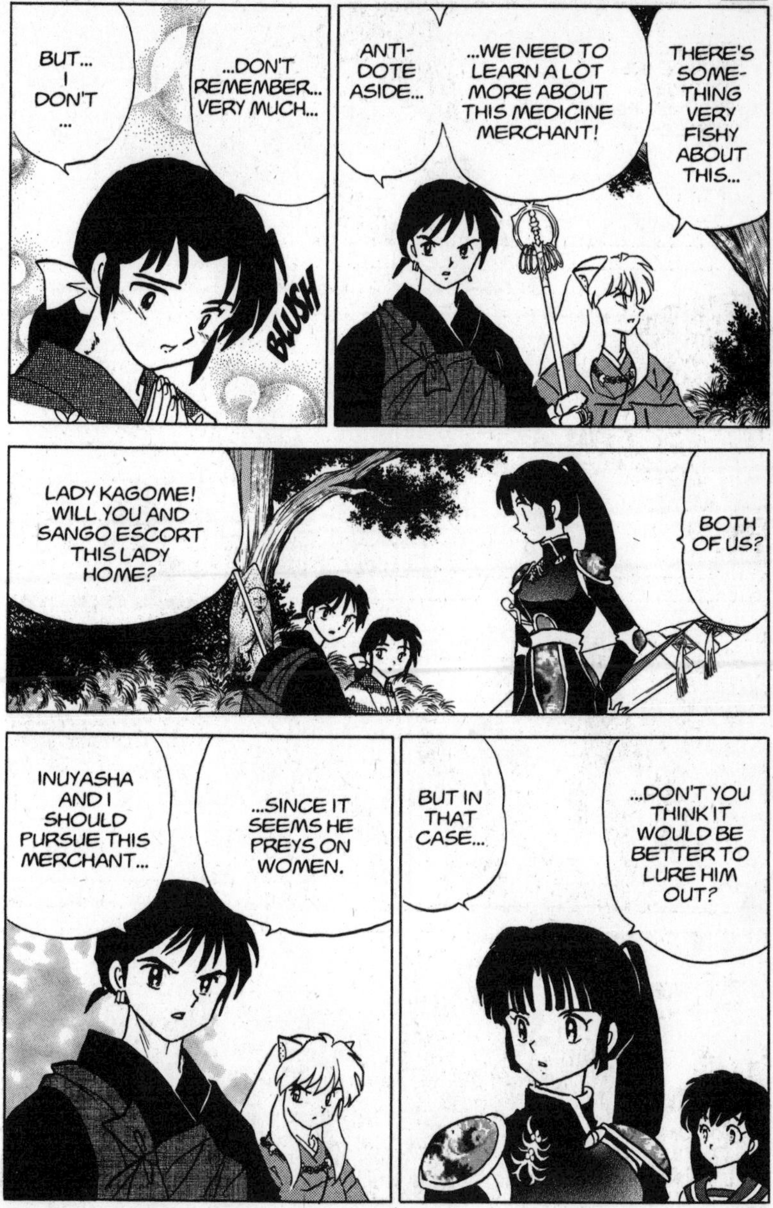
BUT... I DON'T ...
...DON'T REMEMBER... VERY MUCH...
BLUSH
ANTI-DOTE ASIDE...
...WE NEED TO LEARN A LOT MORE ABOUT THIS MEDICINE MERCHANT!
THERE'S SOME-THING VERY FISHY ABOUT THIS...
LADY KAGOME! WILL YOU AND SANGO ESCORT THIS LADY HOME?
BOTH OF US?
INUYASHA AND I SHOULD PURSUE THIS MERCHANT...
...SINCE IT SEEMS HE PREYS ON WOMEN.
BUT IN THAT CASE...
...DON'T YOU THINK IT WOULD BE BETTER TO LURE HIM OUT?

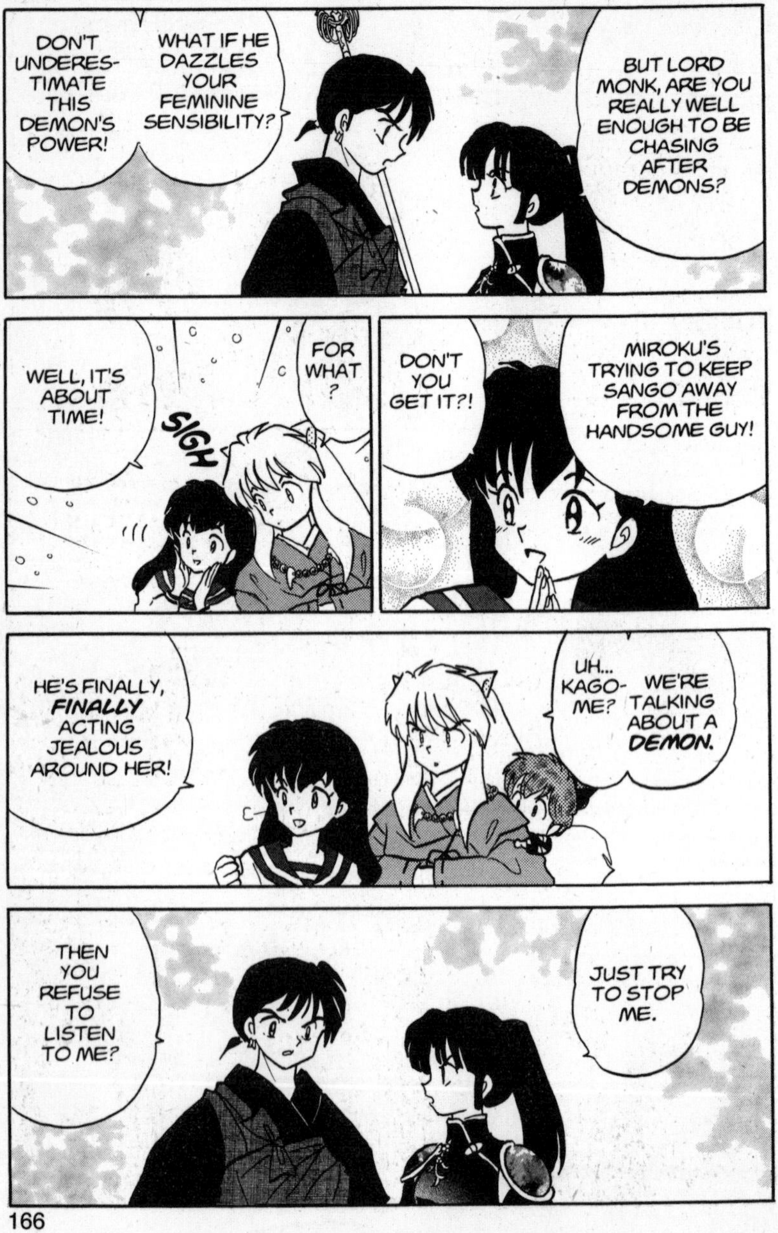
DON'T UNDERES-TIMATE THIS DEMON'S POWER!
WHAT IF HE DAZZLES YOUR FEMININE SENSIBILITY?
BUT LORD MONK, ARE YOU REALLY WELL ENOUGH TO BE CHASING AFTER DEMONS?
WELL, IT'S ABOUT TIME!
SIGH
FOR WHAT ?
DON'T YOU GET IT?!
MIROKU'S TRYING TO KEEP SANGO AWAY FROM THE HANDSOME GUY!
HE'S FINALLY, FINALLY ACTING JEALOUS AROUND HER!
UH... KAGO-ME?
WE'RE TALKING ABOUT A DEMON.
THEN YOU REFUSE TO LISTEN TO ME?
JUST TRY TO STOP ME.

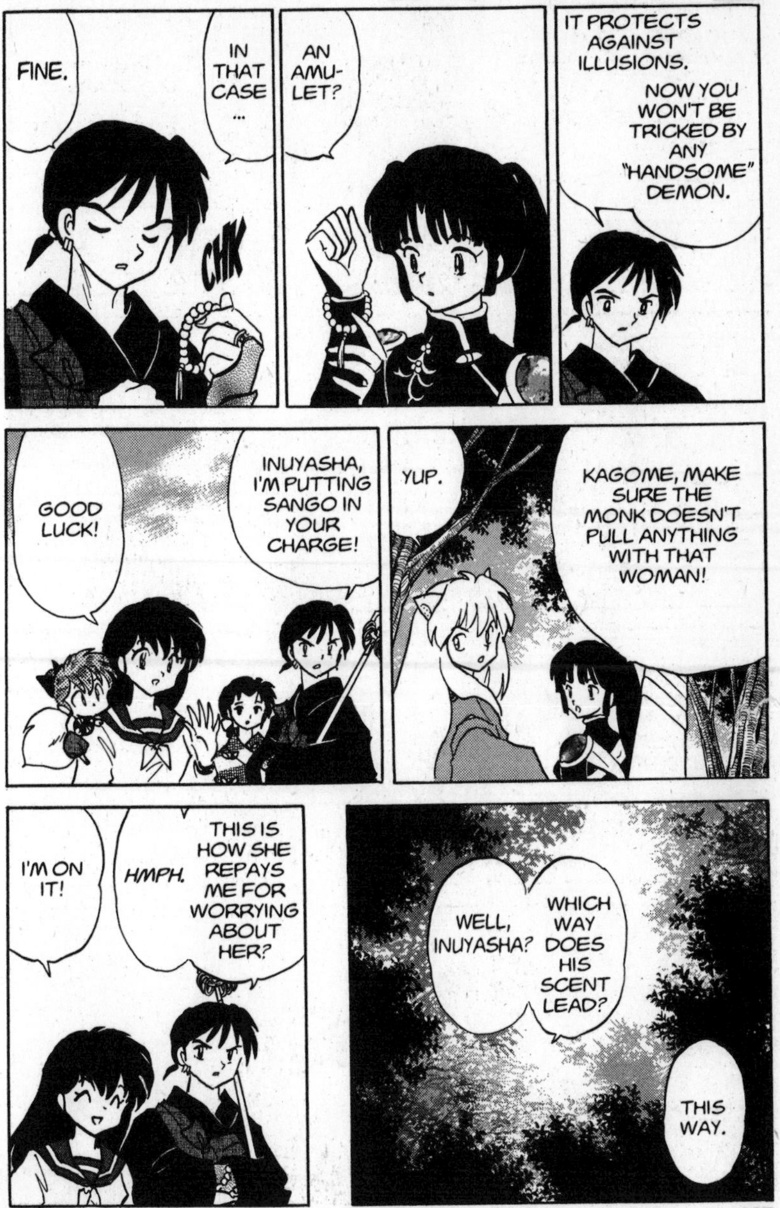
FINE.
IN THAT CASE ...
CHK
AN AMULET?
IT PROTECTS AGAINST ILLUSIONS.
NOW YOU WON'T BE TRICKED BY ANY "HANDSOME" DEMON.
GOOD LUCK!
INUYASHA, I'M PUTTING SANGO IN YOUR CHARGE!
YUP.
KAGOME, MAKE SURE THE MONK DOESN'T PULL ANYTHING WITH THAT WOMAN!
I'M ON IT!
HMPH.
THIS IS HOW SHE REPAYS ME FOR WORRYING ABOUT HER?
WELL, INUYASHA?
WHICH WAY DOES HIS SCENT LEAD?
THIS WAY.

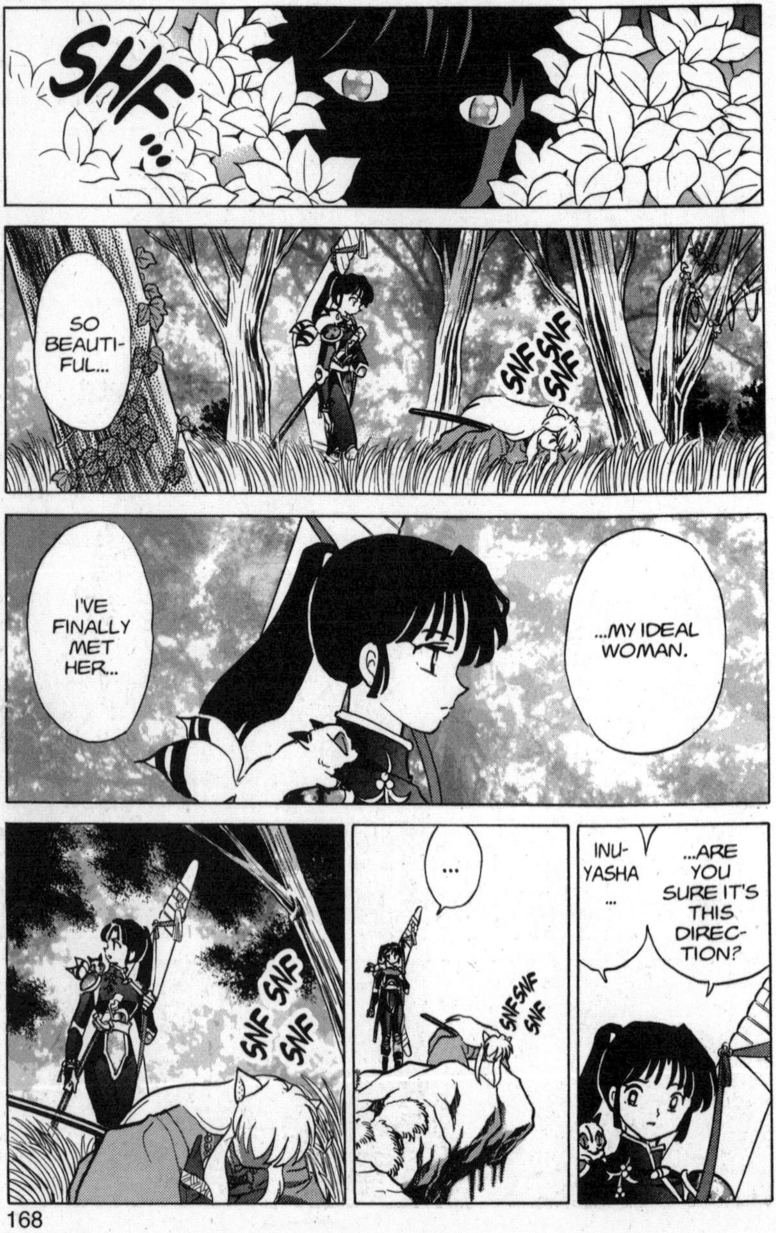
SHF...
SO BEAUTIFUL...
SNF SNF SNF
I'VE FINALLY MET HER...
...MY IDEAL WOMAN.
SNF SNF SNF
...
SNF SNF SNF
INU-YASHA...
...ARE YOU SURE IT'S THIS DIRECTION?

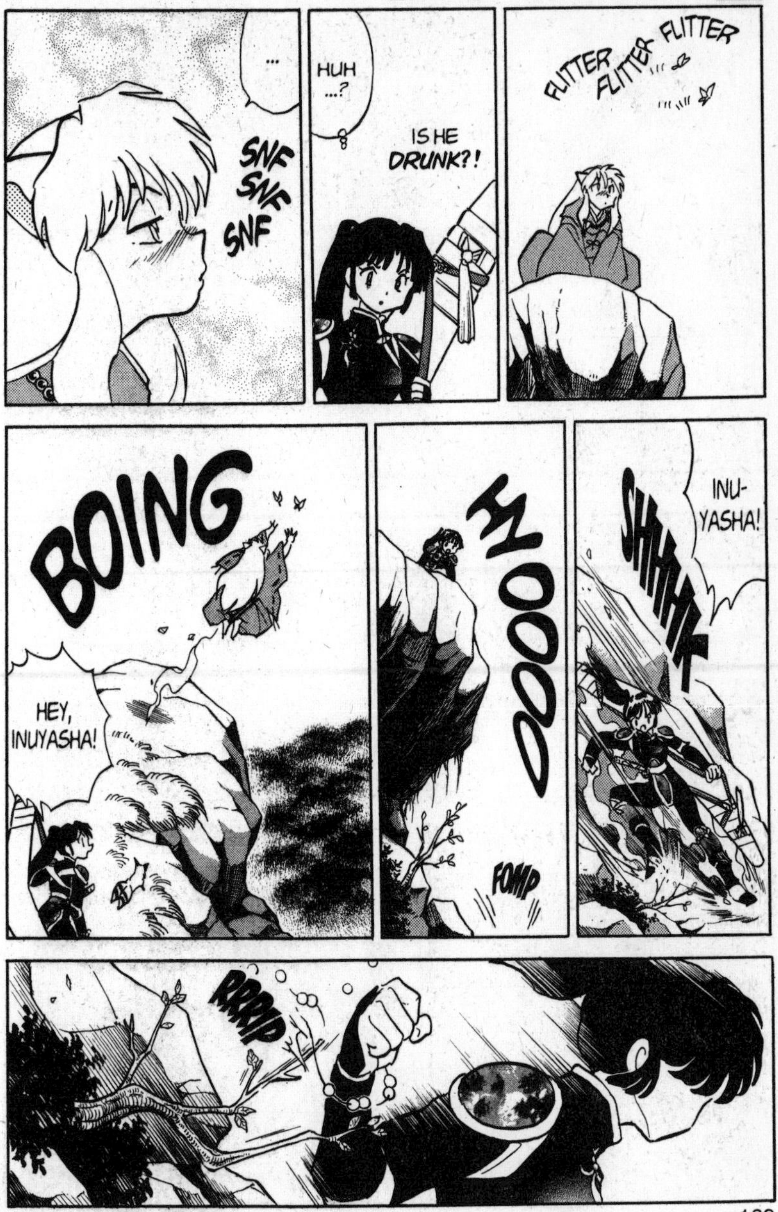
...
SNF
SNF
SNF
HUH ...?
IS HE DRUNK?!
FLITTER
FLITTER
FLITTER
BOING
HEY, INUYASHA!
HYOOOO
FOMP
SHHHK
INU-YASHA!
RRRIP

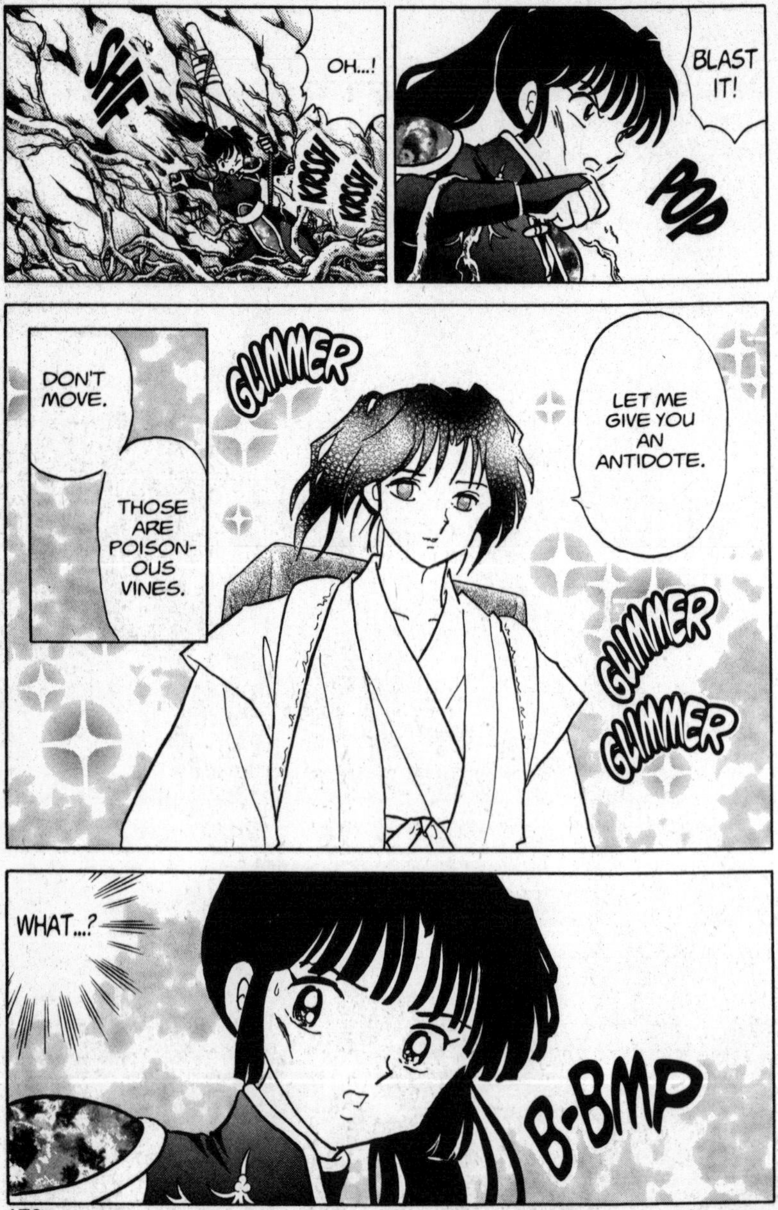
SHF
OH...!
KRSSH
KRSSH
BLAST IT!
POP
DON'T MOVE.
THOSE ARE POISONOUS VINES.
GLIMMER
LET ME GIVE YOU AN ANTIDOTE.
GLIMMER
GLIMMER
WHAT...?
B-BMP

SCROLL 10
ILLUSION

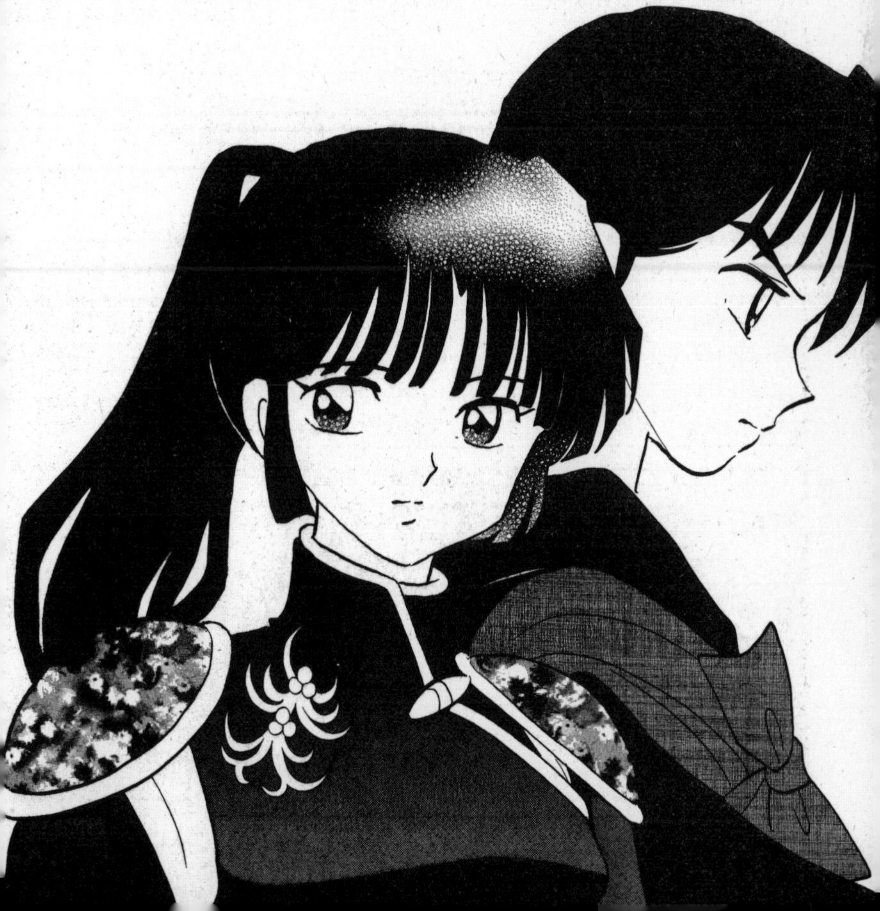

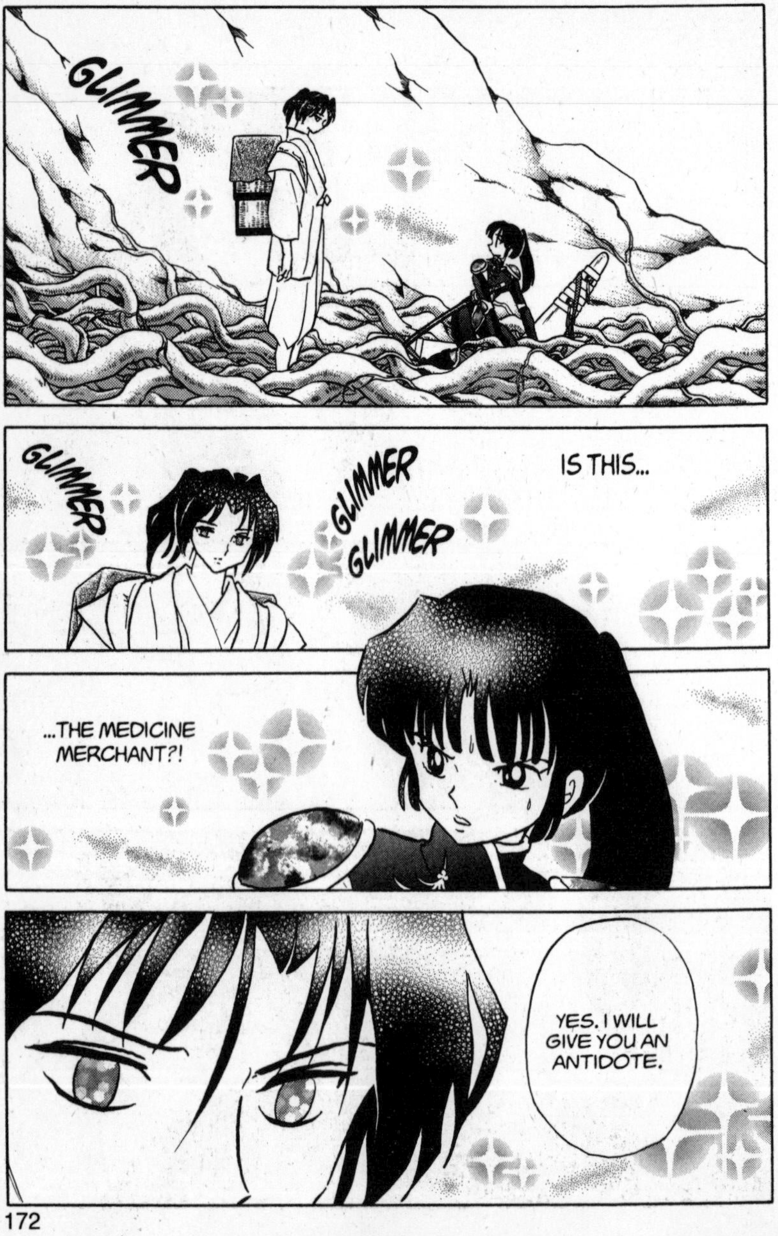
GLIMMER
GLIMMER
GLIMMER
GLIMMER
IS THIS...
...THE MEDICINE MERCHANT?!
YES. I WILL GIVE YOU AN ANTIDOTE.

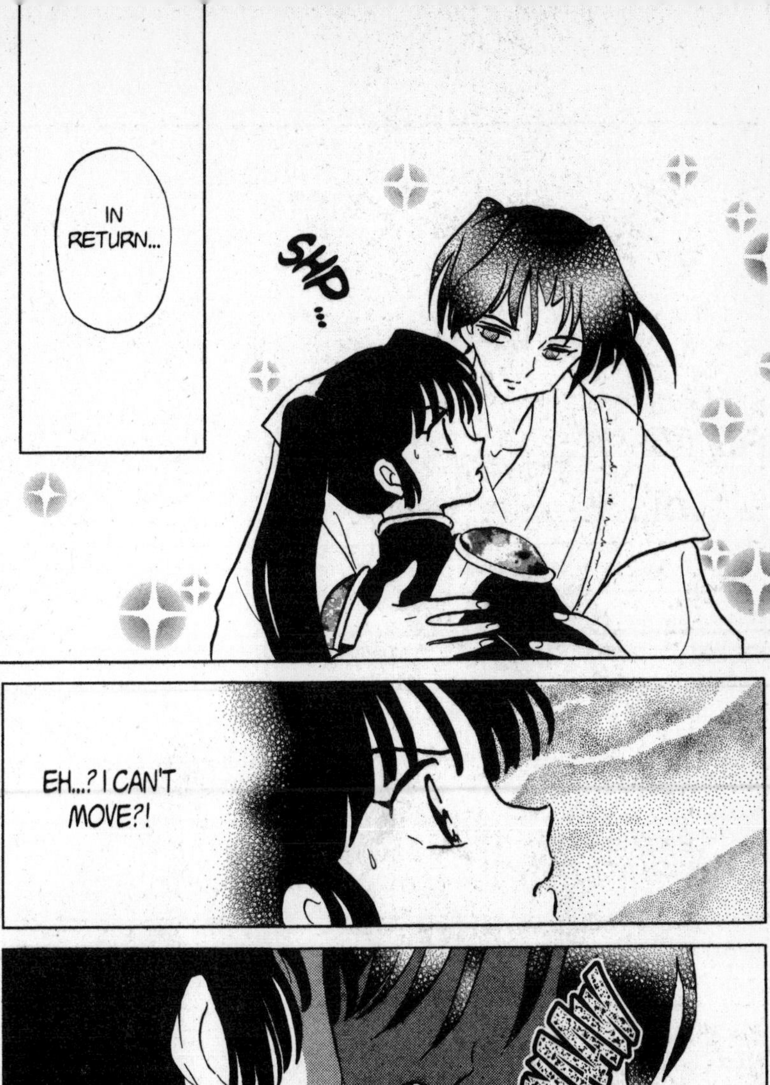
IN RETURN...
SHP..
EH...? I CAN'T MOVE?!

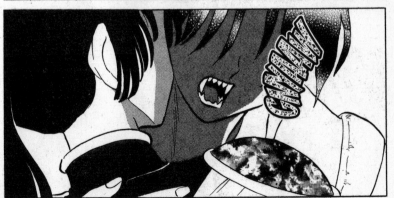

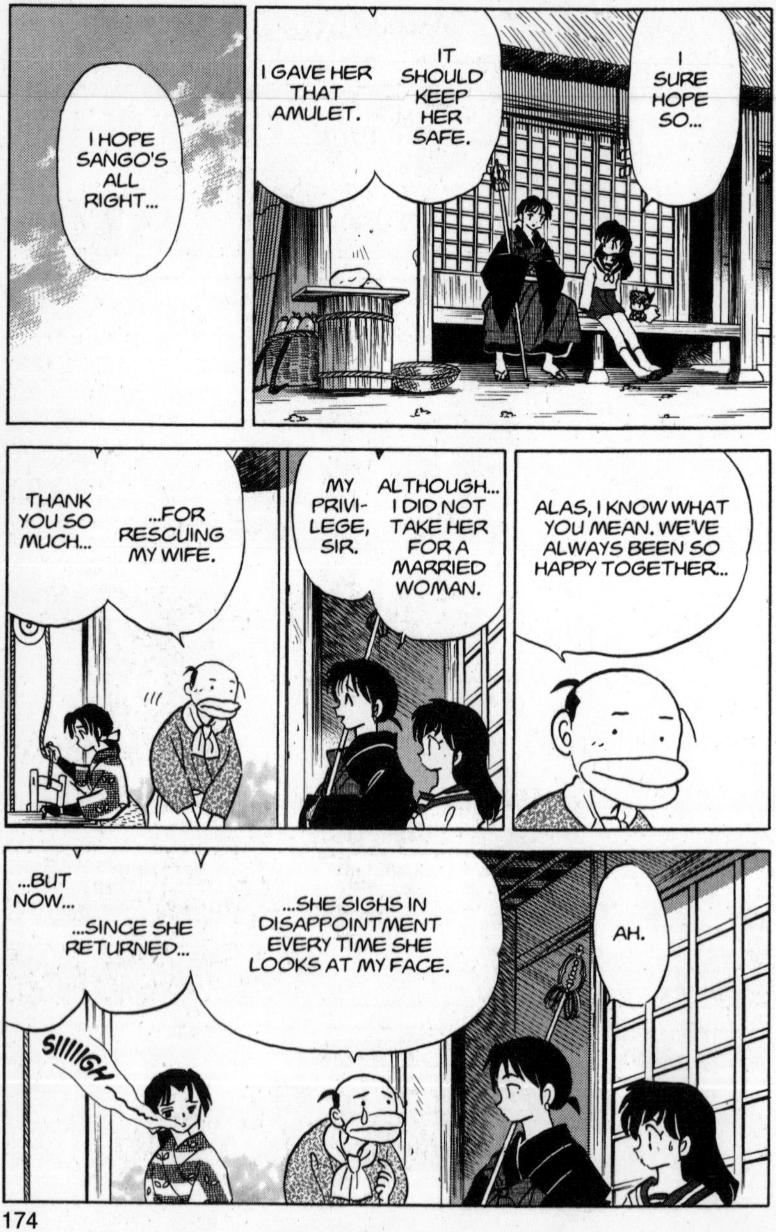
I HOPE SANGO'S ALL RIGHT...
I GAVE HER THAT AMULET.
IT SHOULD KEEP HER SAFE.
I SURE HOPE SO...
THANK YOU SO MUCH...
...FOR RESCUING MY WIFE.
MY PRIVI-LEGE, SIR.
ALTHOUGH... I DID NOT TAKE HER FOR A MARRIED WOMAN.
ALAS, I KNOW WHAT YOU MEAN. WE'VE ALWAYS BEEN SO HAPPY TOGETHER...
...BUT NOW...
...SINCE SHE RETURNED...
...SHE SIGHS IN DISAPPOINTMENT EVERY TIME SHE LOOKS AT MY FACE.
AH.
SIIIIGH

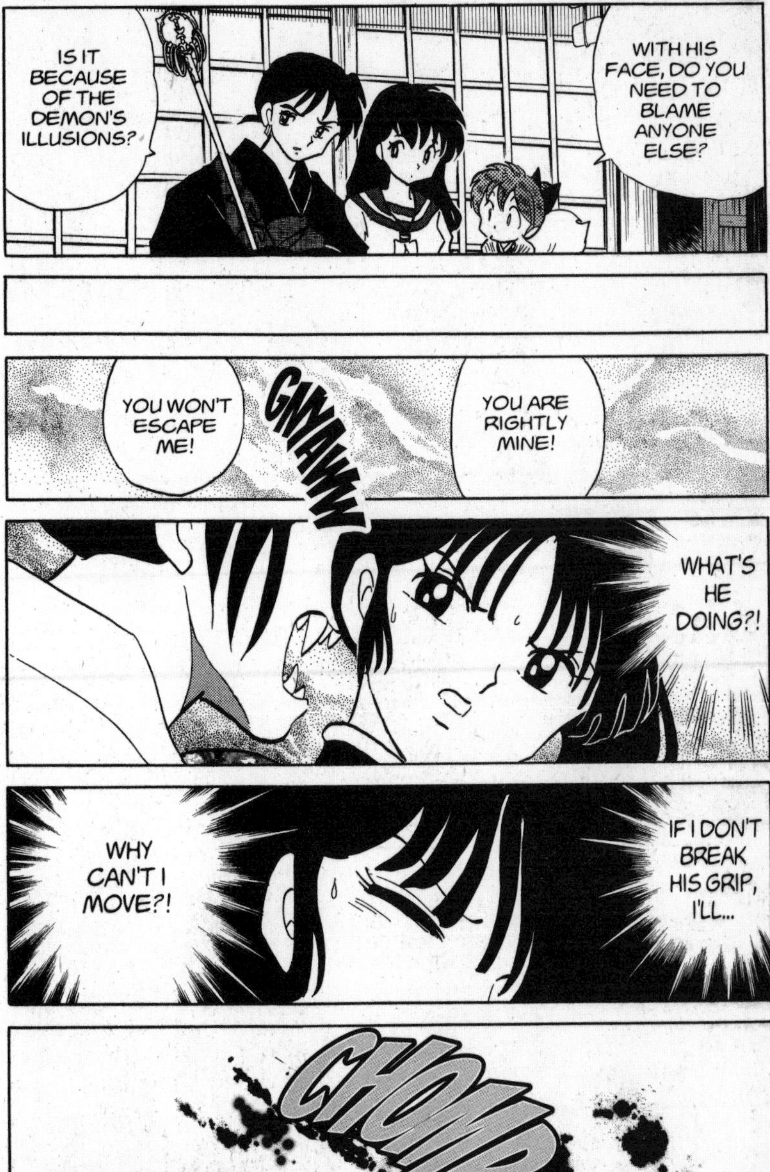
IS IT BECAUSE OF THE DEMON'S ILLUSIONS?
WITH HIS FACE, DO YOU NEED TO BLAME ANYONE ELSE?
YOU WON'T ESCAPE ME!
GNYAWWW
YOU ARE RIGHTLY MINE!
WHAT'S HE DOING?!
WHY CAN'T I MOVE?!
IF I DON'T BREAK HIS GRIP, I'LL...
CHOMP

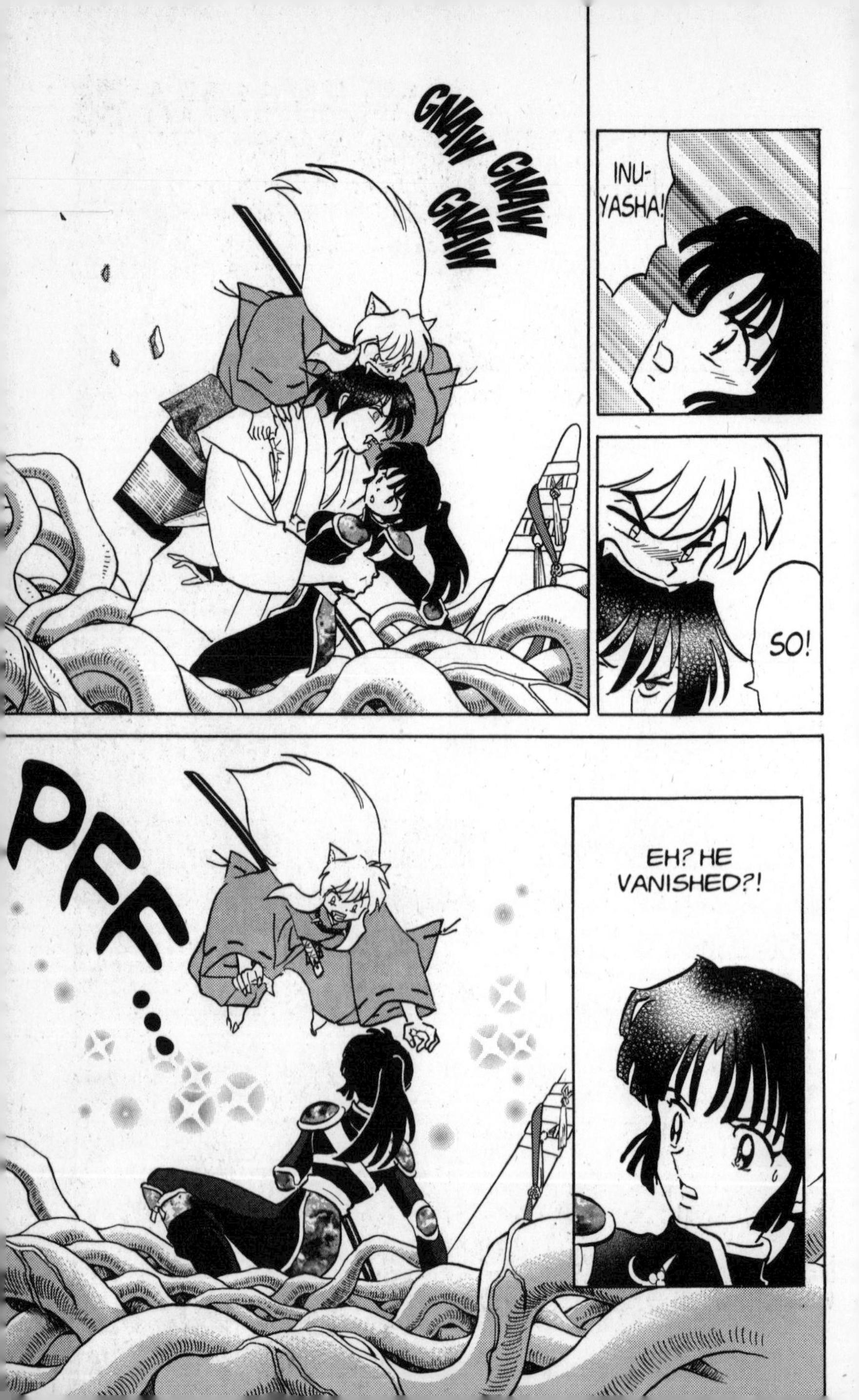
GNAW GNAW GNAW
INU-YASHA!
SO!
PFF...
EH? HE VANISHED?!

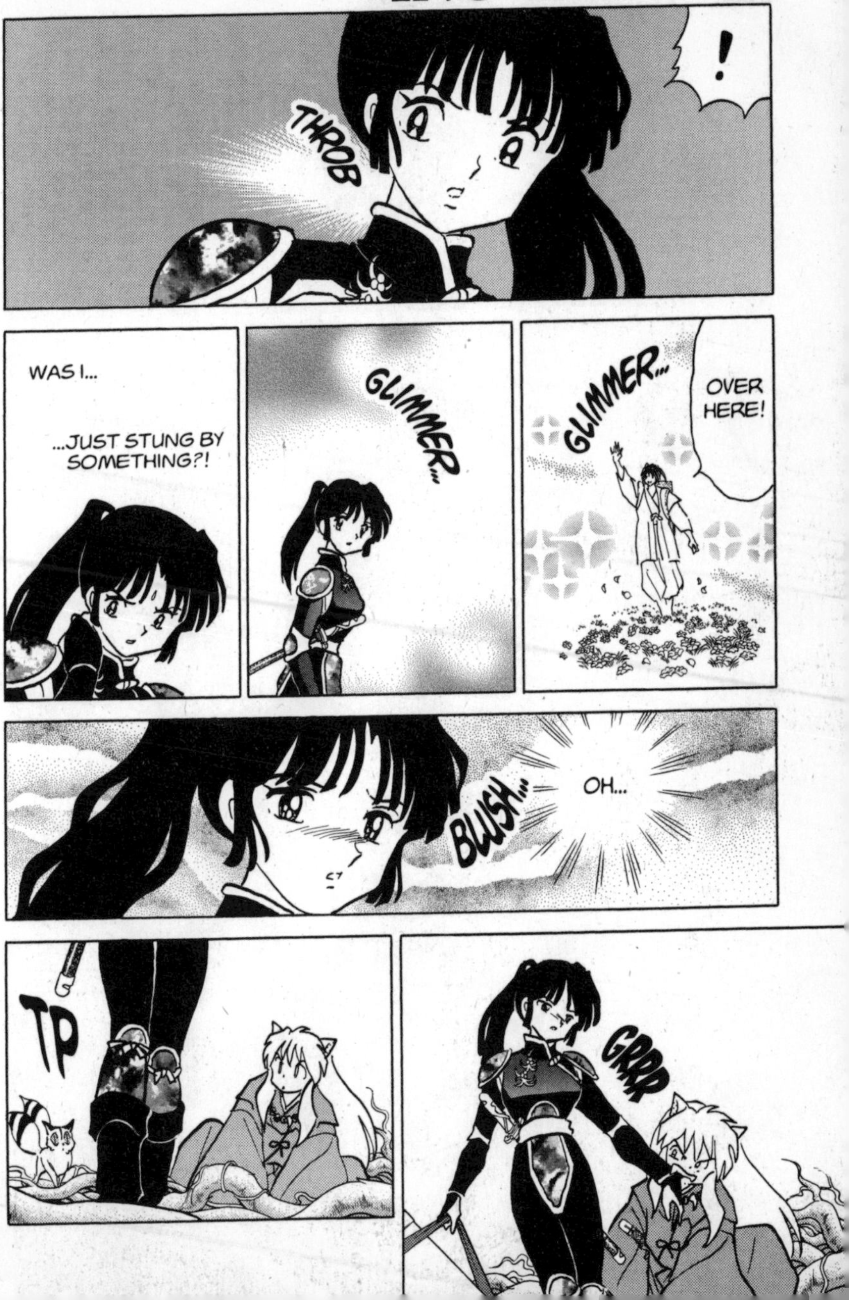
THROB
!
WAS I...
...JUST STUNG BY SOMETHING?!
GLIMMER...
GLIMMER...
OVER HERE!
BLUSH...
OH...
TP
GRRR

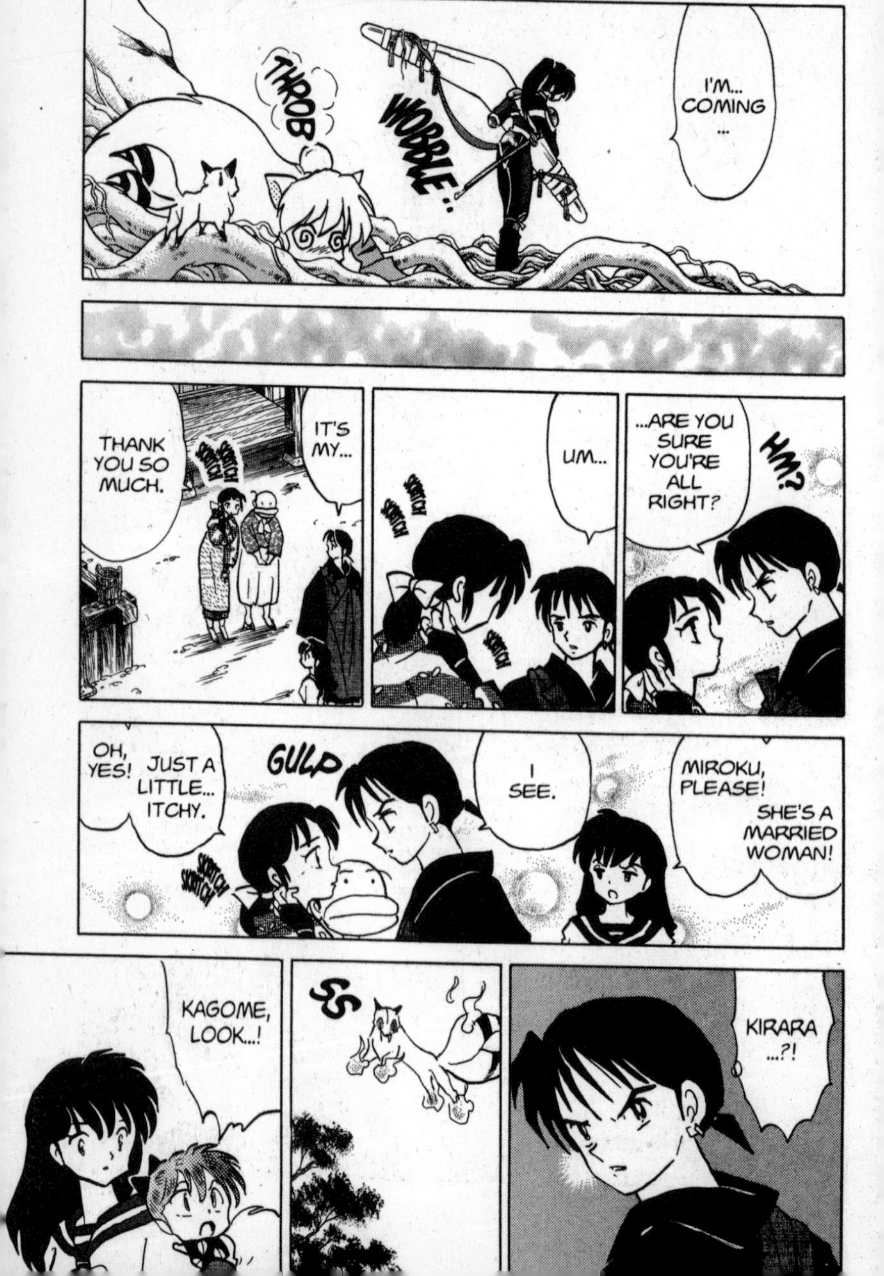
THROB
WOBBLE..
I'M... COMING ...
THANK YOU SO MUCH.
SKRITCH SKRITCH
IT'S MY...
SKRITCH SKRITCH
UM...
SKRITCH
...ARE YOU SURE YOU'RE ALL RIGHT?
HM?
OH, YES!
JUST A LITTLE... ITCHY.
GULP
SKRITCH SKRITCH
I SEE.
MIROKU, PLEASE!
SHE'S A MARRIED WOMAN!
KAGOME, LOOK...!
SS
KIRARA ...?!

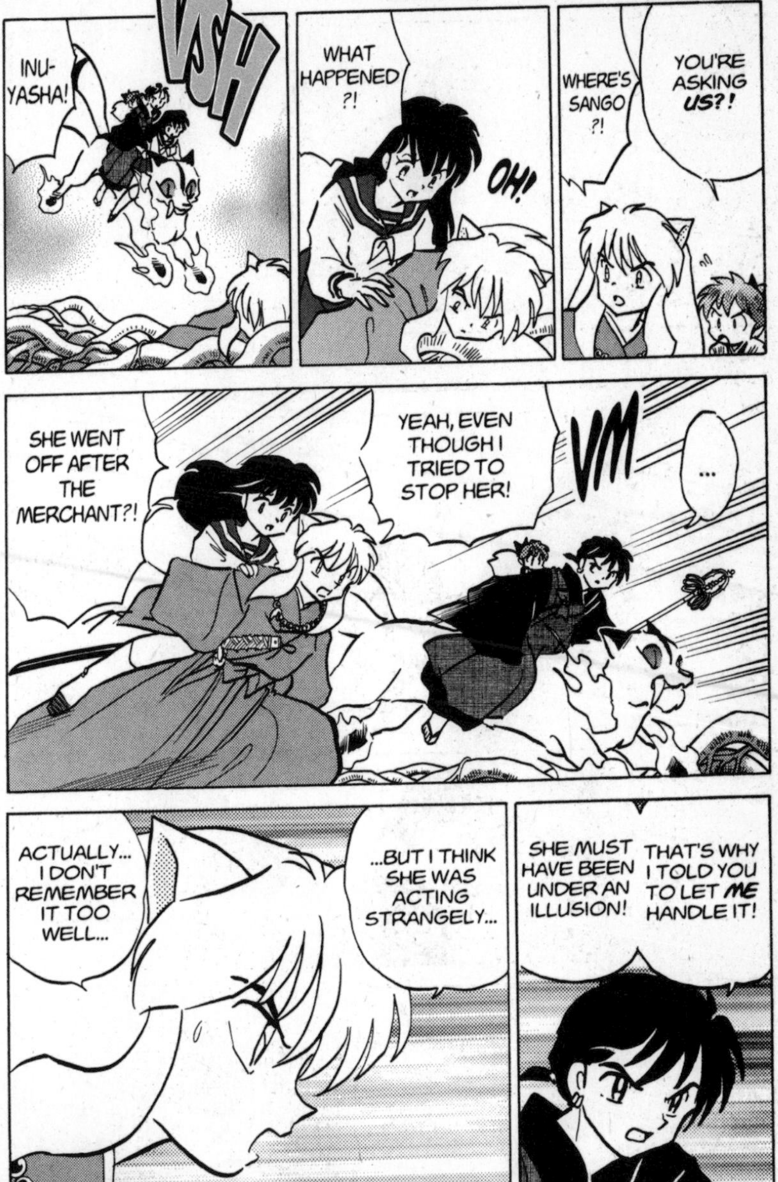
INU-YASHA!
VSH
WHAT HAPPENED ?!
OH!
WHERE'S SANGO ?!
YOU'RE ASKING *US?!*
SHE WENT OFF AFTER THE MERCHANT?!
YEAH, EVEN THOUGH I TRIED TO STOP HER!
VM
...
ACTUALLY... I DON'T REMEMBER IT TOO WELL...
...BUT I THINK SHE WAS ACTING STRANGELY...
SHE MUST HAVE BEEN UNDER AN ILLUSION!
THAT'S WHY I TOLD YOU TO LET *ME* HANDLE IT!

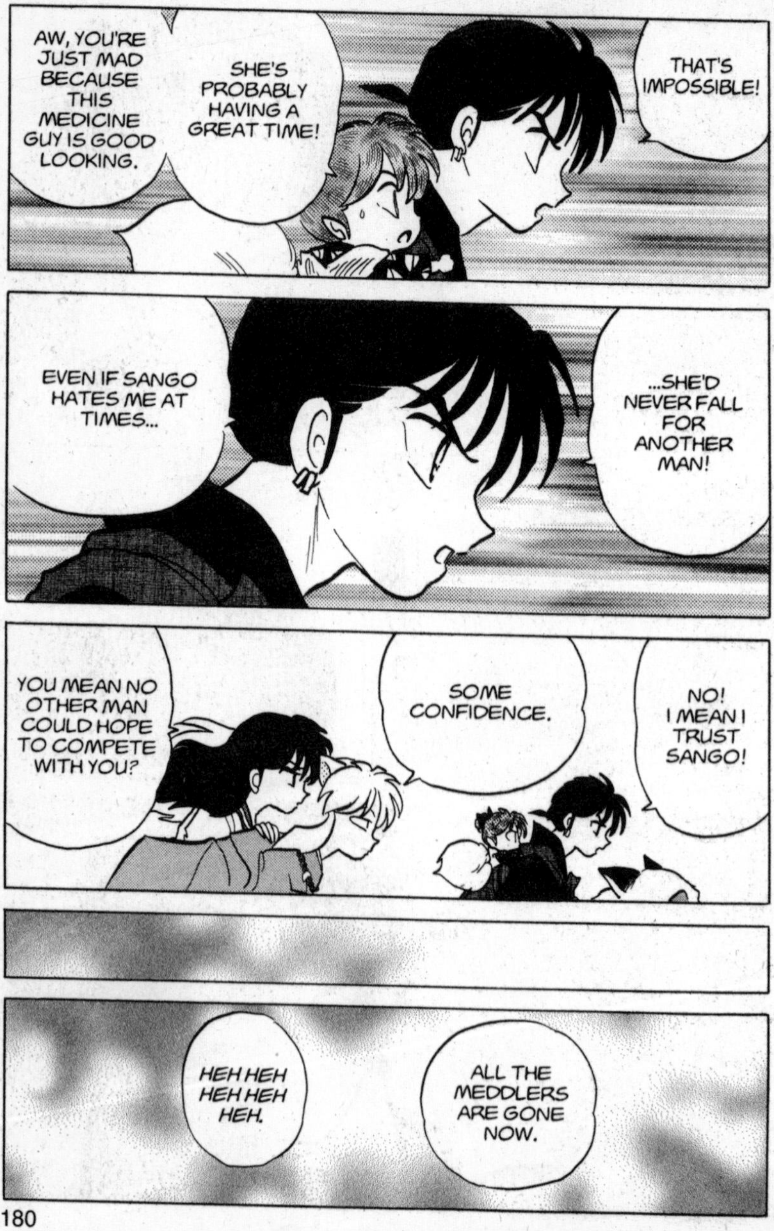
AW, YOU'RE JUST MAD BECAUSE THIS MEDICINE GUY IS GOOD LOOKING.
SHE'S PROBABLY HAVING A GREAT TIME!
THAT'S IMPOSSIBLE!
EVEN IF SANGO HATES ME AT TIMES...
...SHE'D NEVER FALL FOR ANOTHER MAN!
YOU MEAN NO OTHER MAN COULD HOPE TO COMPETE WITH YOU?
SOME CONFIDENCE.
NO! I MEAN I TRUST SANGO!
HEH HEH HEH HEH HEH.
ALL THE MEDDLERS ARE GONE NOW.

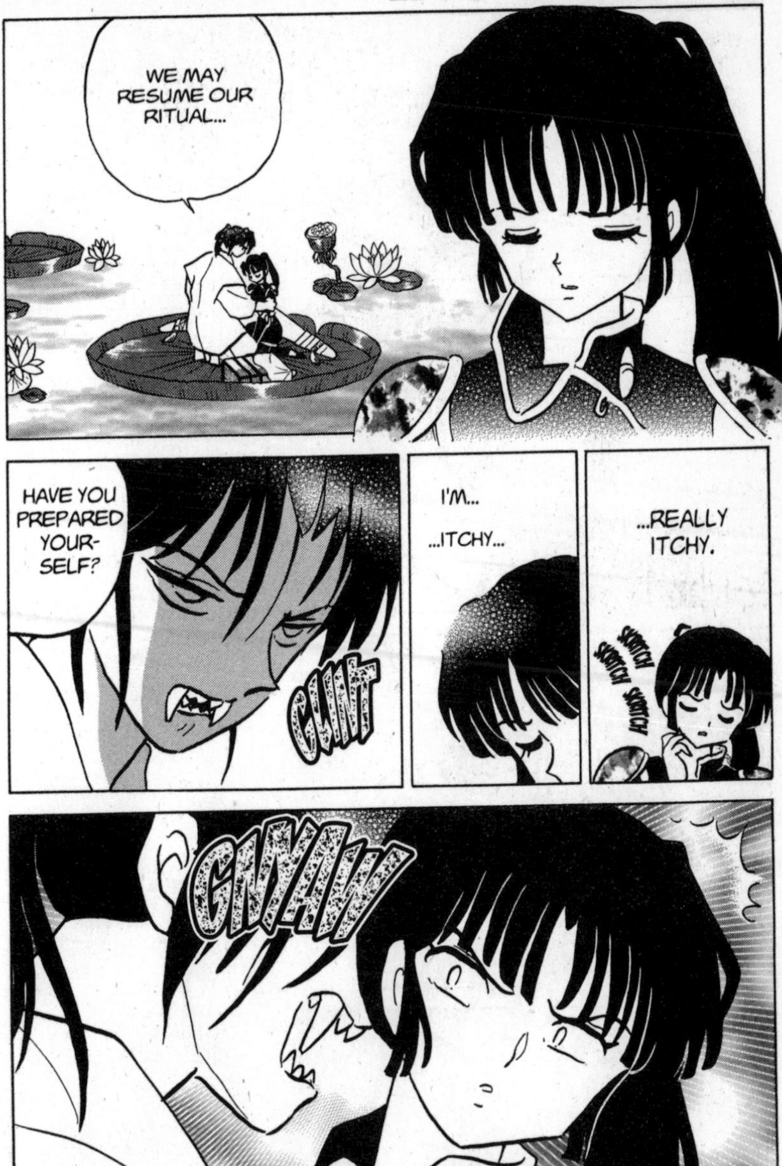
WE MAY RESUME OUR RITUAL...
HAVE YOU PREPARED YOUR-SELF?
CLINT
I'M...
...ITCHY...
...REALLY ITCHY.
SCRATCH SCRATCH SCRATCH
GNAW

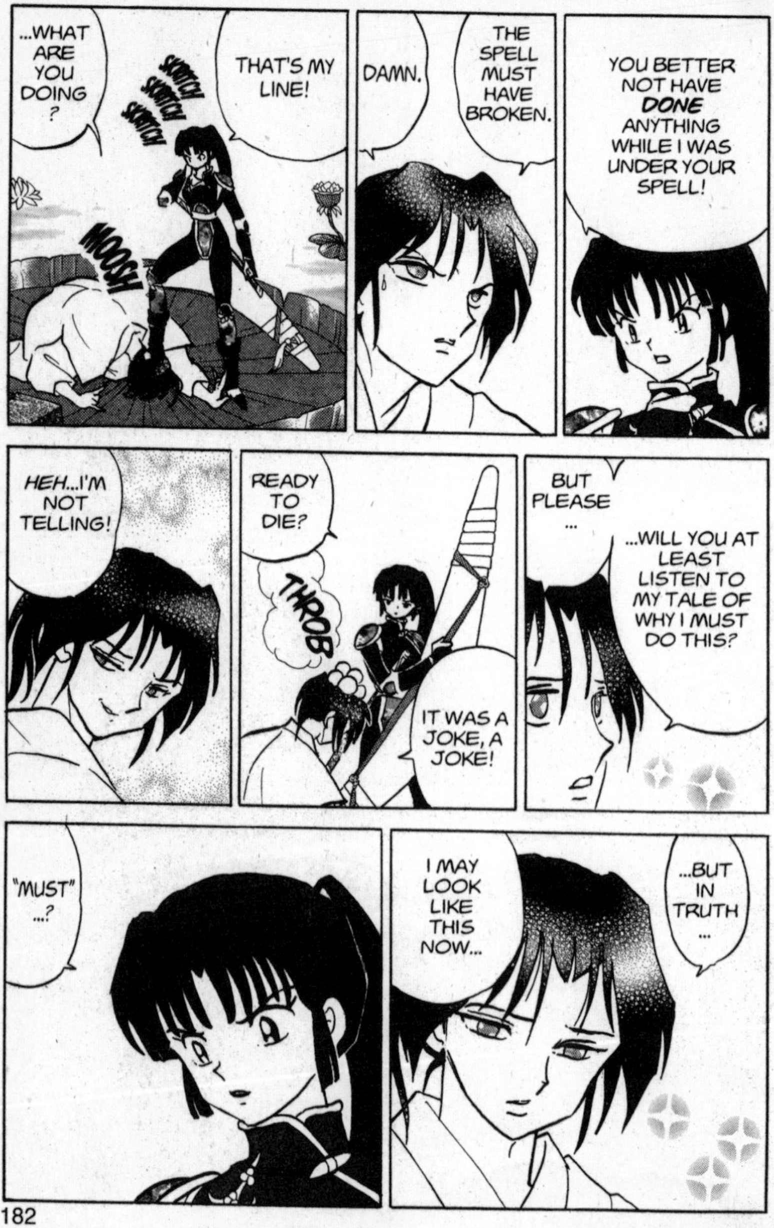
...WHAT ARE YOU DOING?
SCRITCH SCRITCH SCRITCH
THAT'S MY LINE!
WOOSH
DAMN.
THE SPELL MUST HAVE BROKEN.
YOU BETTER NOT HAVE **DONE** ANYTHING WHILE I WAS UNDER YOUR SPELL!
HEH...I'M NOT TELLING!
READY TO DIE?
THROB
IT WAS A JOKE, A JOKE!
BUT PLEASE...
...WILL YOU AT LEAST LISTEN TO MY TALE OF WHY I MUST DO THIS?
"MUST"...?
I MAY LOOK LIKE THIS NOW...
...BUT IN TRUTH...

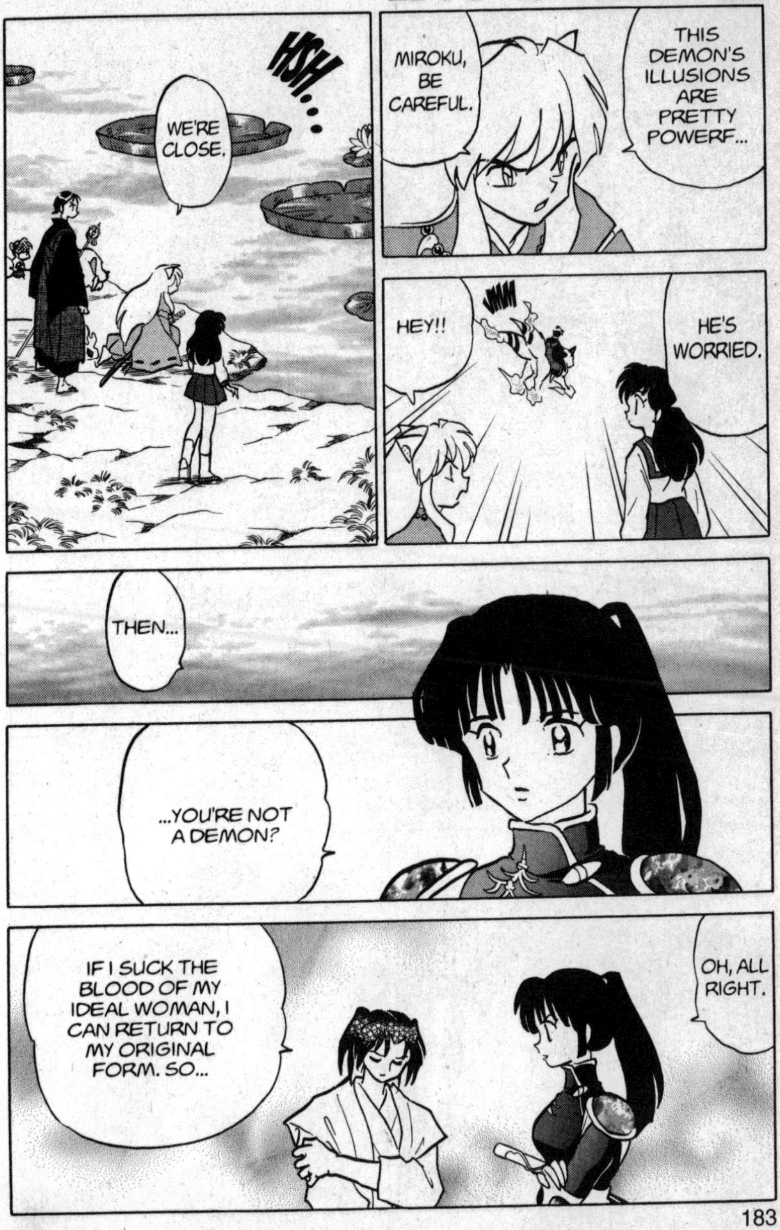
HSH...
WE'RE CLOSE.
MIROKU, BE CAREFUL.
THIS DEMON'S ILLUSIONS ARE PRETTY POWERF...
HEY!!
HE'S WORRIED.
THEN...
...YOU'RE NOT A DEMON?
IF I SUCK THE BLOOD OF MY IDEAL WOMAN, I CAN RETURN TO MY ORIGINAL FORM. SO...
OH, ALL RIGHT.

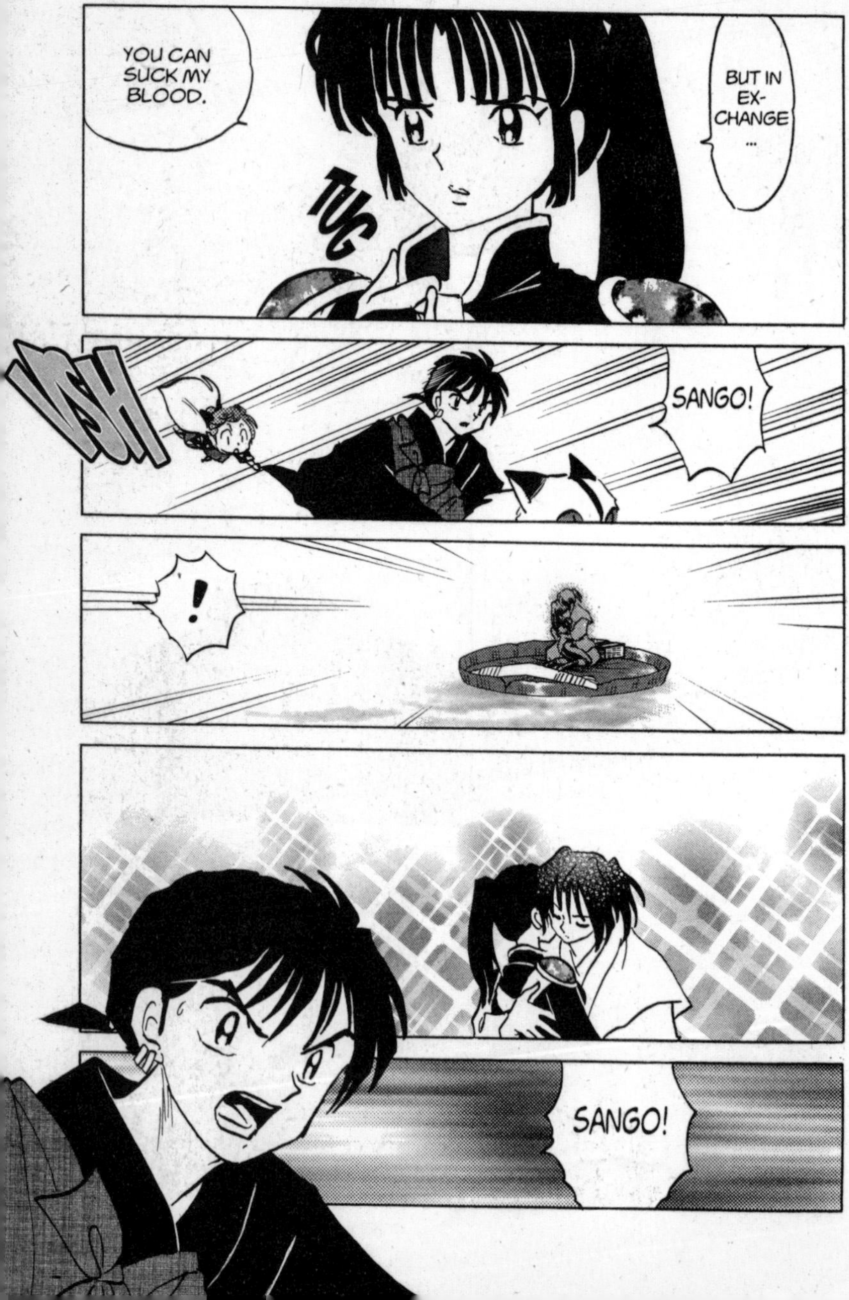
YOU CAN SUCK MY BLOOD.
BUT IN EX-CHANGE ...
TUC
WSH
SANGO!
!
SANGO!

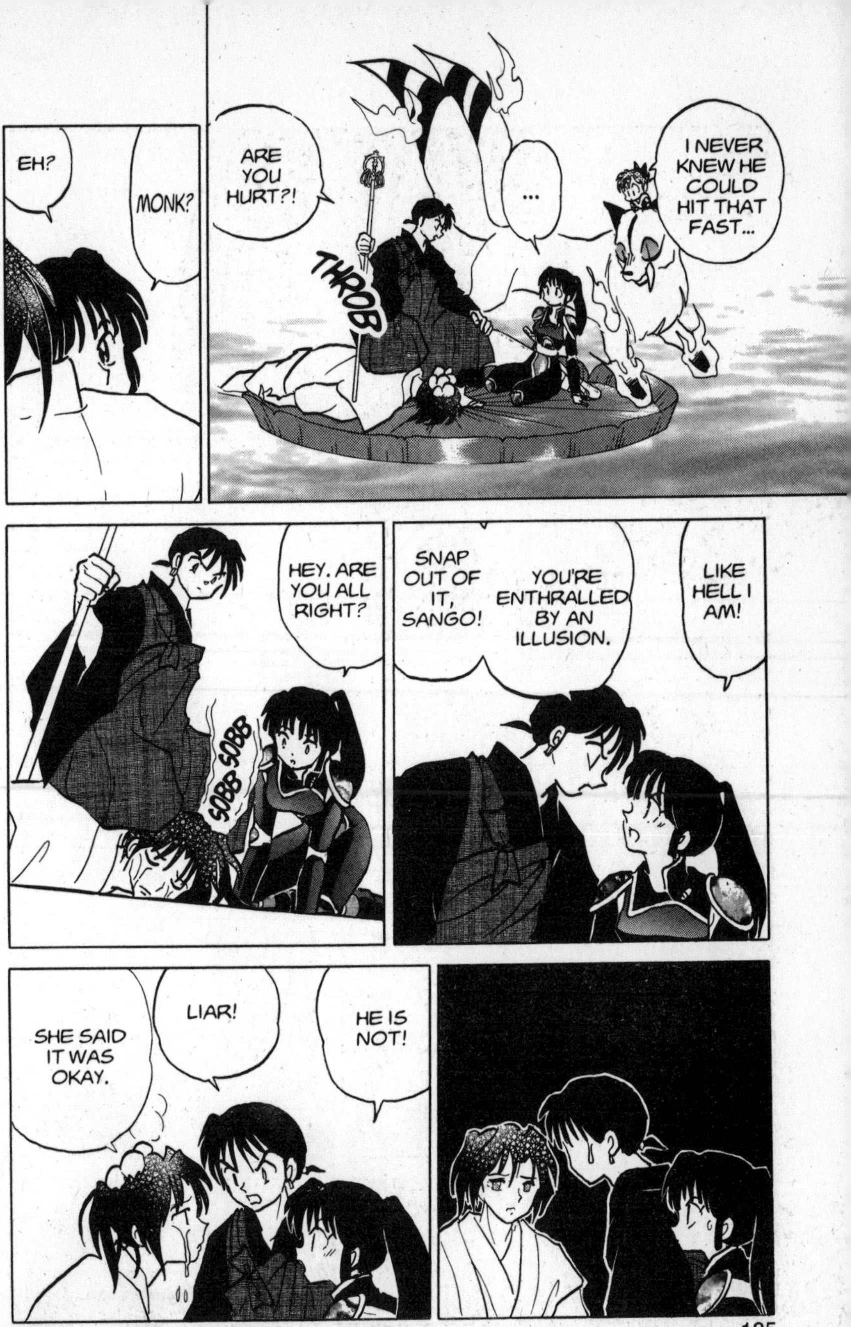
EH?
MONK?
ARE YOU HURT?!
THROB
...
I NEVER KNEW HE COULD HIT THAT FAST...
HEY. ARE YOU ALL RIGHT?
SOBB SOBB
SNAP OUT OF IT, SANGO!
YOU'RE ENTHRALLED BY AN ILLUSION.
LIKE HELL I AM!
SHE SAID IT WAS OKAY.
LIAR!
HE IS NOT!

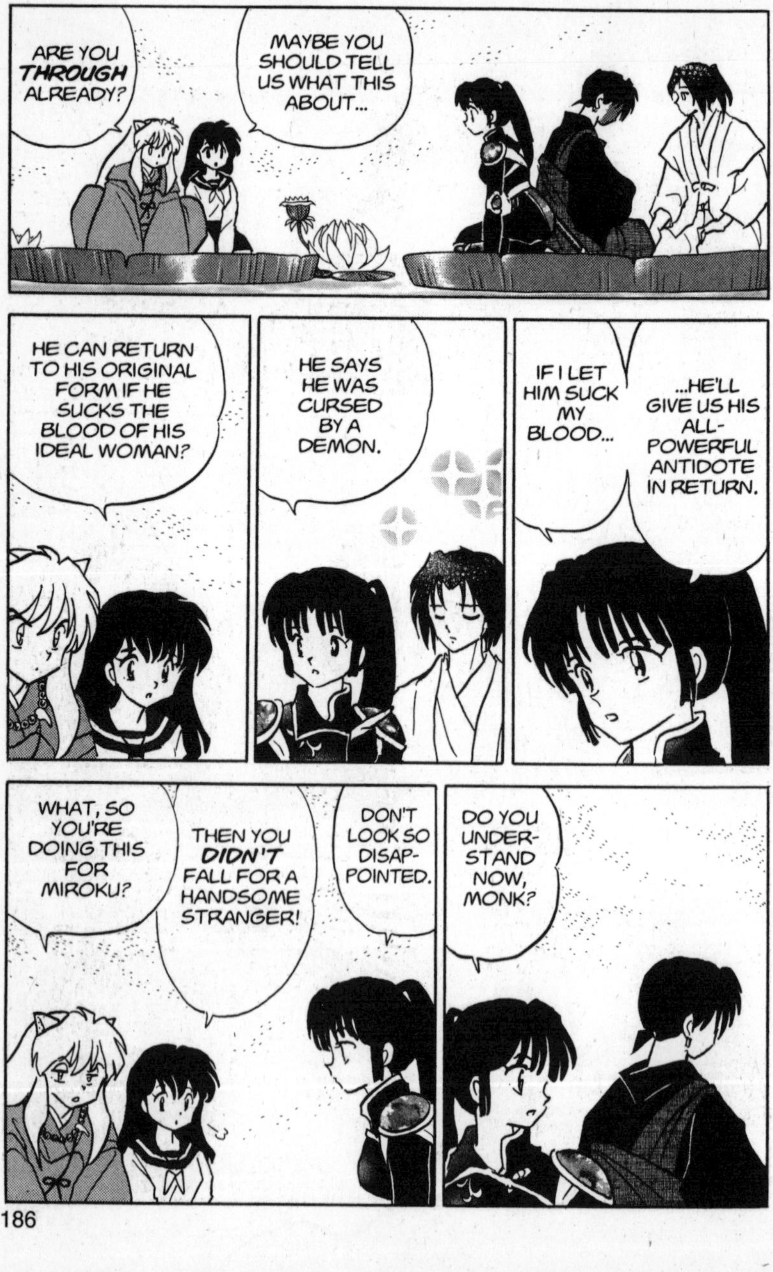
ARE YOU THROUGH ALREADY?
MAYBE YOU SHOULD TELL US WHAT THIS ABOUT...
HE CAN RETURN TO HIS ORIGINAL FORM IF HE SUCKS THE BLOOD OF HIS IDEAL WOMAN?
HE SAYS HE WAS CURSED BY A DEMON.
IF I LET HIM SUCK MY BLOOD...
...HE'LL GIVE US HIS ALL-POWERFUL ANTIDOTE IN RETURN.
WHAT, SO YOU'RE DOING THIS FOR MIROKU?
THEN YOU DIDN'T FALL FOR A HANDSOME STRANGER!
DON'T LOOK SO DISAP-POINTED.
DO YOU UNDER-STAND NOW, MONK?

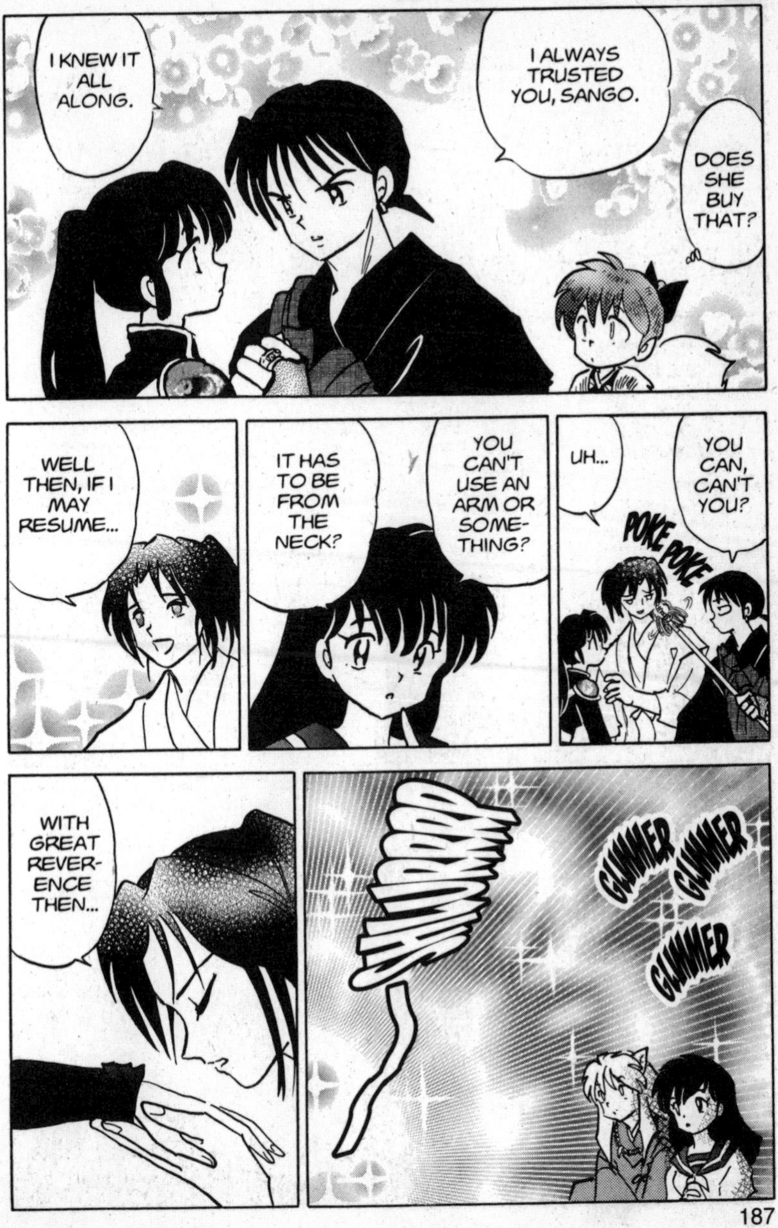
I KNEW IT ALL ALONG.
I ALWAYS TRUSTED YOU, SANGO.
DOES SHE BUY THAT?
WELL THEN, IF I MAY RESUME...
IT HAS TO BE FROM THE NECK?
YOU CAN'T USE AN ARM OR SOME-THING?
UH...
YOU CAN, CAN'T YOU?
POKE POKE
WITH GREAT REVERENCE THEN...
SMOOCH
GLIMMER GLIMMER
GLIMMER

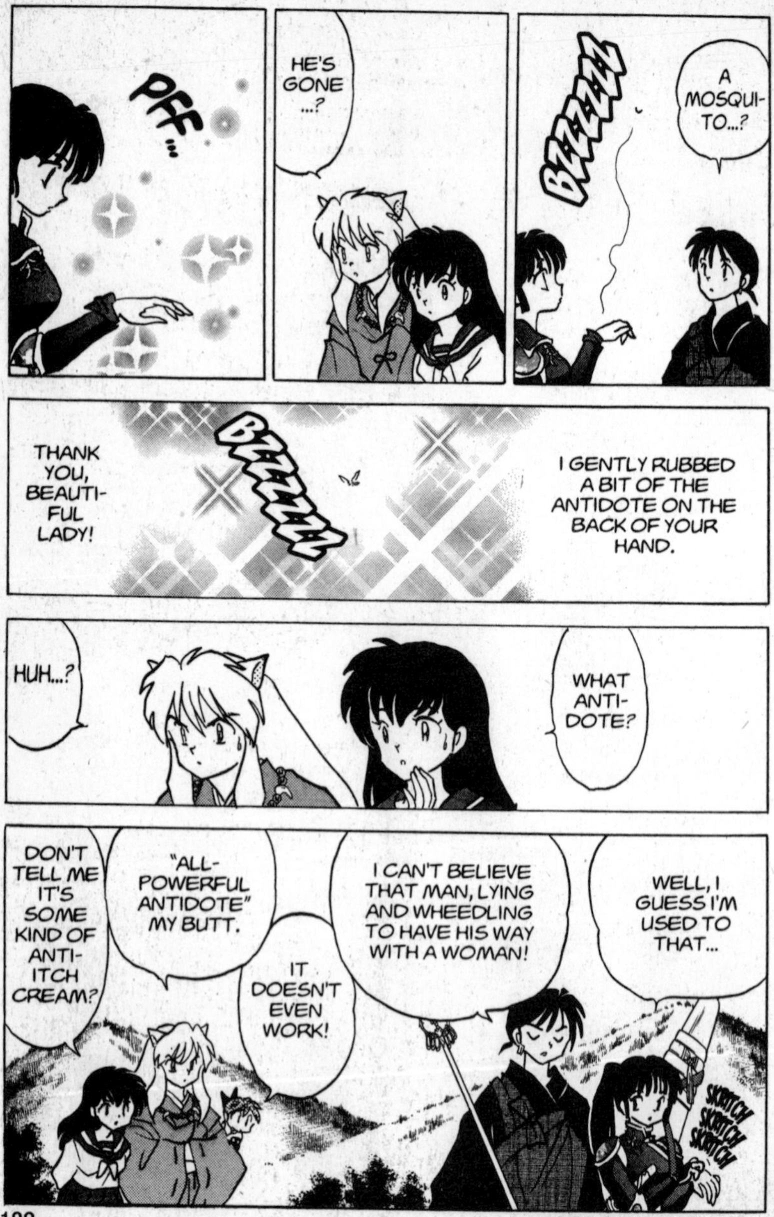
PFF...
HE'S GONE ...?
BZZZZZZZ
A MOSQUI-TO...?
THANK YOU, BEAUTI-FUL LADY!
BZZZZZZ
I GENTLY RUBBED A BIT OF THE ANTIDOTE ON THE BACK OF YOUR HAND.
HUH...?
WHAT ANTI-DOTE?
DON'T TELL ME IT'S SOME KIND OF ANTI-ITCH CREAM?
"ALL-POWERFUL ANTIDOTE" MY BUTT.
IT DOESN'T EVEN WORK!
I CAN'T BELIEVE THAT MAN, LYING AND WHEEDLING TO HAVE HIS WAY WITH A WOMAN!
WELL, I GUESS I'M USED TO THAT...
SKRITCH SKRITCH SKRITCH

TO BE CONTINUED...

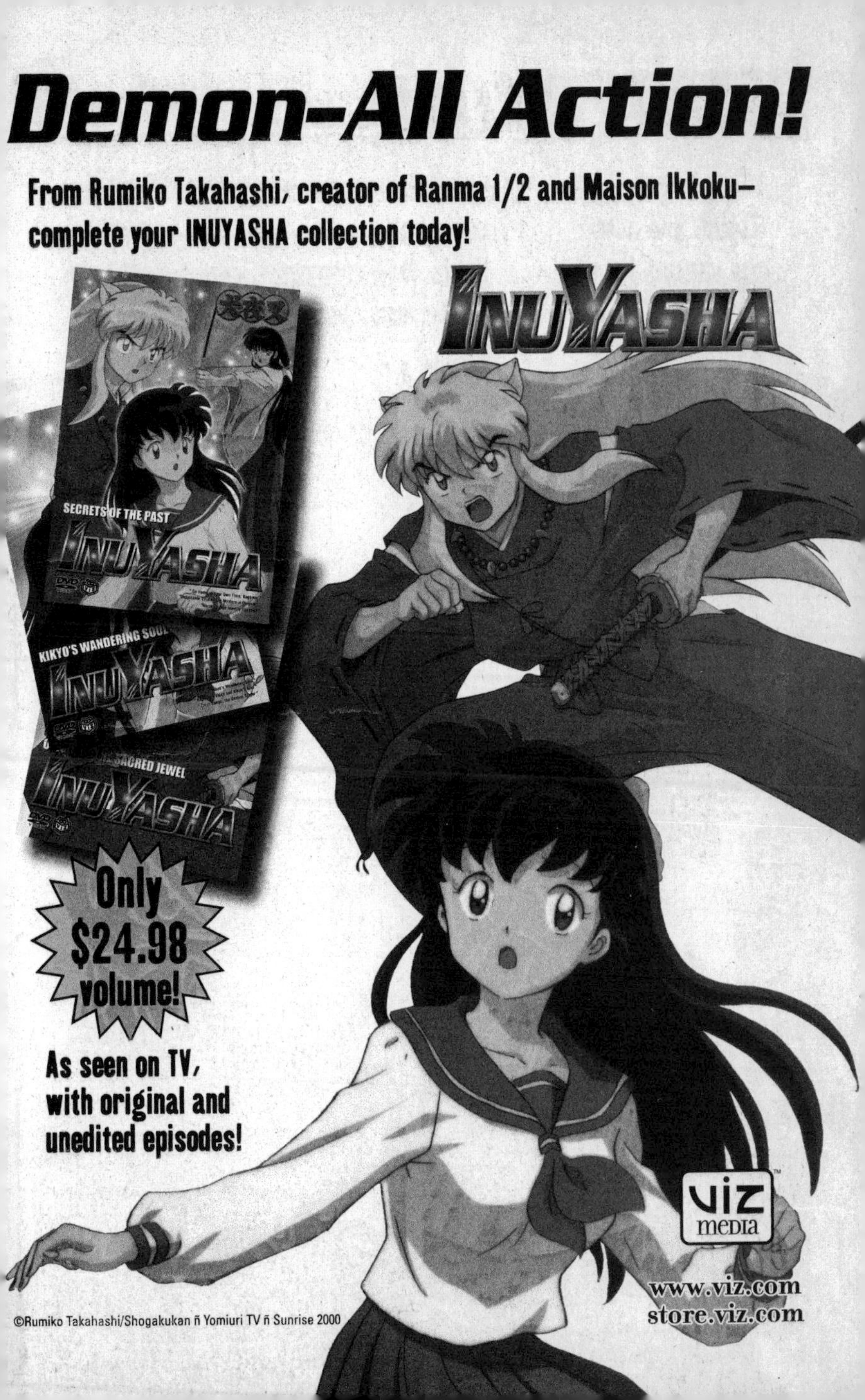
Demon-All Action!
From Rumiko Takahashi, creator of Ranma 1/2 and Maison Ikkoku–
complete your INUYASHA collection today!
INUYASHA
SECRETS OF THE PAST
INUYASHA
KIKYO'S WANDERING SOUL
INUYASHA
SACRED JEWEL
INUYASHA
Only
$24.98
volume!
As seen on TV,
with original and
unedited episodes!
viz media
www.viz.com
store.viz.com
©Rumiko Takahashi/Shogakukan ñ Yomiuri TV ñ Sunrise 2000

LOVE MANGA?
LET US KNOW WHAT YOU THINK!

OUR MANGA SURVEY IS NOW
AVAILABLE ONLINE. PLEASE VISIT:
VIZ.COM/MANGASURVEY

HELP US MAKE THE MANGA
YOU LOVE BETTER!